AF540270

HYPNOSIS

About the Editors

Renu Sharma is Ph D in Psychology and is currently serving as Reader in the Department of Psychology, The M. S. University of Baroda, Vadodara. She is also the faculty and coordinator of the course "Diploma in Clinical and Applied Psychology" run by the department. She is a practicing hypnotherapist and has several publications to her credit.

Contact: renusharma56@yahoo.co.in

B. M. Palan, M D taught Physiology at Medical Colleges for 20 years, headed the Psychosomatic Medicine and Hypnotherapy Clinic, S. S. G. Hospital, Vadodara and guided M D/Ph D students at The M. S. University of Baroda for more than 10 years. He is also a Yoga Teacher. He is the first doctor in India to have obtained Diploma in Clinical Hypnosis from the American Board of Medical Hypnosis. He is conducting self-development and stress management workshops ("tranceformation" and Towards Success and Excellence) in various industrial and academic organizations since 1986.

Dr. Palan has contributed widely at national and international level in the academic journals and books in the areas of stress management, psychosomatic medicine, yoga and hypnotherapy.

Contact: drpalan@gmail.com

HYPNOSIS

Psycho-Philosophical Perspectives and Therapeutic Relevance

Edited by

RENU SHARMA

and

BHUPENDRA M. PALAN

CONCEPT PUBLISHING COMPANY, PRIVATE LIMITED, NEW DELHI-110059

ISBN: 13-978-81-8069-727-2

First Published 2011

Published and Printed by

Concept Publishing Company Pvt. Ltd.
Regd. Office:
A/15-16, Commercial Block, Mohan Garden
New Delhi-110059 (India)
Phones : 25351460, 25351794, *Fax* : 091-11-25357109
Email : publishing@conceptpub.com
Website: www.conceptpub.com

Editorial Office:
H-13, Bali Nagar, New Delhi-110 015, India.

Cataloging in Publication Data--*Courtesy:* D.K. Agencies (P) Ltd. <docinfo@dkagencies.com>

National Conference on Hypnotherapy : the Therapy of New Millennium (7th : 2009 : Vadodara, India)
Hypnosis : psycho-philosophical perspectives and therapeutic relevance / edited by Renu Sharma and Bhupendra M. Palan.
p. cm.
Includes bibliographical references and index.
ISBN 9788180697272

1. Hypnotism--Congresses. 2. Hypnotism--Therapeutic use--Congresses. I. Sharma, Renu. II. Palan, Bhupendra M. III. Title.

DDC 615.8512 22

Preface

Hypnosis: Psycho-philosophical perspectives and therapeutic relevance is being published as a compilation volume of selected papers presented at the "Seventh National Conference on Hypnotherapy : The Therapy of New Millennium" held at The Maharaja Sayaji Rao University of Baroda, Vadodara during January 9-11, 2009. These articles present a practical way of some key aspects of Hypnotherapy for medical and psychological health practitioners, besides an insight on psycho-philosophical issues.

Since 1990s, several techniques for behaviour modification have been researched. Hypnotherapy too, has been extensively explored in the West, and has emerged as an effective tool in behavioural change, opening several new exciting possibilities in the field of psychology, psychiatry and medicine. Proof of its efficacy in the medical field has made hypnotherapy one of the prime methods used in complementary medicine, and this is one of the reasons of its popularity. Hypnotherapy is flexible, briefer and time efficient, making it a treatment of choice in today's fast times. It is no longer an "alternative" form of therapy but rather has challenged traditional therapies by becoming more goal oriented, clearly focussed and centered on the development of the patient's existing strengths and abilities.

In India, Dr. Hrishikesh Jana (1928–2006) may be considered as the pioneer of medical hypnosis. He established Indian Society for Clinical and Experimental Hypnosis in early seventies. The first National Congress of Hypnosis and Psychosomatic Medicine was organized at N. H. L. Municipal Medical College, Ahmedabad in 1984. Subsequently five other national conferences were organized at different institutes of India, for example in Government Medical College, Baroda

(1986 and 1994), and at All India Institute of Medical Sciences (AIIMS), New Delhi (1988) and at National Institute of Mental Health & Neurosciences, Bangalore (1997). Seventh National Conference was successfully organized in January 2009 at The M. S. University of Baroda. This book is compilation of some selected papers presented during the Conference.

The conference emphasized mind-body continuum as a singularity, so that psychopathology as well as its reversal through psychodynamic manipulations that bring about transformation in the body systems could be understood within the current scientific knowledge. Part I of the book contains papers on the history and theoretical aspects of hypnosis/ hypnotherapy. Part II of the book has papers on case studies highlighting the hypnotherapeutic practices.

To get a wider view on the subject a parallel Seminar on the theme 'Psycho-Philosophical Perspectives of Hypnosis' was organized as a part of the Conference. It was felt that cross-fertilization between Indian philosophy, hypnotherapy and other therapies could act synergistically, and the amalgamation of the fundamental principles of these fields would have a salutary effect contributing to the pursuit of excellence and creativity enhancement on the practices of psychology, psychiatry and medicine. Some selected papers of philosophical background are arranged in Part III of the book.

The articles provide clinicians-in-training, as well as experienced clinicians, with most clinical friendly presentation of intervention strategies and treatment methods, which have immediate clinical utility. Since considerable clinical skill is required to apply hypnotherapy most effectively, case studies in this book provide a detailed description of actual treatment protocols and verbatim which experienced clinicians follow while conducting hypnotherapy. Our hope is that practicing hypnotherapists and clinical students everywhere will benefit from acquaintance with these details.

We are confident that this book will be very useful source book to psychologists and medical practitioners. We recommend, however, that those who intend to acquire and use hypnotherapy skill must attend formal training as no book alone can provide the practical skills necessary for effective practice. We also believe that the book will be quite useful to those whose main interest is philosophy. Hypnosis is an example how subjects emanating from philosophy have entered mainstream science. Readers would appreciate that it is a huge task to bring so many experts from varied fields of specializations, and from different regions to contribute for a book. We hope that the book benefits practicing hypnotherapists, clinicians, students, psychologists/ psychotherapists and those who follow philosophy.

Our personal thanks go out to the contributors who have made this laborious job a most enjoyable experience. We would like to express our profound gratitude to Dr. Bhaskar Vyas and Dr. Rajni Vyas who have been our guide and inspiration. We also thank Indian Society of Clinical and Experimental Hypnosis (ISCEH) for its generosity and financial help in supporting us for the larger cause of Hypnotherapy. We appreciate the constant encouragement and help from Dr. Radhamohan, President, and Dr. Alok Prapanna, Secretary, ISCEH.

Renu Sharma, PhD
Bhupendra M. Palan, MD

Contents

Part II
Therapeutic Perspectives : Some Case Studies

Part III
Philosophical Perspectives on Consciousness

Contributors

K. Ramakrishna Rao, PhD : Chairman, Indian Council of Philosophical Research, New Delhi and President of the Institute for Human Science & Service, an experimental institution in Gandhian education to link learning and classrooms with community centres of service, India. He is former Vice Chancellor of Andhra University, and former Vice Chairman of Andhra Pradesh State Planning Board. He is renowned scholar of Indian psychology and has several books and articles to his credit.

Bhaskar Vyas, MD : Plastic surgeon in private practice and visiting professor of Hypnotherapy at Department of Psychology, The M. S. University of Baroda. He has been a pioneer in the field of plastic surgery by way of establishing plastic surgery unit at the Medical College, The M. S. University of Baroda. He is also a scholar on Buddhism and has several scholastic contributions on the subject.

Aruna Lakdawala Thakur, MBBS, FRCP (C) : Clinical Director, Department of Psychiatry, Ellis Hall, Saskatoon, SK, Canada. She is also consultant Psychiatrist in St. Paul's Hospital. She is member of the Board of Directors and a founding member of the Foundation of Canadian Psychiatric Association. She is in the Board of Directors, Hope Medical Institute, Canada.

Ilana Eli, DMD : Faculty at the Maurice and Gabriela Goldschleger School of Dental Medicine, Tel-Aviv University, Israel. Prof. Eli specializes in the field of behavioural sciences in dentistry, including treatment of patients with various oro-related behavioural dysfunctions, psychosocial aspects of pain in the dental setting and psychosocial aspects of bad breath (halitosis).

Renu Sharma, PhD, DCAH : Reader in Department of Psychology, The M. S. University of Baroda. She is the coordinator and faculty for the course "Diploma in Clinical and Applied Hypnotherapy."

Anil Lalwani, BA : PG Student, Department of Psychology, The M.S. University of Baroda.

Reena Biswas, PhD, GQHP : Clinical and Transpersonal Hypnotherapist in private practice in UK.

Sanil Mathew, MA : Student Counsellor, Loyola College of Social Sciences, Trivendrum.

Keyur Vyas, MTech : Post Graduate engineer from IIT, Mumbai. He is an entrepreneur and professional in System Design and Process Control.

Rajni Vyas, MD : Obstetrician and Gynaecologist in private practice and visiting professor of Hypnotherapy at Department of Psychology, The M. S. University of Baroda. She has pioneering research in the field of infertility. She has taught at the Medical College, The M. S. University of Baroda. She has studied Hindu and Buddhist meditation. A versatile scientific training has enabled her to advanced understanding of Patanjali's Raj Yoga as well as Vajrayana practice. This understanding of mind-body continuum is visible in her practice.

Geeta Adwanikar, MD, DGO : Obstetrician and Gynaecologist in private practice at Vadodara. She is an avid reader of Indian philosophy and scriptures.

Leena Hathi, MD : Physician in private practice at Vadodara.

Ratubhai Parikh, MD : Former Professor in Social Psychiatry, The M. S. University of Baroda, Vadodara.

B. M. Palan, MD, D Clin. Hypno. (USA) : Physiologist and Hypnotherapist in private practice and visiting professor of Hypnotherapy at Department of Psychology, The M. S. University of Baroda. He has taught Physiology in Medical College and has headed the Psychosomatic Medicine and Hypnotherapy Clinic at the S. S. G. Hospital, Vadodara.

Maitri Shah MD, DCAH : Associate Professor, Department of Obstetrics and Gynaecology, Medical College, The M. S. University of Baroda, Vadodara.

Sejal Thakkar MD, DCAH : Associate Professor, Department of Skin and V. D., Medical College, The M. S. University of Baroda, Vadodara.

Urmi Nanda Biswas, PhD, DCAH : Reader, Department of Psychology, The M. S. University of Baroda, Vadodara. Honorary Senior Research Fellow, Centre for Clinical & Health Psychology, Roehempton University, London, UK.

Priyanka Kacker, MA : PhD scholar, Department of Psychology, The M. S. University of Baroda, Vadodara.

Ritu Nanda, PhD : Clinical Psychologist and Therapist. Consultant, Ayushman Hospital, Bhopal; Counsellor, Delhi Public School, Bhopal.

Bhupinder Singh, PhD : Reader and Head, Department of Psychology, Barkatullah University, Bhopal.

Bhavana H. Jadav, MBBS, DCCP, DCAH : Physician in Private Practice at Vadodara

Suresh L. Sadhwani, MD, DCAH : Pathologist, Private Practitioner at Vadodara.

Ruta Vyas, MA, DCAH : Teacher and Counsellor, Navrachana International School, Vadodara.

Aarohi Parimu Khar, MA, DCAH : Lecturer, Vivekanand Education Society of Arts, Science and Commerce, Mumbai.

Mukesh Trivedi, MBBS, DCAH, PGCIH, FCGP, FICA (U.S.A.) : Behaviour Psychiatrist and Corporate Trainer, Consultant Physician-Hypnotherapist and Psychotherapist, Stress Management Specialist, Vadodara.

Veena Gupta, MA, DCAH : PhD Scholar, Department of Human Development and Family Studies, The M. S. University of Baroda, Vadodara.

V. N. Jha, PhD : Former Director of Centre of Advanced Study in Sanskrit in Pune, PhD on Vedic Literature, Specialization in Nyaya and Mimansa.

Rupa Vyas, MS, FRCS, MA (Phil.) : Practicing Physician in UK.

Ranjan K. Panda, PhD : Assistant Professor, Humanities and Social Sciences, Indian Institute of Technology, Mumbai.

Shilendra S. Sharma, PhD : Head, Department of Philosophy, Saurashtra University, Rajkot.

C. B. Vadher, PhD : Lecturer, DH Arts College, Saurashtra University, Rajkot.

PART I
History and Psychological Perspectives

1

Hypnosis, Yoga and Psychic Phenomena

K. RAMAKRISHNA RAO

Yoga, psychic phenomena and hypnosis appear to belong to a common family. All the three subject areas had their origin in prevalent practices and have since struggled for an acceptable theoretical niche. They share a long and chequered history; but have a relatively short scientific journey. For long, they were cloaked in mystery and closeted along with supernatural phenomena. About a century ago, a process of demystification and naturalization began giving us a measure of scientific understanding of these areas. In recent years, they have attracted increasing scientific attention and some recognition and yet continue to be academically controversial. Notwithstanding the proven application of scientific method to investigate problem areas, a cloud of conceptual ambiguity and methodological mist hang over these fields.

Their similar histories are in some ways lessons in history and sociology of science. More importantly, apart from their historic commonalities, yoga, psychic phenomena and hypnosis may be seen to share a common ground in human condition that is at once the chilling source of controversies as well as the challenging potential and promise for the future of the humankind. The present exercise is a modest attempt to cover that ground, which I would like to think is the meeting point of mind/consciousness on one side and the body/brain on the other. The implication of this common ground goes beyond the individual disciplines to impact on our understanding of the very basics of human nature.

Historical Roots

First, let us remind ourselves of the common historical roots of these three disciplines that are in some ways shrouded in public misconceptions. What we have come to recognize as hypnosis today was a craft that was widely practiced around the world for millennia by Chinese, Egyptians, Indians, Hebrews, Greeks, and Romans. They were embedded in a variety of healing techniques (Muses, 1972). "Laying on of hands" to heal and stroking of hands to allay pain and induce sleep-like states are older than Christianity. Similarly, yoga has a long history dating perhaps back to pre-Vedic times as a tool of personal transformation and an instrument to gain access to extraordinary abilities. Again, the belief in psychic phenomena is as old as recorded human history. King Croesus of Lydia successfully carried out a field study to test the paranormal abilities of the reputed Oracle at Delphi (Dodds, 1971).

The Biblical "laying on of hands" went through various phases of transformation and naturalization culminating in the advent of Mesmerism. Franz Anton Mesmer (1734-1815) wrote a dissertation as a medical student in Vienna in 1776 on the physical and medical influence of the planets. He theorized that sun, moon and stars influenced our bodies through the medium of a subtle fluid that encompasses the entire universe. Speculations concerning such magnetic fluid were made before him by others like Paraelsus and Van Helmont. As Podmore (1902) points out, "not only did Mesmer borrow his theories ready-made from earlier mystics, but even the name "magnetic" was in common use in the seventeenth and eighteenth centuries to denote the sympathetic system of medicine which was founded on those mystical doctrines" (p. 44). But Mesmer went beyond mere speculation and his experiments convinced him that he had a technique of far reaching therapeutic implications. First, he observed that he could influence a number of physiological functions such as blood flow by passing magnets over his patients. He later found that the magnets were not necessary and that the same effects could be obtained by pointing his fore finger at the patient or by passing any other object which he "magnetized."

In the course of the therapeutic session the patients manifested a variety of bizarre behaviours. Some went into convulsions. Some were seen in a dissociative state. Catalepsy and violent movements were not uncommon. These were regarded as *crisis* states, which were believed to accelerate healing. During the *crisis* states Mesmer noted the instances of what we now call as ESP, that patients responded to signals hidden from them. They had veridical visions and caused physical effects in non-normal ways. Instances of self-diagnosis and diagnosing the illness of others were not uncommon.

Mesmer's technique soon became popular among the rich and the fashionable circles and his practice flourished in Paris. The medical establishment remained, however, skeptical and even hostile. But Mesmer was successful in converting a few prominent people to his enticing art. Among them was Charles D'Eslon, physician to the Court d'Artois, brother of Louis XVI. This royal connection eventually led to the appointment of a Commission in 1784 to inquire into the claims of animal magnetism.

The Commission consisting of four members each from the Faculty of Medicine and the Society Royal de Medicine, and five delegates from the Academy of Sciences including Benjamin Franklin, then American Ambassador in France, observed the practice of animal magnetism by D'Eslon, a friend and disciple of Mesmer.

The Commission did not evaluate the curative effects of mesmeric trance, but concerned itself to examine the evidence for the existence of a physical force which Mesmer and his followers regarded as the agent involved in the healing process. Nine members of the Commission in the first report found no evidence for the existence of such a force and that the effects might be produced by the patient's imagination alone. In a confidential note the Commission even warned of the harmful effects of the practices.

The second report signed five days later belonging to the Society Royal de Medicine said much the same. One of these members, M. de Jussiere, however, disagreed. He thought that the Commission should look also into the alleged physiological and curative aspects of these practices through careful observations and experiments with individual patients. He himself noted what seemed to be cases of action at a distance that patients responded to the movement of a magnetized object which was not seen by them. These observations indicated that these effects seemed to be independent of the patient's imagination. This was a minority view. The findings of the Commission and their implications were unambiguously negative.

The publication of the Commission reports had the expected effect of removing the theories of Mesmer from the arena of scientific inquiry. But it did not stop public interest in animal magnetism or the practice of it by a few. Among prominent practitioners were de Puysegur and J. P. F. Deleuze. Puysegur, a pupil of Mesmer "magnetized" a huge tree on his estate and the patients attached themselves to the tree with ropes. Like Mesmer's patients with the tub, the *baquet,* Puysegur's patients too were being magnetized by their connection to the tree and experienced similar *crisis* period. He also noted the special *rapport* that existed between the patient and the operator so that the former responded only to the latter and no one else in the trance period. Delueze, who believed that the magnetized patients could receive information independent of the conventional senses, thought that the magnetic fluid conveyed the information directly to the mind without the mediation of the senses. It is important to note that neither Puysegur nor Delueze was inclined to attribute the phenomena to anything but natural causes. But there were, of course, others who thought that the trance effects were due to the spiritual world.

A young physician in Paris, Alexander Bertrand, published two important books in 1823 and 1826, which reviewed trance phenomena and the various theories offered to explain them. He concluded that the belief in the existence of a fluid, whether celestial or magnetic, is a myth and that the trance effects are due to the suggestion. His own observations of trance behaviour led him to believe that on occasions the somnambulists exhibited phenomena indicating action at a distance and a faculty of paranormal perception. Some of them were able to accurately describe the symptoms of ailments in great detail when placed in *rapport* with the sick person. Bertrand, unlike Delueze, rejected the physical explanations of trance phenomena and preferred a psychological interpretation.

After an acrimonious debate in December of 1825, the Royal Academy of Medicine at Paris appointed the Second French Commission to examine the somnambulistic trance phenomena. The Commission presented the report in June of 1831, which essentially upheld the genuineness of the somnambulistic trance state and suggested that it could be an important adjunct to medical practice. This was an important step in rehabilitating Mesmerism. The history of hypnosis, as it has come to be known, shows, however, a series of ups and downs before it finally came to be accepted as genuine phenomena worthy of scientific study.

Modern Spiritualism

In a sense, Mesmerism was a precursor of modern spiritualism as it first arose in U.S.A. and later in the British Isles and Europe. While many of the practitioners of Mesmer's art adhered to a naturalistic interpretation of the trance phenomena, there were others who attributed the somnambulistic utterances of entranced patients to spirit agencies.

Some philosophers in Germany readily saw in trance phenomena more cogent evidence for mystical belief in spirits. In Sweden, attempts were made to show how the spiritistic interpretation of trance utterances was consistent with the Swedenborgian view of man's intercourse with the spirit world.

First, Joseph du Commun and, a few years later, Charles Poyen introduced Mesmerism in America. Their lectures especially those of Poyen in Boston in 1836 attracted the attention of a few physicians and some medical students. Soon the strange phenomena spread across the country by "travelling magnetists" who were no more than stage entertainers who demonstrated the phenomena for a fee. At the same time there arose magnetic healers some of whom proclaimed the intervention of spirits in their practice. Prominent among them was Andrew Jackson Davis who published in 1847 a treatise entitled *Nature's Divine Revelations* that at once became a sourcebook of spiritualism.

Davis was seventeen years old and was apprenticing in a shoe shop when a travelling magnetist Stanley Grimes came in the fall of 1843 to Poughkeepsie, N.Y., the native town of Davis. Grime's visit created a lot of excitement. Davis met Grimes who did not find Davis a good magnetic subject. Davis soon came into contact with a local tailor and an amateur mesmerist by name William Levington, who not only magnetized Davis but also discovered that Davis had clairvoyant abilities and that he could in a trance state diagnose ailments in people. Encouraged by their success they soon gave up their trades to become full-time magnetic healers. Davis, in addition to diagnosing the disease of those present, practiced remote diagnosis. By holding the hand of a friend or relation of an absent patient, Davis attempted to diagnose the ailment and prescribed a remedy. This he did while he was magnetized and put in a trance state by Levington.

In 1845, Davis broke up with Levington and began working with Silas Lyon as his magnetizer until the spring of 1847 when he realized that he could exercise his clairvoyant and diagnostic skills without being magnetized and that he could at will receive and recall messages from the other "world."

Convinced that he was an instrument for transmitting divine revelation, Davis arranged to transcribe his trance utterances bearing on philosophical and spiritual issues. William Fishbough, a Universalist minister was hired for this purpose. Davis who had little schooling and obviously no great learning gave a series of philosophical and theological lectures. Fishbough edited and put them in a publishable form. They were published in 1847 under the title *Nature's Divine Revelations : The Principles of Nature, Her Divine Revelations and a Voice to Mankind*. The book, which ran through four editions in the first year of its publication, received considerable attention and made Davis a minor celebrity.

Davis claimed to be in communion with spirits of deceased persons and that he was inspired while in trance state by the spirits of the Greek physician Yalen and Emanuel Swedenborg to practice healing and preach spiritual philosophy. He was clearly instrumental in many ways in promoting spiritistic philosophy through his writings and magazines like *The Universoleum* and *Spiritual Philosopher* he had helped to establish. The birth of modern spiritualism, however, is not traced to Andrew Jackson Davis, but to the strange happenings in an obscure hamlet in upstate New York in 1848.

John D. Fox moved in December of 1847 with his wife and children, to a farmhouse in Hydesville, N.Y. The Foxes had seven children. Three of them, Margaret and Catherine who were living with them at the time and Leah who lived in Rochester and taught for a living, were involved in the happenings that led to the outbreak of spiritualism.

Margaret was about ten years old and Kate, her sister, was seven when strange happenings began at their house in March of 1848. Noises of unknown origin were heard in all parts of the house during nights, but not during the day. These strange sounds included light rappings, knocks, footsteps and walking noise. The family felt that the house was haunted. One night, it is told, Kate challenged the spirit. She asked Mr. Splitfoot to do what she did; count one, two, three by clapping with her hands. Raps appeared following Kate's command. When asked to count ten, there appeared ten strokes from apparently nowhere. The family was convinced that the source of the sounds was the spirit of a peddler who was believed to be murdered and buried in the cellar of the house.

Convinced that the problem was connected with the house, the family moved to the house of David Fox, which was about two miles away. But the raps followed them to the David's house. They soon discovered that the raps occurred only in the presence of Catherine. Then, they decided to send Kate to live with her elder sister Leah in Rochester. The very first night Kate and Leah arrived in Rochester, the disturbances appeared there also. Soon the "spirits" began answering questions by an ingenious method. Some one would recite the alphabet. The spirit would rap to indicate the proper alphabet. The alphabet so retrieved would give a message ostensibly from the controlling spirit. Back in Hydesville the rappings did not stop with Kate leaving for Rochester. They continued, but now in the presence of Margaret.

As one would expect, the happenings in Hydesville and Rochester attracted the attention of a lot of people some of whom did believe that spirits were behind these strange events. Leah sensing the prospects of commercializing the phenomena associated with her sisters, Margaret and Kate arranged private sittings with clients for a fee. She also hired a large auditorium in the city of Rochester to demonstrate to the public. Each night a committee was selected to inquire into the phenomena. The first two committees heard the raps and found no evidence of fraud. The third committee too found no way of explaining the raps even though it felt that trickery was a strong possibility. The final meeting itself ended in a pandemonium when rowdies took over and the police had to escort the Foxes home. This incident did not, however, prevent the Fox sisters going around Auburn, Albany, New York and Buffalo giving sittings and holding public demonstrations and collecting handsome fees.

The public interest in the phenomena exhibited by the Fox sisters was high. Reports of similar happenings had sprung up in many parts of the country. But then there were also skepticism and allegations of trickery and deceit. For example, three professors from the University of Buffalo who observed Leah and Margaret had no doubt that it was all fraud. They believed that the raps emanate from the knee joints of the sisters. When cushions were placed under the heels and legs stretched full length, they observed no raps. These observations they thought, were sufficient proof that the raps came from the voluntary action of muscles on knee joints. Rev. Potts gave a demonstration on the stage to show how he could snap his toes to produce strange sounds. C. C. Burr and his brother Herman went on lecturing to expose the Foxes until Leah sued them for slander. The skepticism was reinforced when Mrs. Norman Culver who was related to the Fox family signed a sworn affidavit claiming that Kate had confessed to her of trickery in producing the manifestations. There were also those like E. W. Capron who defended the sisters by alleging that Culver's statement was a fabrication. Again, there were other manifestations in the sittings of the Fox sisters that cannot be explained by the knee joint hypothesis.

Several important and influential persons who witnessed the performances of Margaret and Kate were duly convinced that the Foxes were not hoaxes. Among them were those who seemed to believe in the spiritual origin of those raps such as Judge J. W. Edmonds of New York and Governor Nathaniel Tallmadge of Wisconsin. Though Horace Greeley of *New York Tribune* did not fully accept spiritualism, he did visit the Foxes, arranged for their sittings in his home and could never find a normal explanation for the phenomena he witnessed.

Despite the notoriety and ridicule in some quarters, the interest in the phenomena manifested in the presence of the Fox sisters was no doubt high. The interest spread well beyond the New York state to as far as St. Louis. Also mediums appeared in various parts of the country, sometimes producing far more interesting phenomena than the raps and knocks. Trance speaking and automatic writing became more common and popular than wrappings. Even musical spirits and drawing mediums appeared. Speaking in languages unknown to the medium was also not uncommon. Thus there was a growing variety of "spiritual" phenomena by the mid-fifties.

As the decade came to a close, spiritualism was still flourishing, but the fame of the Fox sisters faded partly because Leah got married and retired from spiritual practices and Margaret had withdrawn. Also, there were too many mediums producing far more dramatic phenomena than the Fox sisters. As the sisters went into the background, Davis emerged as the main spokesperson for spiritualism. He travelled and lectured extensively and organized the Harmonial Brotherhood to promote spiritualism. He gave up magnetic healing and concentrated on the discussion of the philosophical and theological implications of spiritualism. He feared that the popular preoccupation with mediumistic phenomena might undermine the basic tenets of spiritualism and their benefits to humankind.

Spiritualist phenomena of the kind manifested by Fox sisters was of less interest compared to a variety of phenomena appearing in the séance rooms of celebrated mediums in the US, UK and in some other parts of Europe. This led to a number of prominent scientists like Sir William Crookes, President of Royal Society, to undertake the study of psychic phenomena. In 1882, the Society for Psychical Research was established in England soon followed by similar societies in USA and France. Prominent scientists and scholars such as Oliver Lodge and William James were associated with them. It is interesting to note that hypnosis and psychical research appealed to some of these scientists for the same reasons. A number of telepathic studies were undertaken with hypnotized subjects by the SPR members. Charles Richet (1850-1935), the French Nobel laureate in physiology, carried out experiments in hypnosis as well as ESP. In fact, he was the first to use mathematics of probability to evaluate experimental ESP results. Richet also published an article on hypnosis (induced somnambulism) in 1875 and, in some ways, he was instrumental in introducing Jean Martin Charcot, who later became the leader of hypnosis in Paris. Again, in more recent years, there are people like Charles Tart who made significant contributions to hypnosis as well as psychical research which currently goes under the name of parapsychology.

Hypnosis and ESP

Hypnosis figures in parapsychological research on two counts. In some of the early studies, hypnosis was only an effect produced by telepathy. Gibert (Myers, 1903) for example, was reportedly successful in inducing somnambulistic trance in Madame B, a subject of Pierre Janet, by mental suggestion, i.e., telepathy. Myers also refers to a number of other cases such as that of Madame D, who was hypnotized from a distance by

Hericourt, an assistant of Richet, and of Adams who described how a guest of his twice succeeded in hypnotizing a servant at a distance of fifty miles. Myers was himself so convinced of the genuineness of telepathic hypnotization. He wrote, "It has now ... been actually proved that the hypnotic trance can be induced from a distance so great, and with precautions so complete, that telepathy or some similar supernormal influence is the only efficient cause which can be conceived" (1903, p. 207). Platonov, Ketkov, and Vasiliev have also been known to have successfully induced hypnosis by means of telepathy. Vasiliev (1963) reported, a few years before his death, his studies with hypnosis made in the 1930s. According to the reports, he was highly successful in inducing hypnotic trance in his subjects through mental suggestion from great distances.

If there is any element of paranormality in the above cases, it is difficult to discern what precisely is the role of hypnosis. It is likely, since the subjects almost invariably had been hypnotized prior to these tests, that there existed between the subject and the experimenter a kind of relationship that is commonly characterized as *rapport* which might have facilitated a type of extrasensory induction.

Cases of apparent thought transference between hypnotizer and his hypnotized subject are not uncommon. Azam observed, for example, that one of his patients in a hypnotic state responded to an unspoken thought of his. These observations naturally led to the investigations of hypnotic states (Rhine, 1947). Mrs. Sidgwick, using two digit numbers, experimented with hypnotized subjects, and satisfied herself that telepathy between the agent and the percipient was involved even when they were in two different rooms (Sidgwick, Sidgwick & Smith, 1889).

The methodological limitations of the earlier experiments using hypnosis apart, one does not know too much from these results what precisely is the role of hypnosis. To say that significant results are obtained in tests using hypnosis does not mean very much. Other tests without hypnosis also yielded similar or even better results. Any systematic evaluation of results of hypnotic studies of psi (a general term for psychic phenomena) should attempt to answer the following questions.

1. Does psi manifest when the subjects are in a hypnotic state?
2. If it does, is it any more pronounced or reliable than in the waking state?
3. Is the success obtained in hypnotic states attributable to increased motivation either due to explicit suggestion or otherwise?
4. Or does hypnosis produce any specially favourable state of mind or a level of awareness that is appropriate to heightened psi activity?

Here are some of the reports of experimental work on ESP with hypnosis. Using ESP cards, Grela (1945) tested eleven subjects in four sessions. One of them was without hypnosis and the other three were with hypnosis. In the three hypnotic sessions, positive, neutral, and negative suggestions were given one at a time. His subjects obtained a significant deviation in the sessions where positive hypnotic suggestion was given. They had their lowest scores when negative suggestion was given.

But Rhine (1946) reported that his subjects who were scoring well above MCE before hypnosis dropped way below in the post-hypnotic test period. This was contrary to his suggestion. He concluded : "The important finding, and one that stands out fairly clearly, is that there *was* an effect. The hypnosis did something, even though in four out of six cases it was a reversal of the intended effect" (p. 138).

A similar result was also reported by Nash and Durkin (1959) who gave two of their subjects 300 trials each with single digits as targets in the waking state and an equal number of trials under hypnosis with positive suggestion. The subject obtained a positive deviation when they were working in the waking state and a negative deviation under hypnosis. There was a statistically significant difference between the scores of the two states.

Fahler (1957) obtained significant positive results when his subjects were hypnotized. They scored only at the chance level during the waking state. Another experiment by Fahler and

Cadoret (1958) at Duke, gave similar results confirming the former's findings in Finland.

Lawrence Casler (1964) unlike Fahler, gave explicit suggestions for improvement in scoring. Both the preliminary and the main experiments involving a large group of subjects gave significant scores when the subjects worked under hypnotic suggestion. Casler (1964, p. 86) thinks that 'the induction of hypnosis, in essence, opens up potentialities of communication which may give the individual's psi capacities the opportunity to express themselves.' In an earlier study where the subjects were given no suggestions, Casler (1962) observed that scoring in the hypnotized runs was significantly higher than in the waking state.

Hypothesizing that hypnosis might help accentuate ESP in both directions (positive and negative), Charles Honorton (1964) divided his subjects into predicted low-scorers and predicted high-scorers on the basis of a fourteen-item interest inventory. He found that the predicted low-scorers obtained negative deviation which was higher during the hypnotic condition than in the waking condition, and that there was a significant difference between the predicted high and low-scorers in the hypnotic condition alone. A subsequent study by him confirmed these results (Honorton, 1966).

I used hypnosis in some of my studies not with an intention to test whether the subjects do any better during that state, but to create through suggestion a specially favourable psychological state in which ESP may be obtained more readily. In one experiment (Rao, 1964) my subject did two runs in each session in her normal state and followed them with two runs in a relaxed state created with the help of hypnotic suggestion. I found that the subject scored significantly more hits in the relaxed state than in the pre-relaxed period. It is difficult to draw any confident conclusions from this study which involved only one subject and did not rule out experimenter motivation as a relevant factor.

The cumulative effect of all the experimenters of that period was very well summarized by R. H. Thouless (1963). 'Some experimenters', he wrote, "have reported better scores under hypnosis, some have obtained worse scores in that condition, and in some experiments scores have not been affected by hypnosis. In no case has anything been reported that suggests that we are within sight of the goal of producing reliably high psi scoring by the use of hypnosis."

However, the work of Ryzl has now opened up new potentialities. Milan Ryzl (1962) thinks that with the aid of hypnosis the subjects can be trained to produce psi at will under experimental conditions. Miss J. K., who had shown no ESP abilities prior to her hypnotic training, gave fantastically high scores with the help of the training that she received from Ryzl. Ryzl (Ryzl & Ryzlova, 1962) also trained another outstanding subject, Pavel Stepenek, who did not show any psi ability before undergoing hypnotic training. An important feature of Pavel's work is that once he was able to obtain highly significant scores in a state of self-induced hypnosis, he continued to do so even during waking states. He was able to produce significant results without hypnosis in the presence of visiting parapsychologists from other counties (Ryzl & Pratt, 1962). It is interesting to note that hypnotic training proved very fruitful in the case of J. K. as well as Pavel, however, for Pavel once he acquired the ability, hypnosis was no longer necessary.

Ryzl's method of training is quite simple. The training process has four stages. In the first stage, the subject is simply hypnotized with a view to increase "his suggestibility as much as possible . . . . to obtain the necessary inhibition of cerebral activity and convincing him that he is (will be ?) able to acquire the ability of extrasensory perception..." (Ryzl, 1962). The second stage consists in producing visual hallucinations. During the third stage, the subject is trained to hallucinate ESP targets and to distinguish veridical hallucinations from false ones resulting either from misinterpreting experimenter's suggestions or from a variety of other unconscious or subliminal sources. Finally, the subject is trained to do these things independently of the experimenter. I interpret the first stage as one of creating faith and self-confidence in the subject. The second is one of conditioning the subject to a peculiar stage of mind whose chief characteristic is one of receiving hallucinatory images. The third and the most important stage is two-pronged, consisting of introspective search for recognizing the veridical stages and of conditioning himself to them so that he can produce them at will. Here, we find in practice the important suggestion of Tart, a learning paradigm. The secret of Ryzl's success may well be this, i.e., the creation of a receptive state in which the subject conditions himself to successful responses. When his subject Pavel apparently lost his ability, Ryzl helped him to regain it, at least temporarily, by asking him to practice at home with a set of target cards, guessing and checking so that he would know after each call whether it was a correct or an incorrect one.

Ryzl's work was thus the most hopeful of all the studies involving hypnosis. I recognize that Ryzl's case is not conclusive, and that the outstanding success of one or two subjects of the many he had doubtless tested and attempted to train may well have been due to factors other than the training itself. I also note that attempts by John Beloff and Mandleberg (1966) to repeat Ryzl's work were not successful. My hope, I believe, has two justifications, however. First, Ryzl's is the only outstanding case that suggests the possibility of training for ESP through hypnosis. And second, his method seems to have certain similarities with the technique of yoga that has traditionally been credited in the East with helping the practitioner to obtain supernormal abilities.

Now, the answer to our first question, whether psi occurs in hypnotic states, the answer is clearly in the affirmation. Yes, it does. However, what this really means is not that clear. Does it occur more pronouncedly and reliably in a hypnotic state? A review of all the available studies of hypnosis and ESP in 1977 by Honorton showed that 22 of 42 studies that investigated ESP using hypnosis provided significant evidence in support of ESP hypothesis. The proportion of significant studies (52%) when you expect 5 per cent by chance is statistically highly significant, suggesting a positive relation between ESP and hypnosis. A more systematic meta-analysis of the experimental studies of ESP and hypnosis by Ephraim Schechter (1984) confirms that subjects tend to obtain higher ESP scores in hypnotic state than in a controlled waking state. Ten years later, Rex Stanford and Adam Stein (1994) published another meta-analysis of ESP-hypnosis studies. They also found significant evidence for ESP in the hypnosis condition. They caution, however, against any definitive conclusions from the current database for two reasons. First, they note that the observed difference in ESP scores between hypnotic and the contrast conditions is significant only when the comparison condition preceded the hypnotic condition. Second, they call attention to the fact that there is significant psi-missing in the control condition, i.e., subjects obtained significantly fewer hits than expected by chance in the control condition, which requires an explanation beyond the facilitative effect of hypnosis on ESP scoring.

Now, if indeed hypnosis has a facilitative effect on ESP, as the evidence indicates, the question arises as to why that it is the case. What do we know about hypnosis that is likely responsible for its being a psi conducive state? Simply, what is hypnosis? What are the essential characteristics of the hypnotic state? Hypnosis is notoriously ambiguous as to what it really is. For this reason, it is said that "hypnosis has eluded a single, simple definition. This is not surprising; the field is far from reaching a consensus about how to explain hypnotic phenomena. What is the essence of hypnosis for one theorist is mere artifact for another" (Lynn & Rhue, 1991, p. 3). Theories of hypnosis range from Pavlovian "suggested sleep" (Pavlov, 1923) to neodissociation theory of E. R. Hilgard (1977). Then, there are, of course, the socio-psychological and cognitive models that stand in opposition to the dissociation models (Spanos & Barber, 1974).

Discussing the nature of hypnosis, Charles Tart (1967) remarks how terribly ambiguous is the word 'hypnosis.' Pointing out several sources of variability in hypnosis which include subject characteristics, demand characteristics of the situation, lack of adaptation to hypnosis and the pseudo-operational definition of hypnosis, Tart calls our attention to a core of important phenomena that can be induced by hypnosis.

Among these are physical relaxation, increased suggestibility and reduction of spontaneous thought processes. There is also an enhancement of internal imagery which enables the hypnotized subject to visualize something with greater clarity than is usual. As Tart points out through hypnosis "you are able to bring about a highly selective deployment of attention. We can alter a subject's perception of himself, his body image, his ego boundaries, and his perception of other people in the environment . . . . You can also alter his perception of object, space, and time. You can induce strong desires, emotions, or needs, and you can even alter his cognitive processes in certain ways. This has been called trance logic : one of its features is the acceptance of incongruities that would be cognitively unacceptable in the waking state. Other interesting features of hypnosis are increased access to unconscious and preconscious material, and altered memory function including total and selective amnesias" (Tart, 1967, pp. 26-27).

Emphasizing relaxation as the basic state of hypnosis, William Edmonston, Jr., adds the following other dependent features : "the dissociation of parts of our cognitive, sensory, and motor activities; the diminution of ego controls; and an occasional amnesic period" (1981, p. 197).

It is observed that people who report spontaneous psychic experiences tend to have dissociative tendencies (Pekala, Kumar, & Marcane, 1995). If hypnotic susceptibility, like psychological absorption, is a dimension of dissociative processes, it makes sense why hypnotic state is psi conducive. Further, parapsychological research has shown that relaxation is also a psi conducive condition.

Relaxation and ESP

Several subjects who have done well on psi tests have claimed that they did their best when they were physically relaxed and their minds were in a "blank" state. Mary Sinclair, whom her husband, novelist Upton Sinclair, found to be an outstanding subject, gave the following advice : "You first give yourself a 'suggestion' to the effect that you will relax your mind and your body, making the body insensitive and the mind a blank" (Sinclair, 1930, p. 180). Rhea White (1964), who reviewed the early literature on this topic, also concluded that attempts "to still the body and mind" are common among the techniques used by successful subjects.

There are 33 ESP studies in which progressive relaxation procedures have been used. Seventeen of these gave significant results. The most extensive work in this area was carried out by William Braud and associates. In the first experiment (Braud & Braud, 1974) there were 16 subjects and the subjects self-rated their degree of relaxation. Braud and Braud report that those who performed well in the ESP tests rated themselves as more relaxed than the poor psi performers. The second experiment consisted of 20 volunteer subjects who were assigned randomly to "relaxation" or "tension" conditions. Those in the relaxation condition went through a taped, progressive-relaxation procedure (an adaptation of Jacobson's) before taking an ESP test, which was to guess the picture being "transmitted" by an agent in another room. The subjects in the other group were given taped, tension-inducing instructions before they did the same ESP test. Each subject's level of relaxation was assessed through electromyographic recordings. The EMG results showed a significant decrease in the EMG activity among the subjects in the "relaxation" group and a significant increase among those in the "tension" group; and as predicted, the ESP scores of the subjects in the relaxation group were significantly higher than those of the subjects in the tension group. Other reports of interest are Braud and Braud (1973), Braud (1975), and Altom and Braud (1976). Confirmation of Braud's results may be found in Stanford and Mayer (1974).

Yoga and Psychic Phenomena

If paranormal phenomena are associated with hypnosis, they are more like an occasional by-product rather than an essential aspect of hypnosis. The case is somewhat different with yoga. With yoga, psychic experiences are believed to be a natural manifestation following practice of yoga. So we find the third part of Patanjali's *Yoga-Sūtras* discussing in great detail paranormal abilities (*siddhis*). Again, like hypnosis, yoga means different things. First, yoga is one of the six systems of orthodox Hindu philosophy. Second, yoga indicates a state of *samādhi*, a focussed and absorbed state of the mind where the normal fluctuations of the mind are under voluntary control. Third, yoga refers to a set of practices that are believed to enable the practitioner to gain mind-body control. There is, however, just not one set of practices, but a variety of them ranging from routine bodily exercises to advanced meditation. In popular mind, yoga is a regimen of bodily and breathing exercises, systematized differently by different yoga writers and teachers. If one follows the tradition of Patanjali, there are eight distinctive steps. Patanjali combines in his *Yoga-Sūtras*, the theory as well as practices of yoga.

In brief the psyche (*citta*), according to yoga, is ordinarily in a state of continuous fluctuations. As a result of these fluctuations, we perceive, reason and obtain valid knowledge, as well as experience illusions and acquire false knowledge. Imagination, sleep, and memory are also resultant experiences of the fluctuations in the psyche. The fluctuations in the psyche are caused by the external stimuli and internal forces which include the *samskāras* and *vāsanas* of this life as well as of the previous life. But there is power (*sakti*) stored up in the psyche, which is capable of acting on its own. In order that the psyche can act on its own, it is necessary that the fluctuations of the psyche are controlled. Yoga formulates a psychophysiological method which would help us restrict the fluctuations that obstruct the psyche from acting independently of the senses. As is well known, Patanjali defines yoga as that which controls the fluctuations of the psyche (I.2). The yoga method has become so popular in India that the word yoga has come to be synonymous with the method itself. Not only do other schools of thought in India advocate the practice of yoga, but many in other countries and a few other faiths also believe in it (Dechanet, 1960).

The first-two steps in the eight-fold yoga practice are *yama* and *niyama* which include certain moral commandments such as truthfulness, non-stealing, continence, cleanliness and contentment. The next two, *āsana* and *prāṇāyāma*, are physical exercises that involve practicing certain physical postures and practicing breath control. The fifth state, *pratyāhāra*, is simple internally focussed attention designed to understand the workings of the psyche. The last three *dhārana* (concentration), *dhyāna* (meditation), and *samādhi* are the most important ones in attaining the yogic state. They together constitute meditation proper.

The first-five are preparatory and indirect aids to yoga whereas the last three are essential yoga. The need for the ethical and physiological practices in the yogic training is not difficult to understand. Desires and sensory indulgence encourage further involvement in the sensory processes that result in the constant fluctuations of the psyche which are precisely those yoga seeks to control. The physical exercises are also designed, on the one hand, to control internal processes in the body from causing fluctuations in the psyche and, on the other, to reduce the sensory input from outside. The practice of breath control, for example, could result in a greater control of the physiological processes in the body. The *pratyāhāra*, the internal attention stage is quite important. It is what appears to be the connecting link between the physiological and the psychological exercises. It is by *pratyāhāra* the practitioner of yoga is able to regulate the body to suit the requirements of his mental states. My guess is that this enables the *yogin* to isolate such of his experiences which he is seeking and to produce them later at will.

Now, the objective of all these exercises is to enable one to concentrate. There are some persons who could achieve desired levels of concentration without these exercises. They, of course, could skip them. Concentration or *dhārana* produces in us a state in which the natural wandering of our thoughts or the fluctuations of the psyche are brought under control. In this state of concentration, the psyche attends to one thing so that there is intensification of activity of the mind in one direction. In a state of concentration, the focus of attention is narrowed. This focus is expanded when one goes from the stage of concentration to meditation or *dhyāna*. Meditation helps to concentrate longer and to fix our attention on any object for a length of time. When this is achieved, the psyche progresses to a standstill state, where the mind is steady and becomes one with the object of concentration. The person is completely absorbed in what he is doing.

If the physical exercises help the inhibition of cerebral activities, concentration, it would seem, enables one to reverse the cognitive process. When the desired levels of concentration are achieved, the psyche is no longer affected by stimuli acting on it. Concentration not only helps to inhibit stimuli exciting the psyche and causing fluctuations in it, but enables the individual to focus attention on desired objects. When this is achieved, the psyche can make a contact directly with the object, and obtain supersensuous knowledge. There are thus three important aspects to yoga. Firstly, there is the inhibition of cerebral activity, withdrawing of the senses. Secondly, the psyche is activated by concentration. And, finally, the expansion of concentration reverses the role of psyche from one of receiving impressions through senses to one of acting directly so as to take the form of objects.

From the above, it is clear that the essence of yoga is meditation. If yoga helps to gain access to paranormal abilities, then practice of meditation may be psi-conducive. Do we have any evidence for that, apart from the textual statements and anecdotal reports? There is indeed some evidence; and a few studies we have in this area suggest a strong association between ESP and meditation. At Andhra University, we carried out a study some years ago (Rao, Dukhan, & Rao, 1978). Fifty-nine subjects with varying degrees of proficiency in meditation were administered ESP tests before and immediately after they had practiced meditation. The results showed that subjects obtained ESP scores that are significantly higher in the post-meditation than in the pre-meditation sessions. Other meditation studies include those by Schmeider (1970), Osis and Bokert (1971), and Schmidt and Pantas (1972). Honorton's 1972 review shows that 9 out of 16 experimental studies involving meditation provide significant evidence for ESP. This ratio is comparable to what we have noted in the area of hypnosis and ESP.

Hypnosis and Meditation

It has been said that meditation involves some sort of auto-hypnosis (Zorab, 1963). It may well be. The one-pointed concentration and meditation can cause fatigue and the desired monotony to produce a hypnotic state. There are also unquestionable similarities between the two states. In both, the general cerebral activity can be suppressed at will. In both, the attention can be focussed on the desired object to a degree that is definitely superior to the waking state. I should also think that the yogic concentration in its early phases generates hallucinatory imagery similar to that obtained under hypnosis.

Even if we conclude from these similarities that yogic concentration produces a state similar to hypnotic state, it must be admitted that yoga does more. Yoga involves also further training to which claims of paranormality could be attributed. It is in this context, we may refer to the similarities between yoga and Ryzl's technique. Ryzl (1966) describes the state of mind specially favourable for the manifestation of psi in the following words : "it is a particular state of consciousness, defying adequate description, between sleep and waking, which we most likely could characterize as a state of appeasement of mental activity and of depriving the mind of arrival of normal sensory impressions with a simultaneous intensive directing of attention in one direction." This is precisely what yoga claims to do by means of physical exercises and concentration.

Moreover, it seems to me, the process of hallucinating by the subject is quite relevant to the training. The *modus operandi* involved in creating hallucinations and in having extrasensory perceptions may be the same, even though the source is different. The suggestion of Ryzl that the subject should be able to hallucinate in order that he may be successfully trained to get ESP impressions is, therefore, very important and deserves further explorations.

One obvious underlying state characterizing both hypnosis and meditation is relaxation. Relaxed state of the mind and losening of sensory controls appear to be the basic hallmarks or the ground condition of hypnosis as well as meditation. They are also the conducive conditions for the manifestation of psychic phenomena such as ESP. Apart from the psychological observations we made, there are physiological factors associated with these three disciplines that underscore the common ground. EEG studies of hypnosis have shown greater alpha density with hypnosis (Brady & Rosner, 1966; Edmonston & Grotevant, 1975; Melzack & Perry, 1975). There is also some evidence of theta activity in hypnosis (Tebecis *et al.*, 1975). There is also evidence that basal skin resistance increases in hypnosis (Tart, 1963; Edmonston & Pessin, 1966; Tebecis & Provins, 1976). These suggest that hypnosis is a non-aroused relaxed state. Similarly we have data to show alpha abundance in the meditative state and also some theta activity (Lutz *et al.*, 2007). Again, there is evidence to suggest a positive relationship between ESP and alpha activity (Rao, 2001). While electrophysiological research has yielded some other interesting results in the area of hypnosis as well as yoga and meditation, the results are not consistent enough to generalize across all types of mediation or hypnosis. It would seem that advanced forms of meditation enable the practitioner to gain a measure of control over the autonomic activity. Consequently, the meditating subject could alter her neuro-physiological processes so that she could arouse or depress the sympathetic and parasympathetic systems. Therefore, what is crucial are not the neurophysiological correlates of meditation or hypnosis, but the mechanisms involved that enable one to gain control over the autonomic processes. I have reviewed these studies elsewhere (Rao, in print).

One of the widely held views in parapsychology is that sensory noise reduction enhances ESP. For example, subjects appear to give consistent evidence for ESP in the ganzfeld which provides for continuous uniform and unpatterned stimulation such as the one obtained by focussing a uniform red light on the subject with halved ping-pong balls fastened to her eyes (Bem & Honorton, 1994). From all the above, it is clear that hypnosis, yoga and psychic phenomena have several interesting commonalities that indicate some interconnectedness among them. Perhaps they belong to a common family and follow a common rationale.

Conclusion

I will not be surprised if some people specializing in hypnosis are not comfortable with the association I am suggesting with psychic phenomena. It is natural for those who themselves are struggling to find a niche in the world of science to steer clear of the controversial areas like parapsychology.

Let me hasten to add that the reluctance is not one sided. Many parapsychologists would be reluctant to forge any joint front with researchers in hypnosis area. This is again for the same reasons. They see a good deal of hypnosis research methodologically soft and conceptually weak. They consider several of the clinical applications of hypnosis are unsupported by the available data.

Many of my colleagues in Indian psychology would be dismayed at the suggestion of any commonality between yoga and hypnosis. Here, value considerations dominate. There is the fear of undermining the exalted position of yoga as a sacred discipline by vulgarizing *samādhi* as suggestive sleep or a dissociated state of the mind. It is understandable, therefore, if some of the readers consider what I am saying now is somewhat irrelevant and unhelpful. However, my justification for this overview is four fold. First, hypnosis and psychical research share the same roots and have similar developmental histories, which would be unwise to disown. Second, the two disciplines seen in a broader and holistic context may fit into a model that may have a more wholesome implications for theory and testing in both. Third, the possibility of receiving necessary recognition and support is likely to be greater in a combined effort rather than by a fragmented approach. Fourth, the commonalities outlined are the ground conditions of a model closely akin to yoga psychology that would not only make good sense of these disciplines, but also point to new directions of research.

Hypnosis, ESP and meditation, it would seem, are interconnected links in the chain of human science. The three basic participating parts that constitute the person are the gross body, mind and consciousness. The person is consciousness embodied. The body has two dimensions—the gross and the subtle. The gross body includes the brain. The subtle body refers to the mind in its multifold functions. Thus the person is a continuum with body at one end, consciousness at the other, and the mind in the middle. Hypnosis is primarily concerned with the link that connects the two forms of the body, the gross and the subtle, the brain and the mind. Yoga goes beyond to explore the link between mind and consciousness. Psychic phenomena are by-products emerging out of the cultivation of the mind and its transactions following its interconnectedness with body on one side and consciousness on the other. Hypnosis, yoga and psychic phenomena together provide massive evidence against the cerebro-centric model. Man is more than a brain driven machine. The mind influences the processes in the brain. Consciousness is beyond the mind connecting it with extraordinary resources for personal transformation. I hope and trust that psychology in India would take inspiration from the classical Indian texts like *Yoga-Sūtras* and be in the forefront in forging a synthetic psychology of body-mind-consciousness.

Centrality of consciousness is the defining characteristic of Indian psychology. The chief concern here is with the "person." The person is consciousness embodied. In this view, mind and consciousness are qualitatively different. Mind is the interfacing instrumentality that is connected with consciousness at one end and with the brain at the other. Therefore, mind influences and is influenced by brain processes and at the same time holds a special relationship with consciousness. As embodied consciousness, the person becomes the instrument of individualized thought, passion and action. From such individuation arise subjectivity, rational and relational thinking, and the relativity of truth and values.

The methodological implication of the view is that, for a complete and appropriate understanding of how we humans function, it is necessary that we supplement the bottom-up approach with top-down methodology, because extraordinary phenomena may not be properly understood in terms of the ordinary. This is the essential message of Indian psychology. The researchers in the area of hypnosis as well as psychic phenomena have something to learn from the Indian model.

REFERENCES

Altom, K., & Braud, W.G. (1976). Clairvoyant and telepathic impressions of musical targets. *Research in Parapsychology* (pp. 171-174). Metuchen, NJ: Scarecrow Press.

Beloff, J., & Mandleberg, I. (1966). An attempted validation of the "Ryzl technique" for training ESP subjects. *Journal of the Society for Psychical Research, 43*, 229-249.

Bem, D.J., & Honorton, C. (1994). Does psi exist? Replicable evidence for an anomalous process of information transfer. *Psychological Bulletin*, 115, 4-18.

Brady, J.P., & Rosner, B.S. (1966). Rapid eye movements in hypnotically induced dreams. *Journal of Nervous and Mental Disease*, 143, 28-35.

Braud, W.G. (1975). Psi-Conducive States. *Journal of Communication*, 25, 142-152.

Braud, W.G., & Braud, L.W. (1973). Preliminary Explorations of psi-conducive states: Progressive Muscular Relaxation. *Journal of the American Society for Psychical Research*, 67, 6-46.

Braud, W.G., & Braud, L.W. (1974). Studies of psi facilitating states: Hypnosis, Muscular Relaxation, and an Experimentally Induced Hypnagogic State. *Proceedings of the First International Congress of Parapsychology and Psychotronics*, 204-207.

Casler, L. (1962). The improvement of clairvoyance scores by means of hypnotic suggestion. *Journal of Parapsychology*, 26, 77-87.

Casler, L. (1964). The effects of hypnosis on GESP, *Journal of Parapsychology*, 28, 126-134.

Dechanet, D. (1960). *Christian Yoga*. London: Burns & Oates.

Dodds, E.R. (1971). Supernormal phenomena in classical antiquity. *Proceedings of the Society for Psychical Research*, 55, 189-237.

Edmonston, W.E., Jr. (1981). *Hypnosis and Relaxation: Modern Verification of an Old Equation*. New York: Wiley.

Edmonston, W.E., Jr., & Grotevant, W.R. (1975). Hypnosis and alpha density. *American Journal of Clinical Hypnosis*, 17, 221-232.

Edmonston, W.E., Jr., & Pessin, M. (1966). Hypnosis as related to learning and electrodermal measures. *American Journal of Clinical Hypnosis,* 9, 31-51.

Fahler, J. (1957). ESP card tests with and without hypnosis. *Journal of Parapsychology,* 21, 179-185.

Fahler, J., & Cadoret, R.J. (1958). ESP card tests of college students with and without hypnosis. *Journal of Parapsychology,* 22, 125-136.

Grela, J.J. (1945). Effect on ESP scoring of hypnotically induced attitudes. *Journal of Parapsychology,* 9, 194-202.

Hilgard, E.R. (1977). *Divided Consciousness: Multiple Controls in Human Thought and Action.* New York: Wiley.

Honorton, C. (1964). Separation of high and low scoring ESP subjects through hypnotics preparations. *Journal of Parapsychology,* 28, 250-257.

Honorton, C. (1966). A further separation of high and low-scoring ESP subjects through hypnotic preparation. *Journal of Parapsychology,* 30, 172-183.

Lutz, A., Dunne, J., & Davidson, R.J. (2007). Meditation and the Neuroscience of Consciousness: An Introduction. In P.D. Zelazo, M. Moscovitch, & E. Thompson (Eds.), *The Cambridge Handbook of Consciousness.* New York: Cambridge University Press.

Lynn, S.J., & Rhue, J.W. (1991). Theories of hypnosis: An Introduction. In S.J. Lynn & J. W. Rhue (Eds.), *Theories of Hypnosis: Current Models and Perspectives.* New York: The Guilford Press.

Melzack, R., & Perry, C. (1975). Self-regulation of pain: The use of alpha-feedback and hypnotic training for the control of chronic pain. *Experimental Neurology,* 46, 452-469.

Muses, C. (1972). *Consciousness and Reality.* New York: Dutton.

Myers, F.W.H. (1903). *Human Personality and Its Survival of Bodily Death* (Vol. 1). New York: Longmans & Green.

Nash, C.B., & Durkin, M.G. (1959). Terminal salience with multiple digit targets. *Journal of Parapsychology,* 23, 49-53.

Osis, K., & Bokert, E. (1971). ESP and changed states of consciousness induced by meditation. *Journal of the American Society for Psychical Research,* 65, 17-65.

Pavlov, I.P. (1923). The identity with sleep and hypnosis. *Scientific Monthly,* 17, 603-608.

Pekala, R.J., Kumar, V.K., & Marcano, G. (1995). Anomalous/paranormal experiences, hypnotic susceptibility, and dissociation. *Journal of American Society for Psychical Research,* 89, 313-332.

Podmore, F. (1963). Mediums of the 19th Century. New Hyde Park, N.Y.: University Books, Orig. Publ. under title *Modern Spiritualism,* (1902). London: Methuen.

Rao, Dukhan, & Rao (1978). Yogic meditation and psi scoring in forced-choice and free-response tests. *Journal of Indian Psychology,* 1, 160-175.

Rao, K.R. (1964). The differential response in three new situations. *Journal of Parapsychology*, 28, 81-92.

Rao, K.R. (2001). *Basic Research in Parapsychology*. North Carolina: McFarland & Co. Inc.

Rhine, J.B. (1946). Hypnotic suggestion in PK tests. *Journal of Parapsychology* 10, 126-140.

Rhine, J.B. (1947). *The Reach of the Mind*. New York: Sloane.

Ryzl, M. (1962). Training the psi faculty by hypnosis. *Journal of the Society for Psychical Research*, 41, 234-252.

Ryzl, M. (1966). *Application of Hypnosis in ESP Research*. Paper read at the Parapsychology Seminar, Andhra University, Waltair.

Ryzl, M., & Pratt, J.G. (1962). Confirmation of ESP performance in a hypnotically prepared subject. *Journal of Parapsychology*, 26, 237-242.

Ryzl, M., & Ryzlova, J. (1962). A case of high-scoring ESP performance in the hypnotic states. *Journal of Parapsychology*, 26, 153-171.

Schechter, E.I. (1984). Hypnotic induction *vs.* control conditions: Illustrating an approach to the evaluation of replicability in parapsychological data. *Journal of the American Society for Psychical Research*, 78, 1-27.

Schmeidler, G.R. (1970). High ESP scores after a swami's brief instruction in meditation and breathing. *Journal of the Society for Psychical Research*, 64-103.

Schmidt, H., & Pantas, L. (1972). Psi tests with internally different machines. *Journal of Parapsychology*, 36, 222-232.

Sidgwick, H., Sidgwick, H. (Mrs.), & Smith, G.B. (1889). Experiments in thought-transference. *Proceedings of the Society for Psychical Research*, 6, 128-70.

Sinclair, U. (1930). *Mental Radio*. Monrovia, CA: Sinclair.

Spanos, N.P., & Barber, T.X. (1974). Toward a convergence in hypnosis research. *American Psychologist*, 29, 500-511.

Stanford, R.G., & Mayer, B. (1974). Relaxation as a psi-conducive state: A replication and exploration of parameters. *Journal of the American Society for Psychical Research*, 68, 182-191.

Stanford, R.G., & Stein, A.G. (1994). A meta-analysis of ESP studies contrasting hypnosis and a comparison condition. *Journal of Parapsychology*, 58, 235-269.

Tart, C.T. (1963). Hypnotic depth and basal skin resistance. *International Journal of Clinical and Experimental Hypnosis*, 11, 81-92.

Tart, C.T. (1967). A second psychophysiological study of out-of-the body experiences in a gifted subject. *International Journal of Parapsychology*, 9, 252-258.

Tebecis, A.K., & Provins, K.A. (1976). Further studies of physiological concomitants of hypnosis: Skin temperature, heart rate, and skin resistance, *Biological Psychology*, 4, 249-258.

Tebecis, A.K., Provins, M.A., Farnback, R.W., & Pentony, P. (1975). Hypnosis and EEG. *Journal of Nervous and Mental Disease,* 161, 1-17.

Thouless, R.H. (1963). The control of psi phenomena. *Research Journal of Philosophy and Social Sciences,* 1, 71-74.

Vasiliev, L.L. (1963). *Experiments in Mental Suggestions.* Church Crookham: Institute for the Study of Mental Images.

White, R.A. (1964). A comparison of old and new methods of response to targets in ESP experiments. *Journal of the American Society for Psychical Research,* 58, 21-56.

Zorab, G. (1963). Yoga and parapsychology. *Research Journal of Philosophy and Social Sciences,* 1, 78-83.

2

States of Consciousness

From the Perspective of Meditation and Hypnosis

BHASKAR VYAS

While all of us are conscious, we may have hardly thought how consciousness arises, how does it transform and how and where does it vanish. The matter cannot manifest anything that is not contained in it. If at some stage of biological evolution, the matter were to manifest consciousness as one of its properties, it must be intrinsically contained within it *ab initio.* If the implicate order of the matter is to incorporate consciousness, one has only to find the tools by which implicate, encoded order becomes explicit and unfolded. This epi-phenomenon i.e. consciousness, that is evident in various forms of life is still a mystery though it manifests as self emergent quality of matter.

Expressing itself in the form of self-conscious, personal existence, the consciousness in man is in constant interplay with the phenomenal world. Awareness may be of one's surroundings, as inferred through the sensory inputs or it may be in terms of self-reference. Putting it another way, it involves the contact between the subject and object. And a step further, philosophers like Sri Aurobindo postulate that it is the fundamental attribute of all the matter. Theoretical physicist David Bohm defines consciousness as *an attribute that may be explicitly unfolded as seen in the life forms that are conscious or may be in the form of implicate order that remains unexpressed.*

The biophysics of consciousness (Goswami, 2002) is still obscure; though the brain centres of its origin are well located. However, the play of consciousness seems physically a quantum electro-dynamic field, where the basic quantum currency is a single cell (Vyas & Vyas, 2004). Applied to human beings, it leads to the possibility of infinite number of quantum fields in the process of being conscious (Rossi, 2002; Schwartz & Begley, 2002). This satisfies physical criteria that quantum theory stipulates—infinite degrees of freedom to systems where quantum phenomena are taking place.

This kind of discussion is in the domain of philosophy. Philosophical reflections on the nature of consciousness have a bearing on the attitude of a hypnotherapist to therapeutic application. For instance, this is what Ernest Rossi commented, "*Consciousness is a novelty seeking modality of experiencing that turns on gene expression and brain plasticity.*" An Indian philosopher would have never thought in such a manner: for him consciousness is primordial. On the other hand, hypnotherapist is primarily concerned with how vividly lived experiences in altered state of consciousness can reconstruct and heal the physical brain.

Since hypnosis is an altered state of consciousness, let us review what other states are. To be aware is to be conscious. Awareness may be perceptual of the external world, or it may be self-awareness. It is experienced by all of us in various states of consciousness. Ordinarily, they may be said to be, awake, sleep, and dreaming. Not familiar to all, there are other states of consciousness too. In Patanjali's *Yoga Sutra,* it is said:

Saptadha prantabhumihi pragyna (Patanjali Yogasutra II, 27)

That literally means that there are seven states of consciousness. They are demarcated and yet they are in continuity (as the demarcated geographical areas are). Having said that, Patanjali leaves us to decipher what these seven states are.

As is common to philosophical interpretation of most classical Indian texts, this statement also portends to be discursive with different semantics to word *pragyna.* Most commentaries on Patanjali translate *pragyna* as intellect here, though *pragyna* is variously understood as intellect, discriminative wisdom and, it also means as intelligence in the life forms i.e., consciousness. In support of such semantics, *rishi* of *Aitareya Upanishad* has this to say:

> *That which is known as the heart, the mind...that is consciousness or perception...all these indeed are names of Consciousness* (pragynanam, chinmayanand). *Consciousness is, indeed, the cosmos* (Brahman).

The first three of the seven states of consciousness are awake, sleep and dream. During the experience of all of them, awareness that "I am there" persists. The fourth state is *turya,* which is described as "tranquil settlement in the state of liberation and the state of witness in action." Indian tradition has varying concepts about *turya.* It is most poignantly narrated in *Mandukya Upanishad* as, *that which has no parts, soundless, the incomprehensible, beyond all the senses, the cessation of all phenomena, all blissful and non-dual AUM, is the Fourth, and verily it is the same as the Atman. He, who knows this, merges his self in the Supreme Self—the individual in the total* (Mandukya Upanishad, 12).

This description stops short at the fourth state, describing *turya* as a final submergence into the ocean of consciousness. It does not take the note of other states described in *Yogavaasishtha.*

Since such classic descriptions of *turya* go much beyond what is seen in hypnosis, it might be argued that latter may not be called the fourth state: some say it is nearer the fifth described in *Yogavaasishtha* (Bharti, 2002) as, *abiding in mere nonduality, with all distinction and division extinguished, he is seen as one asleep.*

The Sixth state is described as (Bharti, 2002), *where he dwells "without knot", liberated while living and without conception or ideation. This is "jeevanmuktavibhavana." Having stayed in the sixth state, he can reach seventh state of enlightenment, the state of liberation without the body.*

Here, it is emphasized that narration of esoteric experiential states would differ from Pandit to Pandit. To quote from *Yogavaasishtha* once again, *the sky of pure consciousness is only calm. This Supreme Spirit, some people ascertain as the state of void, certain others, the state of mere knowledge and some others the state of the form of God, they quarrel mutually* (Bharti, 2002). However, to experience any of the states of consciousness is the fundamental attribute of all human beings and, is not culturally restricted or conditioned. William James (1890, 1901-02) said so: *Men involuntarily intellectualize their religious experience. They need formulas about the idea of 'fields of consciousness' with their centre or interest. Fields can vary in width and around what they are centered. These fields can experience incursions from beyond them, leading to sudden conversions marked by ecstatic feelings of happiness that need not be permanent to be critical to our lives.* He describes various characteristics of mystical states such as their ineffability, noetic quality, transience, and involuntariness. He then gives some typical examples of mystical states and points out that while mystical experiences can occur naturally, certain religious traditions like Hindu yoga, Buddhist meditation, Islamic Sufi dance, and Christian prayer systematically cultivate them. Saint Francis and his disciples were, on the whole, of this company of spirits, of which there are of course infinite varieties.

In consonance, Patanjali's *Yoga Sutra* describes different kinds of *Samadhi* (a state of communion where the presence of the observer is completely negated). They are:

1. *Sampragynata Samadhi* (Sutra, I: 17): Dialectic thinking, active mentation, abundance of interests and distinctive individuality are the factors constituting *sampragynata Samadhi* or an experience with thought-habit functioning as a centre.
2. *Asampragynata Samadhi* (Sutra, I: 18): When consciousness retains only impressions of facts without their psychological associations, then is attained *Asampragynata Samadhi*—an experience without any centre of thought habit.

3. *Savitarka Samadhi* (Sutra, I: 42): In this state, there is an experience having thought modification as the centre; there are variable interpretations due to the mind alternating between verbal and conceptual thinking (metaphors used in hypnotherapy illustrate this state).
4. *Nirvitarka Samadhi* (Sutra, I: 43): That is the experience in which the centre of thought modification is nonexistent. This state is attained when perception is clear so that subjective projections by the mind are dropped.
5. *Sabijah Samadhi* (Sutra, I: 46): This also centres round a thought seed.
6. *Nirbijah Samadhi* (Sutra, I: 51): When the very nucleus of identity is destroyed, then there is a complete cessation of all reactive tendency, thus bringing into existence *Nirbijah Samadhi* or an experience in which there is not even a thought seed.
7. *Dharma-Megha Samadhi* (Sutra, I: 29, 32, 34): Here the state of meditation is an end in itself; not a means for the fulfilment of some motive (This is a stark contrast to hypnosis as well as *yoga-nidra*). There is pure and holistic awareness. It is a spiritual experience like benediction. There is infinity of wisdom and the psychological functional entity of three *gunas* (all the defenses of ego) come to an end (so there is complete dissolution of ego, *gunateetam*). There is only that Alone—*Kaivalya*. The consciousness has regained its pristine, pure originality.

It will be of interest to most Indian hypnotherapists to know, understand and if possible to experience these esoteric, spiritual states. For successful practice of hypnotherapy it is not imperative to meditate and experience them. We would now describe as to what is the state of hypnosis.

HYPNOSIS : AN ALTERED STATE OF CONSCIOUSNESS

Since time immemorial, mankind has known a different state of consciousness. This altered/different state of consciousness is the attribute of entire mankind but only a few are aware of it. This state is manifest in hypnosis and meditation. Hypnotic state is widely researched through scientific tools by psychologists, physiologists and medical doctors, and results are well documented. Objective criteria are now available for scientific validation about this subjective, experiential state.

The misconceptions about hypnosis are widely prevalent. This is because of its checkered history. It made its public debut in the West with stage shows by Mesmer in the latter part of eighteenth century. Such stage shows, while claiming to bring about various cures, were motivated by craving for personal power. They indeed resulted in so much myth and mysticism being associated with hypnosis. This caused fear, distaste and dislike.

Mesmer did another mistake. The age of reason had just arrived then. The philosophy of Descartes' and Newtonian discoveries had established the relationship between causality and change. The whole universe was seen as a huge clock and every event was connected to some causative agent like the wheels of a clock. Going by the scientific spirit that was just dawning upon his time, Mesmer tried to postulate a scientific hypothesis. He claimed that the phenomenon of hypnosis and associated cures were because of a field that he called Animal Magnetism. When the Charcot Commission in 1784 failed to find any such field, the baby was thrown with the bath water (It may be noted that after that, there has not been any scientific investigation about the physical nature of hypnosis. Such an enquiry with modern tools is overdue). The hypnosis was discredited and the stigma still sticks in the minds of the lay people. There was enormous empirical data to suggest the existence of a hypnotic state but the misconceived rationalization caused the damage. It attached a further stigma about hypothetical imposition of one's will on the other. Nobody can be hypnotized against his/her will or be made to do actions against his/her will. It put fear and disgust in the minds of people: so much so that subsequent clarification by Abbe Faria that hypnotic phenomena are entirely dependent upon the expectancy and co-operation of the subject, and are, therefore, in the nature of self-hypnosis, was also given a good-bye.

Hypnosis begins by transforming our ordinary consciousness to an altered state of consciousness. It is indeed a different state of consciousness, as much as sleep and dream states are. A sense of differing awareness about the experience is common to all the four states; even in sleep and dreams; the feeling of awareness is there. Hypnosis is not a delusion. It is not anything extraordinary either. Like awareness, sleep and dream state, this is a natural attribute of entire mankind. It is easily accessible by all, may be with a little help initially. Even when not formally told about it, most of us are familiar with it. In ordinary experiences, childhood fairy tales, a beautiful landscape, a piece of fine poetry, an absorbing novel, a magnificent painting, or simply a creative thought has given us a glimpse of this natural attribute. A good glimpse of this not so unfamiliar dimension is obtained in mystic verses from various traditions.

Such intuitive connection remains only a glimpse for most of us, because, caught as we are in the cross traffic of the profit and loss in our worldly trade accounts, we are immediately drawn away from this almost 'other worldly' experience; only to remember it as some precious moments. The memory of the precious moments can and do turn into "ever present now." For this to happen repeatedly, we have the doorway of the altered state of consciousness that is easily provided through hypnosis.

Phenomena in Hypnosis

Hypnosis and all kinds of meditative states begin with the fourth state of consciousness (based on the description of *turya* in *Mandukya Upanishad,* many *gurus* will not agree to hypnosis being called the Fourth state; call it by whatever number, and accepting that hypnosis, *yoga-nidra* and meditation are not the same, there is much common to hypnotic and meditative states as we shall soon see). For the generation of the fourth state of consciousness, most of the traditions rely on reflection, or self-absorption or simple relaxation along with deep breathing. There are sophisticated techniques for each of these but one need not be familiar with them to begin. As the process goes forward, within a few minutes there is spontaneous onset of the fourth state of consciousness.

The characteristics of this state are that the mind is quiet, calm and peaceful. A general sense of well-being prevails. The person is awake but the state is more like sleep than awake. It is a state of alert restfulness. In this state there is focalization on the subject, be it an image or a *mantra* and, the marginal inputs fade. The focal point becomes symbolic, *i.e.,* it gathers content that goes on expanding in its abstract meaning. There is attention on the focalized idea but it is not accompanied by any kind of tension. There may be distraction by the surroundings but there is no disturbance. There is choiceless extensive awareness but it is not exclusive of any thing in particular. Surreal metaphors translate into real.

The subjective time moves slowly and an hour may appear to have been only a few minutes. But if so programmed, the time shall pass very slowly. Or the time may so undulate that the distinction between the past, present and future is lost. There is shift of space location and one can experience oneself at several different locations in space. This is trance. It may be mild, moderate and intense in depth. And in the state of trance, one may experience the space-time dimension to shift. It is possible to regress in time and be at places at times in the past, which may have been forgotten. There can be time progression too. This is utilized in therapy for setting up a goal.

The state has been studied physiologically by Herbert Benson (1975). And there are extensive studies on the physiology of meditative state (Yogi, 1977; Keith, 1970; Orme-Johnson & Farrow, 1976; Tart, 2008). Initially the pulse rate and the blood pressure rise; but soon go below the resting levels. The respiratory rate rises first but soon falls below the resting level and, as the trance progresses, it may be accompanied by small periods of apnea. The metabolic rate falls steeply and it may fall below the level of sleep. The peripheral flow of blood increases and the body and the face may be flushed.

Plasma cortical levels decline. There is increased coherence of functions of both the hemispheres of the brain. In the electroencephalogram there is preponderance of alpha waves. There is increase of the galvanic skin resistance.

For the regular practitioners of self-hypnosis, there are lasting psychological benefits. Overall the stress levels decline. There are better interpersonal relationships. There is realistic goal setting and achievement. There is increase in productivity and creativity. Probably the most important outcome of the process is clarity of perception and the generation of intuitive insight.

Altered states of consciousness are useful tools to clarify perception. In every day living, one is led to several fallacies about perception. What is seen is coloured by various projections of mind. We shall discuss later about this as defenses of ego in terms of Freudian psychology. Before they become diseases of mind, they persist and perpetuate themselves as neurotic compensation thus acting as coping mechanisms in the service of the ego. Such a conditioned mind refuses to accept perceptual clarity. There is a constant striving by the mind to weigh each and every matter in its own favour. In the process, the perception of reality is tilted.

The mind is a mirror that has a tendency to gather dust through stress and strife of everyday life. And this dust must not be allowed to remain. Better still, the dust should not generate and if there is any, it must constantly be wiped out. Meditation is the remedy. J. Krishnamurthy (1979) has explained it thus :

> *How is a mind that has so many problems, to meet new problems? There is problem of time, the problem of space, the problem of relationships, and the problem of living, of earning a livelihood, the problem of disease, health and old age. How is the mind to meet all these problems all at once, not one by one but the whole of them all at once, without effort?...The way we meet them now, our problems are all fragmentary. There is the problem of fear, the problem of boredom, the problem of enjoyment—a multitude of problems*

> *one after the other. Is there a way of meeting all these problems not separately, but totally? For the mind to be totally free from pressure, pleasant or unpleasant, all motives, however subtle or noble, must wither away.*

In contrast, hypnosis is goal oriented and, therefore, circumscribed. What happens to the mind following the experience of meditation is a kind of transformation. It has been variously described as metamorphosis of the self and, mutation of the mind. There is awakening of intelligence (Krishnamurthy, 1970) so that the very ground from where the intelligence arises undergoes a multifold transformation.

This kind of the awareness is different from the ordinary awareness. In this profound state of awareness, one is a participant and a witness too. Of course, on the way further, the participant and the witness both cease to be. Observer and observed also merge (Patanjali *Yoga Sutra,* III : 3) to disappear altogether. One can say this is self-actualization or the peak experience of Abraham Maslow. It is a state of self-realization in the timeless moment !

In this state there is steadiness of perception without any object to hold on and there is total stillness of mind without dependence on any image. It is this new mind that has come out of a radical transformation that can comprehend true nature of time (Patanjali *Yoga Sutra,* III : 16). There is a clear understanding about the perception of time being dependent on the moment of consciousness. While the past and future turn out to be mental constructs, the ever present *now* is just a moment dependent on the consciousness (Reddy, 2003). Since consciousness itself is modulated, the experience of *now* also subjects itself to change. Time dilatation and constriction as well as stoppage of time are the natural outcome.

Anatomy of Consciousness : Physiological Basis

So consciousness seems to be more than a mere function of brain: no matter that we have identified the reticular formation in the mid brain extending down to medulla oblongata as the seat of consciousness. Firing of the cells from the cells located in this region upward to the cerebrum causes the subject to be conscious. However, such an activity does not happen in isolation and the role of genes is being recognized in psychobiology of consciousness. According to Rossi (2002), consciousness can be understood as a series of continuously emerging experiential states that focus attention to evoke activity-dependent gene expression and neurogenesis in the dynamics of self-reflection and co-creation of the self. It should not be long before there is conclusive evidence that the state of hypnosis is gene activity dependent. And we believe the physics of consciousness shall soon be understood in terms of quantum mechanics.

Hypnosis and Meditation

Though there are several features common to both as seen above, meditation is not the same as hypnosis. Meditation, when practiced, begins as self-hypnosis. It happens spontaneously too. And it may extend along an uncharted path to lands without boundaries. Hypnosis is restricted and much circumscribed. Both have been subjected to scientific research but it is difficult to standardize the results since the experience is subjective and input qualitative. On EEG, both the experiential states generate alpha waves and cannot be distinguished by it. Both are royal roads to unconscious mind and can lead to the experience that "a moment reveals what the ages toiled to express." "*Siddhis*" accrue to the meditator. Hypnosis generates creativity. Hypnotherapy alleviates or cures. Let us compare them in a nutshell.

Hypnosis	*Meditation*
1. Scientific and therapeutic	Spiritual
2. Subject of scientific scrutiny	Philosophical

(*Contd.*)

(*Contd.*)

	Hypnosis	*Meditation*
3.	Studied scientifically since last two centuries	Spiritual experience since ages
4.	Fertile ground for research; difficult to quantify the experience	Difficult to quantify
5.	Anyone can learn	A moral and ethical code of living is a prerequisite before initiation and esoteric
6.	Goal oriented	There are many kinds of *samadhis*: goal oriented; goal-less; and nameless experience
7.	Relaxation and deep breathing are utilized as induction tools	Stillness of body and mind is essential; esoteric breathing exercises, *pranayam*, facilitate the experience
8.	Utilized for therapeutic healing and for personality development	Health giving, disease preventing and helps spiritual growth
9.	Self hypnosis is easy to learn and practice and can be taught individually and in group by academicians	Requires a *guru*. Difficult to find a bona fide *guru*.
10.	Archetypal symbols and meaningful images may be utilized	Focalization on a form of sound, *mantra* or visual symbol of a deity
11.	Insight generation and creativity is a step by step process	It is a pathless land where there is no destination, no goal. Enlightenment "happens"

(*Contd.*)

(*Contd.*)

	Hypnosis	*Meditation*
12.	Guided hypnosis is unlikely to do any harm	Meditation has driven people crazy when not practiced under the supervision of a *guru* or a guide.
13.	Freedom from affliction by hypnotherapy	Attainment of *kaivalya*—Journey alone to Alone

Psychedelic State of Consciousness

The altered state arising out of drug ingestion/habit/dependence/abuse is pathological. The damage to self and the civilization are devastating; the use is criminal. Drug abuse is most difficult to treat; in a willing subject, hypnosis promises to be a good adjunct in combination with professional psychiatric help.

The following is only for the sake of academic interest. If this were to be the universal experience, *nirvana* seems to be only a pill away ! No wonder, Arthur Koesler (1975) dreamt of a substance that can be mixed with the drinking water and when consumed, it heightened creativity and sense of peace for the general population !

The highly aesthetic experience is given a poetical description by Aldous Huxley (1954). Huxley was drawn to experiments with altered states of consciousness and was in close contact with Milton Erickson. They closeted themselves for some time and did several experiments to study consciousness at Huxley's home. The home caught fire and the records were destroyed.

Huxley studied Buddhism and had practiced meditation. His description of what happens in the State (induced by ingestion of mescaline) is immaculate. Huxley states, "I was seeing what Adam had seen on the morning of his creation—the miracle, moment by moment, of naked existence. In an instant I experienced in things around me a transience that was yet an eternal life, perpetual perishing, that was at the same moment, pure being. In this state, a simple look at the flower in the vase was to provide the beatific vision of *sat, chit, ananda,* viz. Being, Consciousness and Bliss." He saw the *dharma* body of the Buddha in the flowers. The doors to a new way of perception seemed to be open. Spatial relationships ceased to matter. Instead there was intensity of existence, profundity of significance and relationships within a pattern. He instantaneously realized the experience of Van Gogh in the painting of the Chair. While Huxley gazed at the legs of the Chair, he experienced, "Being my Non-self in the Non-self that was the Chair."

Huxley's above description is following his personal experience with ingestion of mescaline. Hypnosis, meditation and the drug-induced state are not identical. However, one may note many similarities to the experiences.

Summarizing, states of consciousness beyond the ordinarily well known three, are experiential states of esoteric people. The Rishi of *Mandukya Upanishad* was perfect in being brief and not explicit. Patanjali after defining *pragyna* having seven states knew well to leave exposition. *Yogavashistha* (XXXI) after describing *turya* elucidates seven steps to reach the pinnacle of *yoga*. In a broad sweep, he clubs initial three stages as one and describes four advanced stages with enlightenment as the ultimate.

So, call it by any name, or label it as you have experienced. Even to hypnosis, we assign three well documented stages; light, moderate and deep trance. Let us leave philosophic dissection and experience the whole.

REFERENCES

Aldous, H. (1954). *The Doors of Perception*. London: Chatto & Windus Ltd.

Benson, H. (1975). *The Relaxation Response*. New York: Morrow.

Bharati, J. (2002). *The Essence of Yogavaasishtha*. transl. by Samvid (p. 344). Sanskrit and English text. Chennai: Samata Books.

Chinmayananda, S. (1972). *Discourses on Aitareya Upanishad*. Delhi: Chinmaya Publications Trust.

Goswami, A. (2002). *Physics of the Soul*. Charlottesville, V.A.: Hampton Roads Publishing Co.

James, W. (1890). *Exceptional Mental States*. Unpublished Lectures at Lowell Institute.

James, W. (1902). *The Varieties of Religious Experience. A Study in Human Nature*. New York: Longmans, Green & Co.

Koesler, A. (1975). *The Ghost in the Machine*. London: Amazon.

Krishnamurty, J. (1970).*The Awakening of Intelligence*. Madras: Harper Collins.

Maharishi Mahesh Yogi. (1976). *Creating an Ideal Society*. Rheinweiler, Germany: Maharishi European Research University Press.

Mandukya Upanishad, 12.

Mehta, R. (1970). *J. Krishnamurty and the Nameless Experience* (pp.128-153). Delhi: Rector Press.

Orme-Johnson, D.W., & Farrow, J.T. (Eds.). (1977). *Scientific Research on the Transcendental Meditation Programme. Collected Papers* (Vol. 1.). Rheinweiler, Germany: Maharishi European Research University Press.

Patanjali. *Yoga Sutra*.

Reddy, D. (2003). *The Dicey Problem of New Age Science: Einstein, Hawking and God at the Casino*. Chittor.

Rossi, E. (2002). *Dream, Consciousness, Spirit: The Quantum Experience of Self Reflection and Co-creation*. New York: Zeig, Tucker, Theisen.

Rossi, E.L. (2002). *The Psychobiology of Gene Expression*. New York: W.W. Norton.

Schwartz, J., & Begley, S. (2002). *The Mind and the Brain: Neuroplasticity and the Power of Mental Force*. New York: Harper Collins Publishers.

Tart, C. (2008). Altered states of consciousness and the spiritual traditions: The proposal for the creation of state specific sciences, in K. Ramkrishna Rao *et al.* (Ed), *Handbook of Indian Psychology* (pp. 577-605). Delhi: Foundation Books.

Vyas, B., & Vyas, R. (2004). *Space Time Consciousness: The Fifth Dimension*. Delhi: Bhartiya Vidya Prakashan.

Wallace, R.K. (1970). *The Physiological Effects of Transcendental Meditation: A Proposed Fourth Major State of Consciousness*. Doctoral thesis, Department of Physiology, School of Medicine, University of California.

Yogavashishtha, XXXI.

3

Culture and Mental Health

Not A Minor Matter

ARUNA THAKUR

Culture is not a minor matter for several basic reasons. Normal human development demands that we acquire specific culture knowledge and understanding. Without culture, we would not be human. The brain has evolved to be a culture-learning system and its health and dysfunction depends on the coherence and adaptability of our cultural worlds. There is scientific evidence that culture affects every aspect of psychopathology including cause, course, treatment and outcome.

In this century, in contrast to earlier times, large scale socio-cultural change has taken place rapidly around the globe. This has been due to the remarkable improvement of communication systems, such as the postal service, newspapers, radio, television, and now, the internet; as well as improvement of transportation and the subsequent ease of travelling and migration. As pointed out by Zwingle (1999), "Goods move. People move. Ideas move. And cultures change." It is a worldwide phenomenon, as Davis (1999) indicates, "roughly five per cent of the global population (about 300 million people) still remain a strong identity as members of an indigenous culture, rooted in history and language and attached by myth and memory to a particular place. Yet increasingly, their unique visions of life are being lost in a whirlwind of change." Davis notes that throughout the human history, something of the order of 10,000 spoken languages had existed on Earth. But "today of the roughly 6,000 languages still spoken, many are not being taught to children." This is merely one illustration of the formation of a "global culture." However, paralleling this trend toward globalization, in reaction to cultural universalization, many people are working hard to preserve the uniqueness of their cultures.

Increased rates of transnational migration have had significant demographic effects on populations in general (*Economist, 2001)* and on populations presenting to mental health services in particular.

Cultural psychiatry is concerned with understanding the impact of social and cultural difference on mental illnesses and its treatment. Culture has the same transparency as water except, at the junction of cultures where the world is reflected and deflected. The confrontation and intermixing of different cultures has always been part of human experience through travel and economic trend, and the impact has reached a new level of intensity. That makes culture increasingly important for psychiatry.

The changing demography and increasing diversity of Canadian society means that clinical practice and health services must address cultural differences as a matter of basic social equity and effectiveness. Ignoring cultural values, difference and diversity can lead to health disparities at the level of whole populations or communities because people do not have access to effective care. Ignoring culture can lead to tragic errors in everyday clinical practice (errors in making diagnosis, non-compliance with treatment, breakdown in social integrations, etc.).

In my opinion, if in the twentieth century the practice of psychiatry was characterized by a predominately Western/ European approach to treatment of mental illness, the twenty-first century will see a clear change to a more culturally sensitive approach.

Canada has become unmistakably multicultural. Statistics of Canadian demographics clearly show that shift. In the year 2007, 18.38 per cent people were immigrants by place of birth and 20 per cent of the population spoke languages other than English or French. Proportions varied widely between metropolitan areas. Toronto, Vancouver, and Montreal have the largest visible minority populations. Almost two million are of Asian origin according to Statistics Canada 2007 and over a million Canadians identify themselves as First Nations. These numbers clearly indicate the diverse nature of the Canadian Population.

Culture

Now let me define "culture". The British scholar E. B. Tylor (2001), in his pioneer work, *Primitive Culture,* defined culture as "that complex whole which includes knowledge, belief, art, law, morals, custom and any other capabilities and habits acquired by man as a member of society."

For psychiatric practice, perhaps the best definition of culture is the one provided by The National Institute of Mental Health's Culture and Diagnosis Group (Mezzich *et al.*, 1993), which states, "Culture refers to meanings, values and behavioural norms that are learned and transmitted in the dominant society and within its social groups."

Thus, culture refers to perspectives and meanings applied to human experience. Therefore, culture is important because that is what people bring as a part of themselves to the social setting. In fact, in the present world situation many people participate in multiple cultures and have multiple ethnic backgrounds or identifications. Thus it can be seen that culture will powerfully influence cognition, feeling and self-concept as well as the diagnostic process and treatment decisions.

How Culture Affects Mental Health

Culture and society play pivotal roles in mental health, mental illness, and mental health services. The dominant culture for much of Canada focussed on the beliefs, norms, and values of European and British heritage. For Quebec, the focus was French heritage with a different language, legal system, ideology of citizenship (republicanism) and other important cultural differences.

Mental illness can be considered a product of complex interactions among biological, psychological, social and cultural factors. The role of any of these factors can be stronger or weaker depending on the specific disorder or for different patients with the same disorder.

The cultures of racial and ethnic minorities influence many aspects of mental illness, including how patients from a given culture communicate and manifest their symptoms, their style of coping, their family and community supports, and their willingness to seek treatment (McCarty, *et al.*, 1999). Ethnic and racial minorities face a social and economic environment of inequality that includes greater exposure to racism, discrimination, violence, and poverty, which adversely affects physical and mental health. These minorities are at risk for mental disorders such as depression and anxiety (Williams, & Williams-Morris, 2000).

Poverty is linked to poorer mental health (Adler *et al.*, 1994). People in the lowest strata of income, education, and occupation are about two to three times more likely than those in the highest strata to have a mental disorder (Holzer, *et al.*, 1986).

Mistrust of mental health services is an important factor, which deters minorities from seeking treatment (Bhugra, 1989). They fear lack of confidentiality, caregiver's bias and stereotypical approaches. The minorities may deter from using services and receiving appropriate care if clinical environments that do not respect, or are incompatible with, the cultures of the people they serve (Bower, Ojeda, Wyn & Leva, 2000).

These examples indicate that culture plays an extremely important role in Mental Health, Mental Illness and Mental Health Treatment.

Psychiatry itself has a culture that affects how we communicate with patients; becoming aware of the cultural values implicit in psychiatric theory and practice can lead to new innovations in research and clinical practice thus improving our response to everyone.

The implications of this include :

1. Need for more training in cultural psychiatry including how to work with interpreters and cultural-brokers.
2. Need to recognize the cultural diversity of the profession and to encourage trainees and clinicians to think about how to make best use of their language and cultural knowledge and skills.
3. There is a need for accreditation standards in training and in service delivery that require serious attention to culture.
4. Need for continuing research on the impact of cultural variables on psychiatry and on models of mental health care for multicultural societies.

Let me discuss the approaches to cultural psychiatry in some ethnically diverse societies.

Table 3.1 : Approaches to Cultural Psychiatry in Some Ethnically Diverse Societies

Country	*Citizenship and Migration*	*Pattern of Migration*	*Emphasis in recent cultural psychiatry*	*Models of service*
Australia	Multicultural	Immigrant	Language	Mainstream, interpreters
Canada	Multicultural or consociation	Immigrant	Ethnicity	Mainstream
England	Imperial or commonwealth	Colonist	Racism	Anti-racist clinics
France	Republican	Colonist	Traditional Healing	Ethno-psychoanalysis
Germany	Ethnic	Guest workers	Culture-bound syndromes, traditional healing	Undeveloped
Japan	Ethnic	Guest workers	Culture-bound syndromes, traditional healing	Undeveloped
Sweden	Multicultural	Refugees	Stress and trauma, refuge	Trauma service

Castles and Miller distinguish four broad models of citizenship :

1. *The Imperial Model*: Which brings together diverse people under a single ruler (for example the British, Austro-Hungarian, and Ottoman empires).
2. *The Folk or Ethnic Model*: Which defines citizenship in terms of common descent, language, and culture (for example, Germany and Japan).
3. *The Republican Model*: Which defines the state as a political community based on a constitution and laws wherein newcomers who adopt the rules and the common culture are accepted as full citizens (for example, France).
4. *The Multicultural Model*: This shares the political definition of community with the republican model, but accepts the formation of ethnic communities within the polity (for example, Australia and Canada).

These notions of citizenship are not static or entirely consistent within any country either at the level of law and formal policy or in the informal negotiations and accommodations that put these rules into practice.

The cultural society in England has focussed on issues of inequalities in care for immigrants and on providing services that are explicitly anti-racist.

Cultural society in France has been strongly influenced by a psychoanalytic tradition that tends to situate problems in psyche and thus does not directly challenge the states position on culture.

Canada and Australia are immigrant societies with explicit ideologies of multiculturalism. In both cases these are reflected in efforts to respond to cultural diversity in mainstream settings. In Canada, multiculturalism was made an official policy in 1971. Its explicit aims are to maintain ethnic languages and cultures and to combat racism. Culture and ethnicity are viewed positively. Subsequent legislation has attempted to promote pluralism and diversity in the workplace and ensure equal access to health care services.

The United States shares elements of republican and multicultural models. It is an immigrant society but has been profoundly marked by its history of slavery and racism. This painful legacy is masked by the current popular term "diversity" in mental health services but is reflected in census categories and corresponding research on "racial" differences in health care utilization, psychopathology, and psychopharmacology.

Swedish immigrant policy since 1975 has been based on three major principles :

1. Equality,
2. Freedom of choice, and
3. Partnership (promoting working together).

The Country Council of Stockholm sponsored the development of a Centre for Trans-cultural Psychiatry that is conducting specialized clinical consultations and training programmes to improve the quality and accessibility of mental health services for the immigrant and refugee population.

The Impact of Globalization on Psychiatry

Globalization effects psychiatry in three main ways :

1. Through its effect on the forms of individual and collective identity and communal life that interact with psychiatric disorders,
2. Through the impact of economic inequalities on mental health, and
3. Through the shaping and dissemination of psychiatric knowledge itself.

Review of the Literature

Let me review some of the literature, which supports a more culturally sensitive approach to psychiatric practice.

Report of the Surgeon General of the U.S. Department of Health and Human Services, 2001, entitled "Mental Health: Culture and Ethnicity," states "Culture Counts." It points out that with a seemingly endless range of culture subgroups and individual variations, culture is important in how consumers communicate their symptoms and how they report them. Culture is not limited to patients, but also to professionals who provide care to patients. Every group of professionals represents a "culture" in themselves in the sense they too have a shared set of beliefs, norms and values. It concludes that there are racial and ethnic disparities in mental health delivery systems which need to be improved by providing culturally competent services and to build capacity for research and community leadership to meet the needs of racial and ethnic minorities.

Closer to home, the Department of Psychiatry at McGill University has, for some time, been internationally recognized as a leader in the field of cultural psychiatry. Kirmayer *et al.* (2003) have made a strong case for cultural consultation services and have demonstrated the "impact of cultural misunderstandings: incomplete assessments, incorrect diagnosis, inadequate or inappropriate treatment, and failed treatment alliances." It concludes: "The cultural consultation model effectively supplements existing services to improve diagnostic assessment and treatment for a culturally diverse population. Clinicians need training in working with interpreters and culture brokers."

All this leads to another imperative for Canadian psychiatry, i.e. the need for more awareness of cultural diversity in Canadian Psychiatric Residency programmes but sounds cautionary note: "A tendency to rely on informal teaching methods. This may limit the development of culturally competent residents."

Grabovac and Ganesan (2003) point to the need to incorporate two key elements of culture, spirituality and religion, into psychiatric curricula in Canada and recommend the inclusion of a 10-lecture series focussing on an overview of major religions including a review of First Nations traditional spiritual beliefs and practices.

With respect to research, Morton Beiser (2003) has pointed out that there are "at least four implications of culture for the conduct of mental health research. Culture helps define the field of study, assists in identifying research gaps, shapes research paradigms and supports the evolution of a cosmopolitan view of mental health." Furthermore, he notes that research has paid little attention to the role that culture plays in developing mental illness. He states that ethnocultural communities, immigrant and refugee communities, and indigenous peoples' communities need to be the focus of specific study. The needs for care in these communities differ from those in dominant and more powerful societies. Responding to the needs of these communities requires knowledge of the extent and types of those needs, of community expectations for care, and of community resources.

Aboriginal People

With respect to the mental health of aboriginal people, Kirmayer and colleagues (2000) point out that around the world, indigenous people have lost their autonomy on account of a rapid cultural change, global economy and segregation. Culture loss leads to high rates of depression, alcoholism, suicide and violence in many communities, especially amongst the youth.

Also, for any just society, issues of equity in health and well-being of all Canadians, and in particular aboriginal peoples, are important. Research on the problems that aboriginal populations face has important implications for health service delivery, for mental health promotion and for practice in general. Research and programme development must be fully collaborative through partnerships with aboriginal communities.

Women and Mental Health

Mental health and behavioural problems are intricately tied to the social world, as identified in the social roots of poor mental health for women (Canadian Task Force Report, 1988). Various factors affecting women's mental health are: (1) Hunger—under-nourishment affects more then 60 per cent of women in the developing countries; (2) Work issues—women are poorly paid for labour-intensive jobs, often in dangerous work settings; and (3) Domestic violence—surveys in some low-income communities worldwide report up to 50 per cent to 60 per cent of women have been beaten.

According to the Canadian Task Force findings (1988), immigrant and refugee women have more mental health needs than their male counterparts. A few Canadian studies have specifically examined the changing mental health of immigrant women in Canada. They show a high rate of depression among women of four ethnic groups—Chinese, Vietnamese, Portuguese, and Latin American. A review of the literature on childbearing and mental health cited high rates of *post partum* depression among immigrant women. A recent review of Canadian research on the health of refugees identified psychiatric symptoms attributable to trauma, including rape, as an important mental health issue.

Many of the determinants of mental well-being among Canadian immigrant women were systemic and included cultural, linguistic, economic, and informational barriers to care, as well as inadequate social support.

Immigration

According to the Canadian Task Force (1988), the contingencies surrounding the resettlement experience that determine the risk of developing a mental health problem include personal strengths, pre- and post-migration stresses and the availability of family and community support. Pre-migration stresses such as poverty, unemployment and separation from family are frequent components of the refugee and resettlement process that jeopardize mental health. Personal resources such as fluency in the host country language, ethnic pride and positive attitudes towards acculturation together with family and ethnic community support and a positive reception by the host society may buffer the impact of a stressful experience. Sociodemographic characteristics such as age, gender, education, and ethnicity affect the susceptibility to expose the stresses, as well as the availability of personal and social resources.

Elderly people feel the losses of migration more because they leave behind more memories and connections than the younger immigrants and are less able to acculturate and have a high risk of culture shock.

Case Studies

I see many Asian, aboriginal, immigrant, and woman patients. I recognize that each client comes with his or her own cultural background, which requires special approaches and strategies to develop therapeutic alliance and interviewing skills. Let me share a few examples from my own psychiatric practice to illustrate the need for a more culturally sensitive approach to treatment.

Example 1

Mrs. *X*, a housewife from India, immigrated with her husband and accepted a traditional role as a non-earning partner. Soon, the husband recognized the existence of marital discord and sought psychiatric help. Various diagnoses were suggested, including adjustment disorder, personality disorder, and marital discord. She became psychotic and was diagnosed as having schizophrenia. Her husband doubted the diagnosis and flew to India to seek a second opinion. He even argued with my husband, who is also a psychiatrist, about my diagnosis and approach. He insulted me in a social setting, and other general practitioners of the Indian community debated my practice at community gatherings. I soon realized I had to transfer the case to a male colleague. Ten years later, Mrs. *X* and her husband have accepted the diagnosis and see a male psychiatrist of a different ethnic background. She is taking appropriate medications.

There are several issues in describing this case :

(1) My role as a psychiatrist was in question, as was my professional competency, because I am a woman;
(2) Confidentiality was difficult to maintain in a social setting; and
(3) Trust, therapeutic alliance and rapport were difficult to attain in this case because the ethnic background of the patient was the same as mine.

Example 2

My second patient was Mr. *Y*, aged 19 years, of African background who emigrated from Nigeria. Mr. *Y*, a first-year university student, became paranoid towards his father, stating that his father was spying through Mr. *Y*'s glass eye and was following him.

He required admission and was diagnosed as suffering from paranoia schizophrenia. When it was suggested to Mr. *Y*'s father that Mr. *Y* be transferred to an approved boarding home, he reacted with great insult and disappointment. He felt that I did not believe in his capacity as a father to provide care for his son. A few sessions with a community psychiatric nurse facilitated Mr. *Y*'s move into an approved boarding home. Mr. *Y*'s father had tried a few times to take his son home and to re-establish the father-son bond, but failed. Repeatedly, Mr. *Y* was hospitalized to control his paranoid psychotic breakdowns. Now, five years later, Mr. *Y* lives in an apartment with limited supervision, is taking neuroleptic medications and has returned to school. In this case, the cultural expectation of a father to provide unconditional caring to his child was a big problem. A great deal of counselling from the community psychiatric nurse was required in order to deal with his guilt. Once he recognized that his son's illness required special attention and did not reflect on him, he agreed to support the therapy.

Example 3

My third patient is an Iranian woman, Mrs. *Z*, who wore a veil and came with her husband. Mrs. Z did not speak to me for giving sessions and spoke only to her husband in the interviews, looking at him through the veil. It required five sessions to gain the trust of Mrs. Z to see me alone and to request that her husband wait in the waiting room. She was able to remove her veil and talk about the stresses of marriage, finances, language difficulties and her husband's wishes to relocate to a warmer climate with the help of social services assistance. In this case, the husband was an interpreter and historian who was also part of Mrs. Z's problems. Middle Eastern women, perhaps Asian women, take a longer time to develop trust to be able to divulge their problems to an outsider.

Example 4

Approximately 13 per cent of my patients are of aboriginal background. The following is a summary of their problems :

1. There is a significant comorbidity in regard to mental and substance abuse disorders, especially alcoholism, as well as gambling among both native youth and adults. This underscores an important unmet need to provide culturally appropriate treatment of such comorbidities.
2. The majority of my patients are homeless, incarcerated or victims of physical and sexual trauma. Research is needed to understand how the lives of our aboriginal population reach such a stage and to develop appropriate methods for assessing and managing their mental health.
3. Acculturated natives have their own unique problems. They are cast out by their own members and present several psychosomatic and mental health problems.
4. Quite a few of my patients describe painful and unique histories of growing up in residential schools. They are vulnerable to depression and suicidal impulses. They are likely to experience increased need for mental

health care in comparison to non-native population. One example will suffice. An aboriginal patient of mine wept uncontrollable during our first few sessions. When she eventually was able to tell me her problems, she told me she had gone to a residential school. When she was unable to finish a meal, she was forced to eat the unfinished meal. When she vomited, she was forced to consume her own vomit. Is it any wonder, then, that victims of such abuse encounter subsequent severe mental trauma?

Recommendations

These examples strongly indicate the need to adopt a culturally sensitive approach to mental health and mental illness on account of the multicultural nature of our society. Reforms and innovative approaches will be required in the areas of education, training, research and clinical practice.

First, a rigorous review of the curricula is required to ensure that a significant portion of training related to culture diversity is included as a part of every training programme. There is need to develop formal training programmes in cultural psychiatry for psychiatric residents, graduate programmes of psychology, family medicine residents, other mental health and social services professionals. This will include improving the training of mental health practitioners in concepts of culture and strategies for inter-cultural care.

There is a further need to design advanced training for clinicians and scholars who are planning to become qualified specialists in this field as well as particular need to train mental health practitioners to work with interpreters. There is a need for additional training of interpreters and brokers to increase their expertise in mental health issues.

Clinicians and institutions increasingly recognize the role of culture in caring for individuals and families affected by mental illness. However, the mental health research literature has paid less attention to the role culture plays in their research studies. Researchers need to pay attention to culture and to cultural differences in shaping their research paradigms. The researchers working with ethnocultural communities have to recognize that their research should also benefit their communities with whom they choose to work.

Finally, we need to address what changes need to be made in clinical practice. We need to emphasize the clinical application of cultural psychiatry regarding evaluation, diagnosis, management and treatment, and to establish culturally competent psychiatric services into settings other than the hospitals, specialized clinics and private offices in which mental health expertise tends to remain concentrated.

The focus on culture is important in dealing with patients of minority or other ethnic backgrounds, or from foreign countries, and also the majority population of their own society.

Clinicians need to understand and appreciate the multiple aspects of their own cultural identity and that of their patients. They also need to be aware of their attitudes toward their patient's particular ethnicity to assist in engaging and understanding the patient. Thus, the cultural dimensions of therapist and patient deserve full attention with every patient a clinician encounters. Every clinician is expected to provide culturally sensitive, relevant and effective clinical care and treatment for all patients.

(*Editorial Note:* The paper is written in the background of Canadian society. The studies and references are also drawn from Canada. The conclusions are, however, universal. Culture sensitivity is of paramount importance to a therapist for effective psychotherapy/ hypnotherapy. The case studies highlight the relevance of culture and ethnic background in treatment.)

REFERENCES

Adler, N.E., Boyce, T., Chesney, M.A., Cohen, S., Folkmar, S., Kahn, R.L. *et al.* (1994). Socioeconomic status and health: The challenge of the gradient. *Am Psychol,* 49, 15-24.

Baxter, C. (2002). Transcultural psychiatry in Canadian psychiatry residency programmes. *Ann R. Coll Physicians Surg Can,* 35, 492-494.

Beiser, M. (2003). Why should researchers care about culture? *Can J Psychiatry*, 48, 154-60.

Bhugra, D. (1989). Attitudes towards mental illness: A review of the literature. *Acta Psychiatr Scane*, 80, 1-12.

Bower, E.R., Ojeda, V.D., Wyn, R., & Levan, R. (2000) Racial and ethnic disparities in access to health insurance and health care. Los Angeles: UCLA Center for Health Policy Research and the Henry J. Kaiser Family Foundation; Canadian Task Force on Mental Health Affecting Immigrants and Refugees in Canada. After the door has opened: mental health issues affecting immigrants and refugees in Canada—a report. Ottawa: Health Canada.

Cooper-Patrick, L., Gallo, J.J., Gonzales, J.J., Vu, H.T., Powe, N.R., Nelson, C., *et al.* (1999). Race, gender and partnership in the patient-physician relationships. *JAMA*, 282, 583-589.

Davis, W. (1999). Vanishing Cultures. *National Geographic*, August.

Grabovac, A.D., & Ganesan, S. (2003). Spirituality and religion in Canadian psychiatry residency training. *Can J Psychiatry*, 48, 171-175.

Holzer, C., Shea, B., Swanson, J., Leaf, P., Meyers, J., George, L., *et al.* (1986). The increased risk for specific psychiatric disorders among persons of low socioeconomic status. *Am. J. Soc. Psychiatry*, 6, 259-271.

Kaufert, J.M., & Koolage, W.W. (1984). Role conflict among cultural brokers; the experience of native Canadian medical interpreters. *Soc. Sci. Med.* 18, 283-286.

Kirmayer, L.J., Brass, G., & Tait, C. (2000). The mental health of aboriginal peoples: Transformations of identity and community. *Can J. Psychiatry*, 45, 499-508.

Kirmayer, L.J., Groleau, D., Guzden, J., Blake, C., & Jarvis, E. (2003). Cultural Consultation: A Model of Mental Health Service for Multicultural Societies. *Can. J. Psychiatry*, 48, 145-153.

Lopez, S.R., & Guarnaccia, P.J. (2000) Cultural psychopathology: Uncovering the social world of mental illness. *Annual Review of Psychology*, 51, 571-598.

Marcos, L.R. (1979). Effects of interpreters on the evaluation of psychopathology in non-English patients. *Am J. Psychiatry*, 136, 171-174.

McCarty, C.A., Weisz, J.R., Wanitromanee, K., Eastman, K.L., Suwanlert, S., Chaiyasit, W., *et al.* (1999). Culture, coping and context: Primary and secondary control among Thai and American youth. *J. Child Psychol. Psychiatry*, 40, 809-818.

Mezzich, J.E., Kleinman, A., Fabrega, H. Jr., & Parron D.L. (Eds.) (1996). *Culture and Psychiatric Diagnosis: A DMS-IV Perspective*. Washington (DC): American Psychiatric Press.

Prince, R. (2000). Transcultural psychiatry: Personal experiences and Canadian perspectives. *Can. J. Psychiatry*, 45, 431-437.

Sadavoy, J., Meier, R., & Yuk Mui Ong, A. (2004). Barriers to access to mental health services for ethnic seniors: The Toronto study. *Can. J. Psychiatry*, 49, 192-199.

Senate Standing Committee on Social Affairs, Science and Technology. Social 40775-1000—1. Ottawa: Senate Standing Committee on Social Affairs, Science and Technology; May 13, 2004.

Tseng, W.S. (2001). (Ed.) *Handbook of Cultural Psychiatry*. (pp. 26-27), San Diego (CA): Academic Press.

US Department of Health and Human Services. Mental Health: Culture, race and ethnicity—a supplement to mental health: A report of the surgeon general—Executive Summary. Rockville (MD): US Department of Health and Human Services, Public Health Service, Office of the Surgeon General; 2001.

Williams, D.R., & Williams-Morris, R. (2000). Racism and mental health: The African American experience. *Ethnicity and Health*, 5, 243-268.

Zwingle, E. (1999). A world together: Goods move. People move. Ideas move. And cultures change. *National Geographic*, August 12-33.

4

Pain, Placebo and Hypnosis

How Words and Suggestions Affect Patients

ILANA ELI

Pain is a basic and fundamental issue in our existence. There are several forms of pain, which differ from one another not only in its origin, but also in its role in human life and its effect on human emotions and behaviour.

The most basic form of pain is acute pain including acute phasic pain and acute tonic pain. Acute phasic pain is a short duration acute pain occurring at the onset of injury. Its aim is to protect us from further injury and is mainly characterized by withdrawal. After injury has already happened and inflammation starts to develop, we experience acute tonic pain. This form of acute pain can last a while (hours, days or weeks) until recuperation occurs. Its aim is to promote actions directed towards healing, such as immobilization of the injured limb, rest, etc. and is usually associated with such a behaviour.

If pain continues beyond time required for healing (or if healing cannot be achieved), pain becomes chronic. The role of chronic pain in human life is obscure and it is often associated with a significant psychological and social stress, as well as with counterproductive behaviour, such as restlessness, annoyance, etc. The reason for the development of chronic pain conditions is not clear as yet. A lot of medical research is devoted in trying to understand the mechanisms which lead to the development of chronic pain, its prevention and treatment.

The Modern Concept of Pain

The scientific concept of pain evolved only in the middle of the twentieth century when Melzak and Wall (1965) presented their gate control theory, a bio-psycho-social model, for the pain and disease. The gate control theory of pain is a model in which the relation between the stimulus inflicting pain and pain perception and reaction to it is not linear. It involves different sorts of neuron fibres, large diameter and small diameter ones, each reacting differently to the applied, peripheral stimulus. It is the balance of the output of the different fibres which will determine if the stimulus is perceived as pain or is blocked and not be perceived as pain, whatsoever. The model also recognized the importance of central control, namely, that the peripheral stimulus can be blocked (or amplified) also by central effects such as stress, attention, etc.

The bio-psychosocial model shapes the definition of pain as accepted nowadays by the IASP and by the medical and scientific community: Pain is defined as "an unpleasant sensory and ***emotional*** experience associated with actual or ***potential*** tissue damage, or described in terms of such damage" (IASP, 1979). The definition emphasizes that pain is not only a sensory experience but it also bears an emotional component (the mere transmission of the stimulus from the periphery to the CNS is not pain unless it also involves an emotional component). Secondly, pain can also occur even when there is no tissue damage at all, but only a potential of damage exists.

Thus, the experience of pain is comprised from numerous influences, with the pain stimulus being only one of them. It involves the pain stimulus, the receptor system, the perceptual sensory system, the cognitive process, the motivational-affective component, the behavioural response system and the environment.

The gate theory of pain has undergone several developments and elaborations. In the 1990s, the theory was presented in a new form—the neuromatrix theory (Melzack, 1999). According to the neuromatrix theory, when a peripheral stimulus occurs, it is transmitted through several major neural circuits in the brain (somatosensory system, limbic, cognitive system, etc.). The information is shared among the systems and it is the final balance of the shared information which determines if the information is recognized as pain or not. Only then the output is transformed into a conscious perception or blocked whatsoever. Meta analysis and review of PET and fMRI studies provide information about the pain neuromatrix (Apkarian *et al.*, 2007; Tracey & Mantyh, 2007). It shows that the major areas of brain activity under pain are the primary and secondary sensory cortex, insula, anterior cingulated cortex, prefrontal cortices and thalamus (Svensson & Abrahamsen, 2008).

Four major dimensions shape the pain experience. Affecting one or more of these dimensions can alter the subject's pain experience and influence pain perception and reaction. These include: (i) the **Sensory-discriminative** component which refers to the stimulus and its qualities (e.g. intensity, duration, location, quality); (ii) the **Affective-motivational** component refers to the emotional responses to the stimulus (e.g. anxiety, fear, annoyance, despair, depression); (iii) the **Cognitive-evaluative** refers to the way we evaluate the stimulus (e.g. perceive it as threat, expect to experience pain); and (iv) the **effect of the environmental component** which influences the way in which we react to the stimulus in the view of our culture, environment, prior experiences, etc. The different modes to manage pain, be it pharmacological or psychological, refer to and/or are based on the above dimensions.

Psychological Approaches for Pain Management

Last decades brought with it numerous reports regarding psychological approaches for pain management. It is, however, important to remember that not all published material is of an accepted evidence level. This is especially important in the face of the huge, and constantly growing, number of publications which deal with various clinical interventions to manage pain. An evidence pyramid is commonly used as a tool to evaluate the value of such publications. Firstly, we categorize studies according to the type of evidence. Secondly, we consider the strength and consistency of the evidence. The combination of the two gives us an evaluation of the level of evidence as follows (according to Agency for Health Care Policy Research, 1994) :

1. Type of Evidence

Level I—Meta analyses;
Level II—Randomized, controlled, double blind studies;
Level III—Non-randomized, single pre-post, cohort, time series;
Level IV—Non-experimental (e.g. comparative, correlational, descriptive, (case studies); and
Level V—Case reports, clinical examples.

2. Strength and Consistency of Evidence

A—Consistent findings, multiple studies;
B—Some evidence, generally consistent;
C—Some evidence, findings inconsistent; and
D—Little or no evidence.

Fig. 4.1 : Types, Strength and Consistency of Evidence

Thus, levels of IA, IIA indicate the highest level of evidence, while studies categorized as VD, VC—the lowest. Namely, publication of opinions, ideas etc., is rated low at the evidence Pyramid. Also case reports and case series supply us with relatively low evidence base. It is randomized, controlled, double blind studies, systematic reviews and meta analyses of such studies which are accepted as having high level of evidence.

Basically, most of the psychological approaches to pain management refer to the issue—who controls the pain? Is it the physician or the care giver who supplies the patient with the adequate medication or is it the patient who has the main responsibility over the treatment. Most, if not all, of these techniques put the key to pain management in the hands and in the responsibility of the patient.

Different psychological techniques to manage pain refer to the different dimensions of the pain experience :

1. Techniques referring to the sensory component of pain, like hypnosis and placebo. The level of evidence of these techniques is relatively high (IA, IB) for management of both acute and chronic pain.
2. Strategies aimed at the affective component of the pain experience. These include techniques such as relaxation, psychotherapy, support, etc. Although there are numerous publications on these issues, their level of evidence is relatively low.
3. Strategies aimed at the cognitive component (like cognitive behavioural therapy) and at the behavioural component of the pain experience (behavioural therapy) were described mainly as to their effect on chronic pain. Here, too, the level of evidence is relatively low.

Placebo and Nocebo

Placebo ("I shall please") is a well known strategy, aimed to decrease pain. However, sometimes a less beneficial nocebo

("I shall harm") effect might occur, which leads to increase in pain levels. Both are closely connected with the patients' expectations of a specific situation and are strongly affected by physicians' suggestions.

In the potent placebo effect, the mere belief and expectation of analgesia induces discrete physiological changes, leading to relief from pain. This response is probably mediated by endogenous opioids. Namely, the cognitive belief in the efficacy of placebo, initiates the secretion of opiod substances which alleviate pain. The clinical proof for that is that these effects can be reversed by Naloxone, an opiod antagonist. Although we are far from completely understanding all the processes involved in psychological pain management (or in general pain management for that matter) there is enough proof that the psychological processes are associated with some distinct physiological changes which enable pain alleviation.

Positive expectations (placebo suggestions) decrease the transmission in pain pathways and cause activity in numerous brain areas. There are some brain regions that get activated by both placebo suggestions and by opioid drugs (psychosocial effects; pharmaco-dynamic effects), other brain regions are affected by placebo alone (cognitive-evaluative network, pain processing regions) (Colloca & Benedetti, 2005). The brain regions mostly activated during placebo analgesia is the rostral anterior cingulate cortex (Petrovic *et al.*, 2002). The biochemical pathways of placebo suggestions include increased secretion of endogenous opioids and a decreased activation of Cholecystokinin receptors (CCK) (Colloca & Benedetti, 2005), both leading to pain reduction.

On the other side, negative expectations (nocebo suggestions) to experience pain result in the amplification of pain. An expectation to experience pain activates the thalamus, insular cortex, somatosensory cortex, anterior cingulate cortex, and other brain regions (Keltner *et al.*, 2006). It amplifies pain through increased activation of CCK (Benedetti *et al.*, 2006) and decreased activation of endogenous opioids (Amanzio & Benedetti, 1999).

Hypnosis

Hypnosis is defined as "an altered state of consciousness characterized by markedly increased receptivity to suggestion" (Barber, 1996) or "a procedure during which a health professional or researcher suggests that a patient or subject experience changes in sensations, perceptions, thoughts, or behaviour" (The Executive Committee of the American Psychological Association—Division of Psychological Hypnosis, 1994).

Hypnosis enables muscle relaxation which inevitably leads to a decrease in the subject's stress response. It affects also involuntary muscles, controlling the respiratory, alimentary and cardiovascular systems. During hypnosis we can achieve alterations in physical senses (e.g. sight, smell, hearing, pain). We achieve alterations in mental activity, reduction in critical thinking and higher susceptibility to persuasive communication from others or from self.

The amount of information about the ability of hypnosis to manage pain is huge and there is enough scientific evidence in research literature. Hypnosis is a potent tool to block the sensory component of pain and when used properly can reduce, or even totally diminish the need to use local anesthetic agents. A meta-analysis of 18 studies revealed a moderate to large hypnoanalgesic effect, supporting the efficacy of hypnotic techniques for pain management (Montgomery *et al.*, 2000). The brain regions affected by hypnosis include the mid-cingulate cortex, insula, perigenual cortex, pre-supplementary motor cortex, brainstem and thalamus (Faymonville *et al.*, 2006; Faymonville *et al.*, 2000; Hofbauer *et al.*, 2001; Rainville *et al.*, 1997, 1999; Schulz-Stubner *et al.*, 2004). Studies showed that hypnotic analgesia is mediated by an increased functional connectivity between brain areas (Kupers *et al.*, 2005) and is not altered by naloxone (Moret *et al.*, 1991).

It is important to point out that hypnotic analgesia is different from placebo effect. While placebo analgesia is affected by expectation (Montgomery and Kirsch, 1996; Amanzio and Benedetti, 1999; Colloca & Benedetti, 2005) and mediated by opioids (blocked by naloxone); hypnotic analgesia is not affected by expectations (Sharav and Tal, 2004) and not mediated by opioids (not affected by naloxone).

Summary

1. Pain is produced by the output of the neural network in the brain rather than by sensory input evoked by injury.
2. The doctor's words can actually affect the patient's brain (placebo/nocebo suggestions).
3. Placebo and hypnotic analgesia bear distinct qualities.
4. Medical research has provided substantial evidence regarding the efficacy of hypnosis and placebo in pain management.

REFERENCES

Agency for Health Care Policy Research, 1994.

Amanzio, M., & Benedetti, F. (1999). Neuropharmacological dissection of placebo analgesia: Expectation activated opiod systems *versus* condition activated specific systems. *J. Neuroscience,* 19(1), 484-494.

Apkarian, A.V., Bushnell, M.C., Treede R.D., & Zubieta, J.K. (2005). Human brain mechanisms of pain perception and regulation in health and disease. *Eur. J. Pain,* 9, 463-484.

Barber, J. (1996). A brief introduction to hypnotic analgesia, In J. Barber (Ed), *Hypnosis and Suggestion in the Treatment of Pain* (p. 5). New York: Norton & Co.

Benedetti, F., *et al.* (2006). The biochemical and neuroendocrine bases of the hyperalgessic nocebo effect. *J. Neuroscience,* 26(46), 12014-12022.

Colloca, L., & Benedetti, F. (2005). Placebo as painkillers: Is mind as real as matter? *Nature Reviews, Neuroscience,* 6, 545-552.

Faymonville, M.E., Boly, M., & Laureyes, S. (2006). Functional neuroanatomy of the hypnotic stage. *J. Physiol.* Paris, 99, 463-469.

Faymonville, M.E., Laureyes. S., Degueldre., C., DelFiore. G., Luxen, A., & Franck, G. (2000). Neural mechanisms of antinociceptive effects of hypnosis. *Anasthesiolgy,* 92, 1257-1267.

Hofbauer, R.K.A., Rainville, P., Duncan, G.H., & Bushnell, M.C. (2001). Cortical representation of the sensory dimension of pain. *J. Neurophysiol,* 86, 402-411.

IASP Subcommittee on Taxonomy. Pain terms: A list with definitions and notes on usage. (1979). *Pain,* 6, 249-252.

Keltner, J.R. *et al.*, (2006). Isolating the modulatory effect of expectation on pain transmission: A functional magnetic resonance imaging study. *J. Neuroscience,* 26(16), 4437-4443.

Kupers, R., Faymonville, M.E., & Laureys, S. (2005). The cognitive modulation of pain: Hypnosis and placebo-induced analgesia. *Progress in Brain Res.,* 190, 251-269.

Melzack, R. (1999). Pain and stress: A new perspective. In R.J. Gatchel, & D.C. Turk (Eds.), *Psychosocial Factors in Pain* (pp. 89-106). New York: The Guilford Press.

Melzack, R., & Wall, P.D. (1965). Pain Mechanisms—A New Theory. *Science,* 150, 971.

Montgomery, G.H., & Kirsch, I. (1996). Mechanism of placebo pain reduction—an empirical investigation. *Psychol. Sci,* 7, 174-176.

Montgomery, G.H., DuHamel, K.N., & Redd, W.H. (2000). *Int. J. Clin. Exp. Hypn.,* 48, 138-153.

Moret, *et al.* (1991). Mechanism of analgesia induced by hypnosis and acupuncture—Is there a difference? *Pain,* 45, 135-140.

Petrovic, P., Kalso, E., Peterson, K.M., & Ingvar, M. (2002). Palcebo and opioid analgesia—imaging a shared neuronal network. *Science,* 295, 1737-1740.

Rainville, P., Duncan, G.H., Price, D.D., Carrier, B., & Bushnell, M.C. (1977). Pain affect encoded in human anterior cingulate but not sensory cortex. *Science,* 277, 968-971.

Rainville, P., Hobauer, R.K., Paus, T., Duncan, G.H., & Bushnell, M.C. (1999). Cerebral mechanisms of hypnotic induction and suggestion. *J. Cogn. Neurosci.,* 11, 110-125.

Schulz-Stubner, S., Krings, T., Meister, I.G., Rex, S., Thron, A., & Rossaint, R. (2004). Clinical hypnosis modulates functional magnetic resonance imaging signal in pain perception in a thermal stimulation paradigm. *Reg. Anesth. Pain Med.,* 29, 549-556.

Sharav, Y., & Tal, M. (2004). Focussed analgesia and generalized relaxation produce different hypnotic analgesia in response to ascending stimulus intensity. *Int. J. of Psychophysiology,* 52, 187-196.

Svensson, P., & Abrahamsen, R. (2008). Central representation of muscle and pain in hyperalgesia. In T. Graven-Nielsen, L. Arendt-Nielsen, & S. Mense (Eds.), *Fundamentals of Musculoskeletal Pain* (pp. 189-203). Seattle: IASP Press.

The Executive Committee of the American Psychological Association (1994). Division of Psychological Hypnosis.

Tracey, I., & Mantyh, P.W. (2007). The cerebral signature for pain perception and its modulation. *Neuron,* 55, 377-391.

5

Clinical Hypnosis and Yoga

An Integrative Perspective for Spiritual Development

RENU SHARMA

Introduction

Spirituality has been explored throughout the human history as one of the fundamental aspects of human beings (i.e., body, mind, spirit) (Huitt, 2003). In broad perspective, spirituality deals fundamentally with how we approach the unknowns of life, how we define and relate to sacred. The importance of spirituality lies in the fact that, it is a very important component for lasting human happiness.

In Indian tradition, Yoga with its all eight steps as prescribed in *Astang Yoga,* is considered as most effective method of pursuing spirituality. However, in last two decades meditation (one out of eight steps of *Astang Yoga*) has found larger acceptance by Western world and a host of empirical research has been devoted to it. Meditation techniques are drawn largely from Patanjali's *Yoga Sutras* and from Buddhist form of concentrative meditation. Perhaps the elements of Buddhist meditation that are most relevant and intriguing to Western culture are the types of consciousness-altering techniques and their clinical applications in various psychological, medical, and dental specialities. In fact, the non-religious practice of meditation has been popularized in the

U.S in recent years in the name of "visualization" (Brigham, 1996; Fezler, 1989) or "mindfulness meditation" (Hanh, 1999; Kabat-Zinn, 1995). The process is largely similar to contemporary clinical hypnosis having the backing of large scientific research with regard to its efficacy in physical and mental health field (Carlisle, 1988; Edelstein, 1981, 1982; Frederick, 1990, 1992; Malmo, 1991; Newey, 1986; Newey & Newton, 1979; Phillips, 1991; Stewart, 1983; Torem, 1984, 1987).

Hypnosis

Hypnosis is a distinctive, often trance-like mental state that is induced by an organized pattern of suggestions, usually verbal in nature, beginning with the suggestion of relaxation. The suggestions may be directly induced by a hypnotist in the presence of the subject, but may also be self-induced (self-hypnosis or autohypnosis/auto-suggestion).

Although the long held popular view was that hypnosis is a form of unconsciousness, the informed contemporary view is that it is actually a wakeful state of focussed attention and heightened suggestibility, with diminished peripheral awareness. According to the American Psychological Association's Division 30, hypnosis may bring about ". . . . changes in subjective experience, alterations in perception, sensation, emotion, thought or behaviour."

Two aspects of Buddhist meditation—concentration and mindfulness—can be discussed in relationship to hypnosis. Mindfulness training facilitates the investigation of subjective responses to hypnosis. Concentration practice leads to altered states similar to those in hypnosis, both phenomenologically and neurologically (Holroyd, 2003).

Needless to say, both concentration and mindfulness are familiar and crucial elements in hypnosis. Brown & Fromm (1986) elucidate that hypnotic trance is not only characterized by "concentrated and focussed attention" but also by "ego-receptivity." The latter is especially relevant to both hypnosis and meditation for it suggests a temporal suspension of the critical awareness of external reality. In this receptive mode, the ego serves as "the 'gates' to primary process thoughts and images" by "allowing things happen, ... leading to a greater availability of unconscious material" (Brown & Fromm, 1986, p. 203).

Since, hypnosis and meditation have many similarities, the question is—whether hypnosis can be a better technique than meditation for spiritual development, or more importantly whether hypnosis can complement yogic practices. It is author's belief that hypnosis can complement Yoga for effective spiritual development. The idea of cross-fertilization of the current meditational techniques with modern clinical hypnosis is also suggested by Otani (2003), albeit for therapeutic usage. To carry forward the argument, it is imperative to have an overview on the concepts of spirituality and Yoga.

Spirituality

Spirituality can be treated as a psychological dimension of human personality. American Counselling Association (ACA) has defined spirituality as *a capacity and tendency that is innate and unique to all persons. This spiritual tendency moves the individual towards knowledge, love, meaning, peace, hope, transcendence, connectedness, compassion, wellness, and wholeness. Spirituality includes one's capacity for creativity, growth, and development of a value system. Spirituality encompasses a variety of phenomena, including experiences, beliefs, and practices. Spirituality is approached from a variety of perspectives, including psycho-spiritual, religious, and transpersonal.*

The term "spirituality" is rooted in the Latin word *spiritus*, which means "breath of life" (Elkins, *et al*., 1988). Kelly (1995) describes it as "a personal affirmation of a transcendent connectedness in the universe" (p. 4). Shafranske and Gorsuch (1984) call it "the courage to look within and to trust. What is seen and trusted appears to be a deep sense of belonging, of wholeness, of connectedness, and of openness to the infinite" (p. 233). Elkins, *et al*. (1988) describe spirituality as "a way of being and experiencing that comes about through awareness of a transcendent dimension and that is characterized by certain identifiable values in regard to self, others, nature, life, and whatever one considers to be the Ultimate" (p.10). Sri Aurobindo (1970) has presented a detailed perspective on spirituality in terms of 'psychic' phenomenon. These definitions have in common a view of human nature, which recognizes the longing for a reality beyond the physically finite and the search for a deep and abiding meaning to life.

In Indian philosophy, spirituality is seen as a way of life, a process rather than a product, a journey of self-discovery and growth. It is the expression of potential against opposing forces of *karma, samskara* and *guna*. Indian psychology does not accept human life as deterministic; rather, it provides ample freedom of choice and action in its *karmas* to rise above its limitations of *samskaras* and *gunas*. This capacity is rooted in the basic human nature. Indian scriptures, especially the *Astang Yoga* of Patanjali prescribed Yoga as a means of spiritual development whose ultimate result is variously described as the transcendence or *moksha*

Yoga

The *Patanjali Yoga* philosophy, which is one of the six systems constituting Vedic philosophy, is also known as *Astang Yoga* (the *yoga* of eight parts or limbs) and is closely related to Sankhya and Vedantic philosophy. *Ashtanga Yoga* is the practical manifestation of both these philosophies. This practical system attempts to understand the nature of the elusive element known as 'mind'—its different states of being, impediments to growth, afflictions and the methods of harnessing it for the achievement of absolute self-realization.

The central doctrine of Yoga philosophy is that nothing exists beyond the mind and its consciousness, which is the only ultimate reality. The objective of this philosophy is to uproot misconceptions about the existence of external 'realities' from the minds of men. It believes that it is possible to reach this stage of self-realization through regular practice of *Astang Yoga* that brings a complete withdrawal or detachment from all false sources of knowledge and inculcates an inner sense of balanced calm and tranquillity.

Astanga Yoga means purifying the mind through eight steps. These eight steps are—

(i) *Yama: Yama* is described by five universal vows. These vows are guidelines for how one should interact with the outer world and adhere to the social disciplines for better relationship with others. The five vows are truthfulness, non-violence, celibacy, non-covetousness, and non-stealing.

(ii) *Niyama: Niyama* describes how to interact with internal world. Niyama is about self-regulation. It helps to maintain a positive environment in which one can grow naturally. The five *niyamas* are contentment, purity, self-education, austerity, and meditation on the divine.

The *yamas* and *niyamas* help to view ourselves with compassion and awareness. They help us to lead a conscious life. These are about being honest to ourselves and respecting the value of this life.

(iii) *Yogasana: Yogasana* is a posture in harmony with inner consciousness. It helps in attaining a comfortable posture for meditation and balancing the basic structure of the human body. The five basic functions of *asanas* are to develop mental, spiritual, cognitive, and intellectual functions.

Yogasanas help in affecting the mind positively and have various physiological benefits. In regular practice of *yogasanas*, weight is reduced, blood pressure normalized, cholesterol level controlled, and heart performance improved. The *yogasanas* make mind strong to enable one to face mental and physical sufferings.

(iv) *Pranayama: Pranayama* is the maintenance of *prana* in a healthy way throughout our life. Pranayama is controlling the life force or *prana*. The practice of *pranayama* helps in harnessing the *prana* in and around oneself. The *pranayamas* can be classified as: breath retention technique, inhaling through the nostrils, travel of breath between the nose and the heart, and concentrated and fixed breathing exercise.

Pranayama helps to manipulate energies, if practiced correctly. It helps in releasing tensions and develops a relaxed state of mind. It improves mental clarity, creative thinking and physical well-being. It balances the nervous system and increases the amount of oxygen to the brain to improve alertness. *Pranayama* enables the mind to attain ability to concentrate on any given object of attention. When practiced along with *yogasnas* the benefits are more pronounced.

(v) *Pratyahara: Pratyahara* manages senses in a correct way. It goes beyond the senses instead of suppressing them. It involves reining in the senses for better attention.

(vi) *Dharana: Dharana* develops and extends powers of concentration. Attention and mind-fixing skills can be directed and controlled. It also involves concentrating on *chakras* or turning inwards.

(vii) *Dhyana: Dhyana* is the state of meditation. At this state, mind attains ability to concentrate. *Dhyana* is nothing but a state of mind when it attains natural ability to concentrate without distraction.

(viii) *Samadhi: Samadhi* is the total absorption. The individual consciousness becomes pure consciousness. It is the ability to become one with the true self and merge into the object of concentration. The different levels of *Samadhi* are distinguished contemplation, non-distinguished contemplation, deliberated absorption, non-deliberated absorption, reflective meditation, and non-reflective meditation.

The above eight steps are practiced in ascending order. In the vast field of *yoga*, there are many layers, aspects, and dimensions. And while most meditators usually only focus on the most superficial aspect of *yoga*, seeing it as a system of physical postures or breathing exercises designed to bring strength and flexibility to the body, more scholarly experts agree, however, that the essence of *yoga* is given in Patanjali's second *sutra*: *"Yogas citta-vrtti-nirodhah."* In this *sutra, Yoga* is described as both the process of calming and quieting the mind, as well as the end result of possessing a calm and quiet mind. In the third *sutra,* Patanjali describes what happens through the practice and achievement of the second *sutra*: "*Tada drastuh svarupe vasthanam.*" "Then the seer is established in his own essential and fundamental nature." This is the ultimate goal of *yoga*: union with the Higher Self, often referred to as *samadhi,* enlightenment, or pure bliss consciousness (*Satchitananda*) (Tamini, 2001).

Integration of Hypnosis with Yoga

While it is true that *yoga* practice does bring about a more untroubled attitude, to present this as the goal of *yoga,* as the most *yoga* practitioners today believe, is to support a misperception that *yoga* practice is about becoming better adapted to the world. This takes *yoga* out of its spiritual context and diminishes the possibility of the radical reorientation of consciousness necessary for realization of one's true nature. If *yoga* practices are presented outside of their spiritual context, they are no longer *yoga* in strict Indian tradition.

Patanjali's *Yoga Sutras* is considered as the definitive work on traditional *yoga,* and is well known as the first ever written. According to the *Yoga Sutras,* the ultimate aim of Yoga is to reach "*Kaivalya*" (freedom). This is the experience of one's innermost being or "soul" (the *purusa*). When this level of awareness is achieved, one becomes free of the chains of cause and effect (*karma*). In the second and third chapters of the *Yoga Sutra,* Patanjali describes a methodology for the practice of traditional *yoga* called the 'eight-fold path' or the 'eight limbs of *yoga.*'

The first five steps of *Astang Yoga* are called external aids to *yoga* (*bahiranga sadhana*) and the rest three are referred as internal aids (*antarik sadhana*). Sequentially, one has to learn and practice *yama, niyama, asana, pranayama, pratyahara, dharana, dhyana and samadhi.* In its popular usage, especially in the West, the term *yoga* has come to be associated more or less exclusively with the physical postures (*asana*), the regulation of breathing (*pranayama*) and concentration (*dharana*) each in isolation or in combination. This popular usage is not approved in Indian philosophy. An individual who merely practices the postures, the breathing exercises and concentration exercises, without a concomitant consecration to a spiritual discipline and to the goals of *yoga,* is simply practicing a few yogic exercises, and not practicing *yoga* in strict sense.

Yama and *Niyama* are not meant to be a set of rules set up to make life more convenient for parents, teachers and heads of state. They are a direct tool for the liberation of true intellect. *Yama* and *Niyama* are an indispensable base; furthermore, an integral part and starting point of *yoga.*

To move towards spirituality, man must first clear, and then steady, his mind against the fury of illusory passions, and free his life from entanglements. Patanjali very carefully and fully outlines the elements of the support needed by the aspirant, giving invaluable information on how to guarantee success in *yoga.*

The ten restraints (*yama*) and observances (*niyama*) are not optional for the aspiring *yogi*. Shankara states quite forcefully that "following *yama* and *niyama* is the basic qualification to practice *yoga*. Mere desire and aspiration for the goal of *yoga* is not enough." The qualification is not simply that one wants to practice *yoga,* for the sacred texts (*Katha Upanishad*) say: "But he who has not first turned away from his wickedness, who is not tranquil and subdued, or whose mind is not at rest, he can never obtain the Self by knowledge." Similar are the opinion of other texts: "It is in those who have *tapas* (strong discipline) and *brahmacharya* (chastity) that truth is established" (*Prashna Upanishad*). So *yama* and *niyama* are methods of *yoga* in themselves and are not mere adjuncts or aids that can be optional.

In the same way, *asanas and pranayama* should not be confused with mere exercises that help strengthen and develop muscles. The main application of *asanas and pranayamas* is the resolution of problems that appear on the path of meditation. Most of us, especially when we begin meditational practices, become surprised to what extent the mind is restless, unstable and full of various thoughts and desires. Emotions of anger, fear, hate and their derivatives afflict us, while emotions of enchantment, infatuation and attachment and their derivatives delight us. Both kinds of emotions and sensations impede our efforts to enter deep meditative states. Such mental impediments are due to the effect of mental modifications (*vrittis*), which try to find external expression through the sensory organs and, therefore, create emotional confusion. Since *vrittis* are derivatives of endocrine glands, if one can regulate one's (hormonal) secretions through *asanas* and other special *yogic* techniques, one can regulate and control the emotions and the mind. Gradually the mind becomes calm and focussed, i.e., ready for deep meditation.

As said above, practice of only *asana, pranayama* and *dhyana* may be sufficient for the betterment of physical and mental health, however, for spirituality one has to start from *yama* and move upward. In day-to-day life this is very difficult, as *yama-niyama* call for 24-hour self-surveillance or self-regulation. They refer to developing spontaneity in truthfulness, and *ahimsa* to be followed 24 hours a day. To be spiritual, it is essential to transform to such a nature. To develop such a life style is difficult even with a strong will-power. Like moods and emotions, will-power too fluctuates. One day it may be strong and the very next day could be quite a depressing, and will-power diminishes. Unethical habits are rooted in, and perpetuated by the power of imagination. For that reason, such problems cannot be countered effectively by will-power alone. Will-power is a function of the conscious mind, and it is always at the mercy of the subconscious. Because of the problems faced in first-two practices, i.e. *yama* and *niyama*, most modern day practitioners of *yoga* start from *asanas*, which is not advised by the proponents of *yoga* such as Jois (2008) who says, "The starting point of *yoga* studies is not *asanas* and *pranayamas*, but the study of *yama* and *niyama*. If one starts the study of *yoga* ignoring these *yamas* and *niyamas*, he will not be in position to experience the results of studies as expected. One cannot negotiate on this aspect."

It is upon this elementary truth that the techniques of hypnotherapy and self-hypnosis can be adopted to internalize *yama-niyama*. Because of the utilization and manipulation of the force of imagination upon the subconscious, hypnosis or hypnotherapy could become the most effective means of implementing *yoga* as prescribed in literature. Self-hypnosis/ hypnotherapy thereby deserves valid consideration in any effective programme of *yama, niyama* and other limbs of *yoga*. To appreciate the role of *yama/niyama,* one should first understand the life journey of human being in the language of Metzner (1998, p. 258) :

> *"In the first phase [of life], which normally lasts from childhood to middle adulthood, we are becoming individuals, in the sense of learning the ways of the world and involving ourselves in the demands of family, work, and society. In the second phase, which begins, according to Jung, with the midlife crisis, when we may find ourselves, like Dante, 'lost in the middle of a dark forest,' we begin the process of individuation, which involves a turning inward, to reconnect with the Self, the centre of our being. One could say in the first phase you build and develop your ego and in the second phase you transcend it."*

It is this ego-transcending effort that is the prime goal in (*yoga*) *yama-niyama* and can be undertaken through the Ego-state model of Hypnotherapy. There is sufficient research on the efficacy of ego-state hypnotherapy in overcoming the ego issues (Chessick, 1993; Frederick & McNeal, 1999; Phillips & Frederick, 1992; Watkins, & Watkins, 1997).

Ego-state therapy is a psychodynamic approach in which techniques of group and family therapy are employed to resolve conflicts between various "ego-states" that constitute a "family of self" within a single individual. It assumes that any person is really composed of many diverse, fragmentary images of "self" which reflect different personas or life experiences. These images are generally covert, hidden, disassociated or disconnected ego-states that we might not be aware of. These normal fragments of personality are often called "ego-states." Ego-states that are cognitively dissonant from one another or have contradictory goals frequently develop conflicts with one another. However, many such conflicts appear between ego-states only covertly, and are frequently manifested by anxiety, depression, or any number of neurotic symptoms and maladaptive behaviours (Watkins & Watkins, 1993).

Although covert ego-states do not normally become overt except in true multiple personality, they are hypnotically activated and made accessible for contact and communication with the therapist. Any of the behavioural, cognitive, analytic, or humanistic techniques may then be employed in a kind of internal diplomacy. Available evidence of last two decades has demonstrated that complex psychodynamic problems can often be resolved in a relatively short time through Ego-state therapy.

In the context of yogic philosophy the ego-states may be referred in terms of *citta-vrattis*. They refer to the distortion in the true nature of *citta*. Like ego-states, *vrattis* are completely mental and subtle. They are difficult to recognize. However, the physical manifestations of *vrattis* and ego-states is grosser, and, therefore, easier to recognize.

Both *vrattis* and ego-states prevent the full functioning of the individual and thereby hinder reflection of true self. *Vrattis* must be overcome before self is realized. This process needs systematic transformation of *citta*. *Yama-niyama* are prescribed for such a transformation in *Ashtanga yoga*. Incidentally, the ego-state hypnotherapy does exactly same, and possibly more effectively as evidenced in hypnosis research.

As we initiate work on *yama-niyama* through ego-state hypnotherapy initially one must consider the origin of ego-states. Often they were first created when the individual was quite young. The child ego-state was formed to adapt to the conditions of yesteryear, not today, and its attempts to function today often results in maladaptation. As one inquires and secures some information about the time and the circumstances when an ego-state first appeared, one's approach to deal with it can be modified accordingly. This modification can be done without embarrassment and conscious effort under hypnosis.

As therapy progresses, ego-states (*vrattis*) that hold the underlying feelings of emptiness, rage, depression, jealousy, greed, untruthfulness and other unethical habits are able to emerge. With further practice, transformation and maturation of the ego states occur, reflecting the changes in internal structure and dynamics as well as improvement in external interpersonal relationships. The person must learn and feel how he/she has sacrificed him/herself, then mourn his/her losses, rediscover his/her own deeply buried spiritual needs, and attempt to meet them. This is nothing but what Johnson (1994) calls as character transformation—a process of maturation that involves the development of creativity, the acceptance of transience, and development of the capacities for empathy, a sense of humour, and wisdom.

With ego maturity through hypnotherapy, we acquire a clear sense of Self. Knowing where the self ends and the 'other' begins; we replace projection with empathy. When the self is contained and secure in its worth, we as individuals, far from being self-invested, accord the same respect to others as we do to ourselves. When the altruism of 'doing for others' is not motivated by a desire for return or secondary gain, we are close to ego-transcendence (Gagan, 1998, pp. 143-144).

Hypnotherapist can provide empathy, regard, and a safe place for the person to experience his or her pain while sacrificing his old habits as a part of *yama/niyama* practice. In ancient traditional Indian set-up, this support was offered by Guru. Interpretation or reframing can emphasize pain as a signal in such a way as to enhance internal exploration. Interpretation can relate current injuries, anger, and disappointments to earlier failures of the environment to meet the person's spiritual goal, while also providing support for the person's innate capabilities combined with realistic assessment of abilities, resources, weaknesses, and limitations. The hypnotherapist, here, is only a media to train the person in self-hypnosis and relieve him of internal injuries, inflictions, and attachments. The person makes the informed choice to grow up, to accept his humanity, and finally let in the love and acceptance of others and Higher Self. The use of self-hypnosis can further enhance this process in helping him to build internal structure, and consolidate his new spiritual identity.

Spiritual growth and development takes many forms depending on the culture in which one lives. The content of the hypnosis sessions depends greatly on the *vrattis* engrained in belief system of the person undertaking it. Having overcome the problems faced in *yama-niyama* through hypnosis, it would be easier to follow or practice the other six steps of *Ashtanga yoga*. Hypnosis can even be used for *dhyana* for better connection. Integration of hypnosis with *yoga* may have immense influence on the speed of progress on eight-step *yoga*. Further applied research on the integration of hypnosis and *yoga* can open up exciting new possibilities.

REFERENCES

American Counselling Association (2006). *A White Paper of the Association for Spiritual, Ethical and Religious Values in Counselling*. Retrieved on 06/10/2006 from htpp: www.aservic.org/guidelines.htm.

Bhagavad Gita, 6:14.

Brigham, D.D. (1996). *Imagery for Getting Well: Clinical Applications of Behavioural Medicine*. New York: Norton.

Carlisle, A. (1988). *Dreams in Multiple Personality Disorder and Ego-state Conditions*. 5th International Conference on Multiple Personality and Dissociated States, Chicago, IL.

Chessick, R.D. (1993). *Psychology of the Self and the Treatment of Narcissism*. Northvale, New Jersey: Jason Aronson.

Edelstein, M.G. (1981). *Trauma, Trance, and Transformation: A Clinical Guide to Hypnotherapy*. New York: Brunner/Mazel.

Edelstein, M.G. (1982). Ego-state therapy in the management of resistance. *American Journal of Clinical Hypnosis*, 25, 15-20.

Elkins, D.N., Hedstrom, L.J., Hughes, L.L., Leaf, J.A., & Saunders, C. (1988). Toward a humanistic-phenomenological spirituality. *Journal of Humanistic Psychology*, 28, 5-18.

Fezler, W. (1989). *Creative Imagery*. New York: Fireside.

Fraser, G.A. (1991). The dissociative table technique: A strategy for working with ego-states in dissociative disorders and ego-state therapy. *Dissociation*, 4, 205-213.

Frederick, C. (1990). *Rapid Treatment of Obsessive-Compulsive Disorder with Ego-state Therapy*. 5th European Congress of Hypnosis in Psychotherapy and Psychosomatic Medicine, Constance, Germany.

Frederick, C. (1992). *Heidi and the Little Girl: The Creation of Helpful Ego-states for the Management of Performance Anxiety*. 12th International Congress of Hypnosis, Jerusalem, Israel.

Frederick, C., & McNeal, S. (1999). *Inner Strength: Contemporary Psychotherapy and Hypnosis for Ego-strengthening*. Mahwah, New Jersey: Lawrence Erlbaum and Associates.

Holroyd, J. (2003). The Science of Meditation and States of Hypnosis. *American Journal of Clinical Hypnosis, 2,* 46

Hanh, T.N. (1999). *The Miracle of Mindfulness.* Boston: Beacon Press.

Huitt, W.G. (2003). *An Introduction to Spiritual Development.* Paper presented at the 11th Annual Conference on Applied Psychology in Education, Mental, Health and Business. Valdosta, G.A.

Gagan, J.M. (1998). *Journeying: Where Shamanism and Psychology Meet.* Santa Fe, NM: Rio Chama Publications.

Johnson, S.M. (1994). *Character Styles.* New York: W.W. Norton.

Jois, K. Pattabhi. (2008). *Ashtanga Yoga.* (Pg 3) Downloaded on 9/10/2008. http://www.scribd.com/doc/12573685/Ashtanga-Yoga-by-Maharishi-Patanjali.

Kabat-Zinn, J. (1995). *Wherever You Go, There You Are: Mindfulness Meditation in Everyday Life.* New York: Hyperion.

Katha Upanishad, 1.2.24.

Kelly, E.W. (1995). *Spirituality and Religion in Counselling and Psychotherapy: Diversity in Theory and Practice.* Alexandria, VA: American Counselling Association.

Metzner, R. (1998). *The Unfolding Self: Varieties of Transformational Experience.* Novato, CA: Origin Press.

Malmo, C. (1991). Ego state therapy: A model for overcoming childhood trauma. *Hypnos, 28,* 39-44.

Newey, A.B. (1986). Ego state therapy with depression. In B. Zilbergeld, M.G. Edelstein, & D.L. Araoz (Eds.), *Hypnosis: Questions and Answers* (pp. 197-203). New York: Norton.

Newey, A.B., & Newton, B.W. (1979). *Ego-state Therapy: Everyman a Sybil?* 22nd Annual Meeting of the American Society of Clinical Hypnosis, San Francisco, CA.

Otani, A. (2003). Eastern meditative techniques and hypnosis: A new synthesis. *American Journal of Clinical Hypnosis,* 233-240.

Phillips, M. (1991). *The Use of Ego-state Therapy with Posttraumatic Stress Disorder.* 34th Annual Scientific Meeting of the American Society of Clinical Hypnosis, Las Vegas, Nevada.

Phillips, M., & Frederick, C. (1992). The use of hypnotic age progressions as prognostic, ego-strengthening, and integrating technique. *American Journal of Clinical Hypnosis,* 35, 90-108.

Prashna Upanishad, 1:15.

Sen, A.P. (2006). *Raja Yoga: The Science of Self-realization.* New Delhi: Orient Blackswan.

Shafranske, S.P., & Goursuch, R.L. (1984). Factors associated with the perception of spirituality in psychotherapy. *Journal of Transpersonal Psychology,* 16, 231-142.

Sri Aurobindo. (1992). *The Synthesis of Yoga.* Pondicherry: Sri Aurobindo Ashram Trust.

Stewart, D.L. (1983). *Ego-state Therapy and its Relationship to the Peri-natal Period*. First International Congress on Pre- and Peri-Natal Psychology, Toronto, Canada.

Tamini. (2001). *The Science of Yoga*. New Delhi: Theosophical Publishing House.

Torem, M.S. (1984). *Anorexia Nervosa and Multiple Dissociated Ego States*. First International Conference on Multiple Personality and Dissociated States, Chicago, IL.

Torem, M.S. (1987). Ego-state therapy for eating disorders. *American Journal of Clinical Hypnosis*, 30, 94-104.

Watkins, J.G., & Watkins, H.H. (1993). Accessing the Relevant Areas of Maladaptive Personality Functioning. *American Journal of Clinical Hypnosis*, 35(4), 277-284.

Watkins, J.G., & Watkins, H.H. (1997). *Ego States: Theory and Therapy*. New York: W.W. Norton.

Yogacharya Shivaji Mizner. *The Yoga Sutras of Maharishi Patanjali*—a translation and commentary.

Zimberoff, D., & Hartman, D. (1998). Personal transformation with heart-centered therapies. *Journal of Heart-Centered Therapies*, 1(1), 211.

6

Evolving Paradigm in Hypnotherapy

ANIL LALWANI

Introduction

Evolution is not a fad, rather it is a norm. We humans have been evolving right since our inception and so our notions and ideas keep adjusting to new ways that we develop to understand ourselves. In a way, it can be said, whatever starts in a way does not end the same way. Psychology as a discipline, might have started as an enquiry of the soul, but kept changing its emphasis from one epoch to another—from soul to mind, than to consciousness, and finally resorting to behaviour. The current accepted definition as given in the dictionary of psychology (Colman, 2006) defines the psychology as, "the study of the nature, functions, and the phenomena of behaviour and mental experience." Going by the etymology of the word, psychology should have been actually exploring the mind, but much of modern psychology focusses on behaviour rather than the mind, and some aspects of psychology have little to do with mind.

Hypnotherapy is not an exception when it comes to its transitional nature. Attributing its origin to the oriental culture, it was the West that acknowledged its latent therapeutic effect and further explored it. *Atharva Veda* which dates back to about 5000 BC, mentions a specific word, *samvashikaram,* that roughly translates as hypnosis, and its use is given to enhance personality and for treating diseases like epilepsy, hysteria, and consumption (Vyas & Vyas, 2006). The West with its well researched approach of scientific enquiry and experimentations has made great developments in the understanding of hypnosis as an altered state of consciousness, with 'modalities of gene expression' being the latest highlight in the development of hypnotherapy. A development within the researched elements of altered states of consciousness is the adaptation of hypnosis in transpersonal psychology.

This chapter deals with those paradigmatic shifts in psychology and hypnotherapy that have occurred as a part and parcel of the evolutionary times. Within the ongoing conversation about the nature, scope and definition of transpersonal hypnotherapy from the transpersonal movement of 1960s to the present, there have been articles reviewing collections of published definitions of transpersonal psychology (LaJoie, Shapiro & Roberts, 1991; LaJoie & Shapiro, 1992; Shapiro, Lee & Gross, 2002); those reviewing the content and themes of transpersonal hypnotherapy course (Association of Transpersonal Hypnotherapy, Institute of Transpersonal Hypnotherapy); and others offering perspectives of the practice (Milton Erickson, Charles Tart, David Quigley, Carl Jung, Stansilav Grof).

The chapter first orients about the historical background of transpersonal psychology and hypnosis, which is followed by a detailed description of Transpersonal Hypnotherapy. Some techniques used in transpersonal psychology that are based on hypnosis form the next part of this chapter .

The chapter is intended to brief out the contribution to the discussion in the form of brief introduction of current perspectives. The viewpoints represented within come from leading thinkers and practitioners of transpersonal hypnotherapy.

Before dwelling into the intricacies of transpersonal hypnotherapy, it would be appropriate to brief out certain pertinent theorists and their outlooks, certain events that account for the birth of 'Transpersonal' view, at the first place, followed by the accessibility of the creative states within the same viewpoint and the approach towards such creative states of super consciousness through hypnosis. Only by discerning the core of transpersonal perspective, will we be able to comprehend the concept of transpersonal states, their healing potentialities and their derivation from the humanistic school of thought.

Historical Backdrop of Transpersonal Hypnotherapy

In accordance with the above viewpoint, and the importance of it in order to understand the nature of states that one has access to, it becomes indispensable to unravel the basics of transpersonal psychology. The origin of transpersonal psychology can be traced down to the historical transpersonal movement of 1960s that laid the ground for transpersonal psychology and foretold the 'psychology of the future.'

The Human Potential Movement of 1960s

In the history of psychology four well defined periods delineate the evolving trends that existed in defining human nature: the first period beginning between 1900 and the World War I was the departure of the thinking that was largely deductive and philosophical to the accumulation of facts that were based on experience and induction, the result of which was the setting up of the first psychological laboratory by William Wundt and the creation of experimental psychology; during the second period, between the two World Wars, was the era of behaviourism and Gestalt psychology; subsequent to the World War II came the third period, wherein psychology was recognized as a natural science of behaviour; during the more recent fourth period including the late 1950s and 1960s, the humanistic and existential movements came together to begin what has been considered a " tangential reaction." This newly shaped "third force" was clearly differentiated from the earlier forces of behaviourism and psychoanalysis (Simpson, 1977, p. 71).

Within this force has appeared the major emphasis on human nature that accounts for the healthy unity of personality and self-determination, and the primacy of self, as well as the belief in values of creativity, self-actualization and fulfilment, and the idea that conscious processes offer valid data for scientific investigation of human essence. Humanistic psychology brought in newer concepts :

1. Individuality (defined as complexity, richness, and the power of mind and consciousness),
2. Holism of mind, body, and feelings (particularly as emphasized in medicine, education, and sports),
3. Subjectivity as well as objectivity,
4. Growth, self-actualization, self-transcendence as innate human characteristics,
5. Concern for the will and responsibility of others,
6. Use of energy flows and the natural ability of the body to balance itself, and lastly,
7. The spiritual dimension which, as transpersonal psychology, many see as the psychology in the future (Simpson, 1977, p. 76).

It was this dimension that came to be known as Maslow's fourth wave. The very fact why it is named after him indicates the irreplaceable contribution that Abraham Maslow had in formulating what we call transpersonal. Maslow's (1970, 1971) research resulted in the theory of self-actualization: the innate human potential that each of us has, to achieve our potential by using and developing our talents and abilities. Each time we experience such a sense of fulfilment is called a peak experience. This published work of Maslow regarding human peak experiences was a major motivating factor behind the initiative to establish transpersonal psychology. Along with the humanistic movement of the 1960s, gradually the term "transpersonal" was associated with a distinct school of psychology within the humanistic movement (Benson, 1998).

Hypnosis on the other hand, has a historical trip analogous to that of psychology. In the following section, certain popular pertinent theoretical fretworks are mentioned that will suffice for the shifts, hypnosis and its use have undergone since its inception.

Perspectives in Hypnosis—Brief History

The history of hypnosis has had its ups and downs. The ancient use of the technique, as practiced by Celts and Druids as well as the Egyptians, some 4000 years ago, involved implications of hypnosis to induce trance states in which curative suggestions were given. Primitive tribes had shamans who practiced ritual, sleep cures and healing suggestions to remove the influences responsible for illness. The "modern" era of hypnosis dates back to Vienna in the 1700s. The first period beginning in the late eighteenth century with Franz Anton Mesmer and his creation of the first of the several metaphors for what is now called hypnosis—Animal Magnetism. Post Mesmer, two other investigators who majorly contributed in this period are Marquis de Puysegur and Abbe Jose Custodia di Faria. They did so by documenting conditions between hypnotist and hypnotized person that lead magnetic phenomena to occur. They also associated hypnosis to sleep by coining terms such as 'somnambulism' (Puysegur) and 'lucid sleep' (Fraia). In his book of 1843, James Braid, a Manchester surgeon, after following the sleep metaphors proposed by Puysegur and Faria, coined the term "hypnosis", since the term comes from the Greek *hypnos*: to sleep. Till 1950, at a superficial level, phenomena such a sleep walking and talking appear to be duplicated in hypnosis. With the advent of electroencephalogram (EEG) in 1950, the sleep metaphor was discarded.

The second period that prevailed for much of the nineteenth century took hold of the view of suggestibility. This is the belief that hypnosis is a matter of a person's degree of suggestibility. This particular conceptualization implies that response to hypnosis is a matter of gullibility and/or feeble will. In the latter part of the nineteenth century, the sleep metaphor came to be reconciled, to a degree, with suggestibility theory.

For the first-three decades of the twentieth century, interest in hypnosis remained in decline, only to be revived by Hull (1933) whose book entitled, "Hypnosis and suggestibility: An experimental approach" was instrumental in rekindling interest in the topic. World War II, however, provided an unexpected reprieve. In the heat of battle field hospitals often ran short of the drugs needed to treat wounded soldiers. Under often appalling conditions, a small group of clinicians of hypnosis were able to provide pain relief and alleviation of the suffering of their often severely injured patients. Some of these clinicians banded together after the war ended to form the Society for Clinical and Experimental Hypnosis (SCEH); it held its first meeting in 1949.

The period between 1960 and 1990 is likely to be seen by future historians as halcyon days for hypnosis. During this period, the study of hypnosis became international in a manner hitherto not envisaged. The success of hypnosis in the dismissal of symptoms through a reliving of the events of a traumatic experience, created a wave of enthusiasm for hypnotic methods.

The same enthusiasm created, evolved and ended up projecting the use of hypnosis in the transpersonal domain, wherein hypnosis was seen as a method of evoking those latent potentialities in order to reach higher states of consciousness. Out of all the pre-contemporary and contemporary researchers of hypnosis who have contributed to this innovative way of using hypnosis, two names, who have been highly instrumental in adding another dimension to the typical use of hypnosis, stand out. They are briefly discussed in the following section.

Milton H. Erickson : The first person in this sequence is the man who did not come to be known as a transpersonal hypnotherapist, as such, but who relentlessly worked in the innovation of hypnosis. He not only created the backdrop for the adaptation of hypnosis in the transpersonal domain but also indirectly made hypnosis more client-friendly and removed some of the misconceptions that tarnished its image as a valid therapy. In many of his papers Erickson (1980) has emphasized that deep or really satisfactory trance experience depends on the ability to subordinate and eliminate waking patterns of behaviour; that is, to give up some of the learned limitations and habitual frameworks of one's characteristic conscious attitudes. To achieve this end, Erickson evolved many new techniques of induction and stressed the need of careful "hypnotic training" whereby the individuality of each subject was carefully taken into account to maximize the presence of involuntary or autonomous behaviour in trance with as little participation of habitual conscious attitudes and mental frameworks as possible (Erickson, Rossi, & Rossi, 1976, pp. 297, 298, 300). The nature of therapeutic trance as viewed by him could be summarized under the following headings :

(a) Trance viewed as inner directed state.
(b) Trance viewed as highly motivated state.
(c) Trance viewed as active unconscious learning.
(d) Trance viewed as an altered state of functioning.

Of the above four views, two views pertaining transpersonal hypnosis are (b) and (d). The former states the essence of transpersonal medium to enhance human potential. Erickson developed so many unique approaches to hypnotic induction and trance training wherein a person's usual limitations could be altered momentarily so that inner potentials could manifest. Erickson's hypnotic interaction reflects the facilitation of human potentials and unrealized abilities to facilitate a person's development at large, in ways that are creative and surprising. Trance in this sense can be understood as a period of free exploration and learning.

The view of trance as an altered state of functioning has been pondered upon in detail by the second person, Charles T. Tart, who not only theorized but also illustrated potential use of hypnosis through an experiment.

Charles T. Tart: Popularly known as the pioneer in the scientific study of altered states of consciousness and peak experiences, Charles Tart (1970) has added a new outlook to science. With his immense and meticulous research in the area of Parapsychology and Transpersonal psychology, he not only achieved mastery over the different states of consciousness but also managed to imbue a science out of the area of the humanistic and transpersonal. In his presentation at the 7th Annual Convention of the Association for Humanistic Psychology, he sounded as the harbinger of a new perspective of hypnosis by expressing his comments on the transpersonal potentialities of deep hypnosis and bolstering his assertions by referring one of his experiments. He proved through the experiment the possibility of reaching those levels of consciousness that historically have always been associated with the realm of super consciousness. The eye opening experiment is summarized as follows :

A subject was given the required instructions to reach the state of bliss. According to Tart, this particular subject reached a dimension called depth or profundity. He asked his subject to scale the depth of his hypnotic state and to do it intuitively. Following is the actual description as stated by the subject at the level of 50, which indicates profound hypnosis, as contrary to level 0-25, which accounts for ordinary hypnosis.

As the subject goes deeper into trance he sees more and more blackness. On the physical front he reports "No, I cannot tell you how relaxed I am, because my body has reached its limit. It is absolutely relaxed." As far as his body image and identity are concerned, Tart reports :

> *The subject loses touch with the sensory stimulation present around. Body, feeling of peacefulness, holds no more importance for him. He starts out as himself and then his sense of identity tends to become less disturbed through his body and more just his head; just sort a thinking part. He identifies with a new identity, that of potential. He is not anybody in particular, he is potential. He is aware of identifying with this flux of potentiality that could evolve into so many sorts of things. Here, looking at it in a sort of different way, he eventually becomes aware of an infinite amount of potential. Anything is possible. Absolutely anything could be experienced in the kind of existence he is in.*

In the deepest of trance state, the sense of time gets

diminished, as the subject reports time as a meaningless concept. He no longer feels in the kind of space time framework; there are no spontaneous thoughts racing in consciousness and even realization of breathing disappears after some time. Tart reports saying: *I am just me at the lightest levels of hypnosis; at a deeper level, I am no longer Charley Tart. I am just a voice; just something that keeps talking*. And it not only stays that way but finally he says, he exists in infinite consciousness. This very statement elucidates the whole concept of transpersonal hypnosis in a nutshell. Charles Tart has, indeed, paved a way for a new branch of hypnosis. His emphasis on hypnotic behaviour and construction of tools for measuring person's susceptibility to hypnosis and most importantly, his belief that we can expand the scientific framework to take in most of the humanistic phenomena, may be all, makes his work worth mentionable and incomparable to contemporary notion of transpersonal use of hypnosis (Tart, 1999).

Thus, after considering the above historical events and comprehending the intricacy of each periodic development, it is evident that there has been a lucid paradigmatic shift in the way psychology has been shifting its focus and hypnosis has been co-relating with that shift. In further sections author has elaborated Transpersonal Hypnotherapy and posited it in alliance with all four waves of psychology.

Transpersonal Hypnotherapy

We all are familiar with hypnotherapy as a valid therapy and most of us know the root meaning of it as well, whereas the word "transpersonal" is still unversed when it comes to its common use in everyday usage. Hence, at this juncture it becomes important to understand the interpretation of the word "transpersonal" in its psychological context. The word 'transpersonal' can be broken down as the root 'personal' with the prefix "trans", the latter having two meanings: one meaning of trans as 'through' suggests the possibility of going against interconnections of what presently comprises us and our world. Another meaning of trans as 'beyond' reminds us of the something else, the more of ourselves and of the world that we have not yet fully experienced, or actualized (Braud, 1998). Semantically speaking, the word relates to those forms of knowing, being and doing that go beyond of those conventionally recognized—beyond what is available to us, our nature and possibilities. Psychology of such states and experiences that goes beyond the personal is transpersonal psychology. Transpersonal hypnotherapy thus becomes that therapeutic medium that provides an access to go beyond self.

Association of Transpersonal Hypnotherapy terms the same as a profound and highly effective healing practice for behavioural conditions. It is hypnotherapy that transcends ordinary ego mind functioning. It is a holistic therapy which encompasses mind, body and spirit—the physical, the conscious and the super conscious, respectively, and, therefore, it works with the various states of consciousness that are beyond the rational but can precede the mystical.

Institute of Transpersonal Hypnotherapy describes transpersonal hypnotherapy as a natural extension of transpersonal psychology which incorporates the methods of all four waves of psychology. Accordingly, whereas, traditional hypnotherapy is to reprogramme the subconscious mind, transpersonal hypnotherapy is to deprogramme the subconscious mind to allow better access to the higher mind and the wisdom of intuition. In addition to reprogramming the subconscious mind, the Institute asserts that transpersonal hypnotherapy goes beyond the personality to access intuition or inner wisdom. The goal is to increase awareness around personal and societal programming. With increased awareness comes the personal choice to keep or reject these programmes. Once the choice is made to reject these programmes, the undesirable patterns are deprogrammed. This leads to waking up of the spirit.

The transpersonal definition of hypnotherapy assumes that :

(a) We are not who we "think" we are. Who we think we are is our deepest trance state (actually a "bundle" of trance states).

(b) To the degree that our awareness is absorbed in and identified with our thoughts, we are in a hypnotic state—a defined state rather than a spontaneous, "real" state, an "awake" state.

(c) All communication, both intrapersonal and interpersonal, to the degree that it is a sharing of thoughts about reality rather than a direct experience of reality, is a sharing of hypnotic states, "dream" states, even deluded states (Jack, 2003).

The uses of transpersonal hypnotherapy are manifold. Although it is often used to work with issues that relate to spiritual development and other metaphysical experiences of living, it is also extensively used on ordinary, everyday issues in order to bring about significant and often permanent change to behavioural conditions. The goal is to increase awareness around personal and societal programming. It aims to take you beyond the limitations of your ego to enable you to access your own pure inner guidance and healing energies to bring about beneficial change. It is highly effective and can be quite profound.

One of the astonishing feature of this kind of hypnotherapy is that although, being highly humanistic in approach and origin, it assembles with all other waves of psychology. Institute of Transpersonal Hypnotherapy highlights this feature in the following way, which is also adopted as a graded pattern in applying transpersonal hypnotherapy:

At the level of first wave which is developed by Freud, underlying issues are dealt with the unconscious mind. Here, root cause of problems is examined, it is called 'Hypnoanalysis'.

At the level of second wave that comes under the domain of behavioural psychology, habits are altered by making environmental alterations. Here, direct suggestions are given to reinforce a new behaviour and expect a change.

At the level of third wave, which is developed by Abraham Maslow, our personal mastery is acknowledged. Here, various techniques are taught that take us closer to our ultimate striving for self-actualization—a healthy integration of body.

At the last level, that of fourth wave, also developed by Abraham Maslow, our unconscious mind is tapped. Here, meditation combined with hypnotherapy helps us attain self-transcendence and the realization of our spiritual potential.

A typical use of transpersonal hypnotherapy entailing the above mentioned four factors is mentioned below:

Underlying issue—Review, understand and relieve childhood wounds around weight.

A habit to change—Open the refrigerator less.

Personal mastery—Achieve physical, emotional and mental potential around weight issues.

Spiritual potential—Expand perspectives and wisdom.

Transpersonal hypnotherapy ultimately focusses on the fourth wave, spiritual potential, with the goal to help clients wake up and realize who they truly are. One learns how to facilitate one's inner journey and connect with their inner wisdom and intuition (Institute of Transpersonal Hypnotherapy).

Within the transpersonal domain, hypnotherapy has more than just one set of use. Besides, being applied to reach higher states of consciousness (as explained above), hypnotherapy is also used to heal problem areas that occurred in the past (Alchemical hypnotherapy), or those problems that occurred in past life (Past Life Therapy), and to change and replenish existing thinking patterns.

Other Applications of Hypnosis in the Transpersonal Domain

Alchemical Hypnotherapy

Developed in the 1970s by David Quigley, alchemical hypnotherapy combines the use of hypnosis to access the subconscious mind to reveal and heal traumas which occurred in the past, yet affect our present. It also brings in the concept of spirit guides to aid in the healing process. The writings of the Middle Age alchemists indicate that they saw their inner guides as keys to their own transformation. According to Carl Jung, the first modern alchemist, the vehicles of this transformative process were the archetypes, the Inner Guides. Based on Carl Jung's archetypal theory, this kind of hypnotherapy is popularly known as 'Guided Imagery.' According to Jung, imagery is the language of intuition, and the exploration of imagery is thought to allow deeper contact with emotional and intuitive processes than would mere thought about feelings (Kasprow and Scotton, 1999).

In guided imagery therapy, an atmosphere is created that allows imagery to emerge out of a client's unconscious processes. The patient thus enters an altered state of consciousness, which arises from the attenuation of the usual executive activities of the intellect and from the inward-directed focus on internal imagery rather than exterior sensory data. As with all ASCs, such alterations create the possibility of individuals experiencing their circumstances from new and potentially helpful perspectives. Rather than engaging a client's defenses, guided imagery therapy can facilitate the emergence of material underneath and around those defenses and help the client reach his/her hidden potential (Kasprow and Scotton, 1999).

The goal of a typical alchemical hypnotherapy session is to locate the memory and imagery behind an issue, restructure it, and access or create an internal resource which is then anchored to the outer world through post hypnotic suggestion. Alchemical hypnotherapy synthesizes techniques from many modern schools of Transpersonal Hypnotherapy and Psychology. It includes Gestalt psychology, Eastern psychology, Shamanism and other mystical schools of thought.

Past Life Therapy

Quite pejorative in reputation, past life therapy has shown positive results in the past few decades. With pioneers like Brian Weiss (1988), past life therapy has been given place in the pool of contemporary therapies used, nowadays. Some therapists think hypnosis opens a window to the unconscious mind where memories of the past life are stored, courtesy, the belief of reincarnation. Hypnosis then becomes a medium to access memories of the past lives. Although the theory of reincarnation associated with this technique is controversial, past life therapy, like always has been subjected to the accusation of lacking concrete realistic roots and failure of it to be applied universally, especially in cultures where there is no concept of rebirth.

Some transpersonal practitioners also use hypnotic regression to help patients explore spiritual connections between present-day conflicts and purported experiences from past lives. They use this method as a variant of guided imagery therapy, in which recollection of past lives is dealt metaphorically rather than literally (Kasprow and Scotton, 1999).

The therapy works wonders when the person under hypnotic state happens to be having a spiritually sound past life. In such a case, the person may be made to acquaint with his spiritual dimensions of past life, which he can inculcate in present life.

Meditation

This method does not need any introduction as it has been extensively used nowadays by people to combat stress. Within transpersonal psychology, also, meditation is one technique which is highly prescribed, that entails application of hypnotic suggestion to access an altered state of consciousness for therapeutic benefit.

Meditative techniques fall into two general categories: methods that use concentration on a specific object of meditation, either internal or external, and methods that foster undirected, receptive awareness. Most techniques of prayer, yogic meditation, and Christian contemplation fall into the former category; techniques such as Buddhist *vipassana* or insight meditation fall into the latter. Transpersonal meditation happens to be a member of the latter category (Kasprow and Scotton, 1999).

Transpersonal meditation is the amalgamation of traditional hypnosis and the technique of meditation that is used to tap spiritual potential. Relaxation and deep breathing are used as induction tools which facilitate focalization on the form of sound, *mantra* or visual symbol (Vyas & Vyas, 2006).

The benefits of transpersonal meditation are abound, but from a transpersonal point of view, the most significant benefits are suggested by reports from advanced meditators who refer to the emergence of deep feelings of peace, joy, and compassion and transcendent states of consciousness, including trans-egoic states of profound unity. Meditative practices have been widely employed for thousands of years by the non-Western wisdom traditions (Kasprow and Scotton, 1999).

Neuro-linguistic Programming

Neuro-linguistic programming is one of those techniques that happen to have origins in the 'Human Potential Movement.' Milton Erickson, as earlier cited, has contributed immensely to this method. His model, known as the 'Milton Model' makes use of pacing and leading, ambiguity, metaphor, embedded suggestion, and multiple-meaning sentence structures by the communicator and then allowing the listener to fill in their own meaning of what is being said. This has been described as "a way of using language to induce and maintain trance in order to contact the hidden resources of our personality." Once the contact is established, the hidden potential could be used to restructure client's thought patterns and lead him to a more superior development.

Holotropic Breathwork

This method relates more to breathing practices from *yoga*, Taoism, and Buddhism, and more recently has been adapted as a technique for transpersonal therapy. Developed by Stanisilav Grof, a noted psychiatrist and LSD researcher, the theoretical framework of the method was developed through careful observation of thousands of patients undergoing psychotherapy while experiencing the effects of psychedelic drugs. Grof (2009) came out with a kind of therapeutic breathing pattern that induces altered states of consciousness without the use of drugs, as hypnotic suggestions replace intake of drug.

Grof's holotropic breathwork provides sophisticated attention to set and setting, by using hypnotic techniques, using concrete instructions during induction. The intention is to access repressed memories, perinatal experiences, and archetypal imprinting. Attention is given not only to the induction of the ASC, but also to processing the material that arises out of it with the use of group process and art therapy (Kasprow and Scotton, 1999).

Transpersonal Psychology—An Indian Overview

> *In the East we have been aware that the conscious mind is not the only mind. Below it, there is the unconscious mind; then below that is the collective unconscious mind. Then below that is the cosmic unconscious mind. Above it, there is the super conscious mind; above that there is the collective super conscious mind; above that there is the cosmic super conscious mind. And when someone says mind, it means the whole range.*
>
> (Osho, *Beyond Enlightenment*)

Positioning India in relation with transpersonal psychology suggests an obvious action, as India's spiritual heritage far outweighs any other aspect of the country. Known as the 'land of the enlightened', India popularly has been the destination for the spiritually inclined. Yet, despite having such rich spiritual history, India is still not acquainted with the paradigmatic shift that has occurred in hypnotherapy.

On one front, India is the unanimous choice for a place of transpersonal practice where traditional beliefs and cultural settings already show proclivity towards strengthening the spiritual and the ultimate. Concepts like reincarnation, inner soul (*antaraatma*), and *yoga* that pertains to past life, alchemical and meditation respectively are banal and are inherent part of country's belief system. In such a case, the task of introducing transpersonal hypnotherapy in Indian context is not much of a task actually. But the reality seems otherwise, as such issues are still attributed to saints and the yogis. Though there have been developments of indigenous psychology, there is however no parallel development of indigenous hypnotherapy. The very land where probably, variations of hypnosis by some other name (*Samvashikaram, p. 3)* were practiced for the first time; India, still has not gained the label of that land where the art of hypnotherapy evolved with the changing times. Except a few diligent and dedicated researchers who keep looking for new dimensions of the art; India, in general, can be said as lying dormant as far as renovation in hypnotherapy, in terms of its transpersonal application, is concerned.

Terms like 'Positive psychology' and 'Spiritual Psychology', still survive in their infancy periods, as far their acceptance in the mainstream psychology is concerned. There are currently no institutes that offer courses in transpersonal psychology, and most of the institutes in India still remain deprived of the existence of a full fledged field of enquiry called transpersonal psychology. Paradoxically, that country which is expected to have adapted and evolved further by now in transpersonal dealings still is transpersonally deprived.

Conclusion

Transpersonal hypnotherapy offers a broadened view of what it means to be human. It acknowledges the developmental stages available to individuals as they grow from infancy to adulthood to levels of connectedness beyond the personal identity. It has its roots in transpersonal psychology, which provides models of these states of consciousness that can assist hypnotherapist in facilitating client's spiritual experiences as a part of therapeutic process. This broadened view of hypnosis may permit holistic healing and may prevent ineffective, unnecessary spiritual inhibitions. The principal therapeutic methods of transpersonal hypnotherapy are well known and include most of the conventional hypnotherapies, but these are applied on the basis of models that take into account developmental stages ignored by ego-oriented or purely biological paradigms. In addition, transpersonal research and practice explores the therapeutic use of altered states of consciousness to facilitate connection with levels of the psyche that are often unavailable through exclusively rational or cognitive approaches. The use of hypnosis and other techniques like imagery, meditation, breathwork, past life experience to produce altered states of consciousness may play a significant role in the advancement of hypnotherapy.

REFERENCES

Aserinsky, E., & Kleitman, N. (1953). Regularly occurring periods of eye motility, and concomitant phenomena during sleep. *Science*, 273-274.

Association of Transpersonal Psychology. (2005). *About Transpersonal Hypnotherapy* Retrieved on October 29, 2008, from http://www.atpweb.org.

Benson, N. (2000). *Introducing Psychology*. Victoria: McPhersons Printing Group.

Braid, J. (1843). *Neurypnology or the Rationale of Nervous Sleep Considered in Relation with Animal Magnetism Illustrated by Numerous Cases of its Successful Application in the Relief and Cure of Disease*. London: John Churchill.

Braud, W. (1998). Can research be transpersonal? *Transpersonal Psychology Review*, 2, 9-17.

Colman, A. (2006). *Dictionary of Psychology*. Delhi: Oxford Publication.

Elias, J. (2003). *What is Transpersonal Hypnotherapy?* Retrieved on October 24, 2008, from http://www.transpersonalhypnotherapy.co.uk/Articles/index.htm.

Erickson, M. (1980). *Innovative Hypnotherapy*, New York: Irvington Publishers.

Erickson, M., Rossi, E., & Rossi, S. (1976). *Hypnotic Realities—The induction of clinical hypnosis and forms of indirect suggestion*. New York: Irvington Publishers.

Grof, S. (2009). Holotropic research and archetypal astrology. *Archai: The Journal of Archetypalcosmology*, 1, 1.

Hull, C.L. (1933). *Hypnosis and Suggestibility: An Experimental Approach*. New York: Appleton-Century-Crofts.

Jack, E. (2003). *Finding True Magic: Transpersonal Hypnosis and Hypnotherapy/NLP*, American Institute of Transpersonal Hypnotherapy/NLP.

Kasprow, M.C., & Scotton, B.W. (1999). A review of transpersonal theory and its application to the practice of psychotherapy. *Journal of Psychotherapy Practice and Research*, 8, 12-23.

LaJoie, D.H., & Shapiro, S.I. (1992). Definitions of transpersonal psychology: The first twenty three years. *Journal of Transpersonal Psychology*, 2(1), 79-94.

LaJoie, D.H., Shapiro, S.I., & Roberts, T.B. (1991). A historical analysis of the statement of purpose. *Journal of Transpersonal Psychology*, 23(2), 175-182.

Maslow, A.H. (1970). *Motivation and Personality* (2nd ed.). New York: Harper & Row.

Maslow, A.H. (1971). *The Farther Reaches of Human Nature*. New York: Viking.

Melzack, R., & Perry, C. (1975). Self-regulation of pain: The use of alpha-feedback and hypnotic training for the control of chronic pain. *Experimental Neurology*, 452-469.

Osho, (2008). Beyond enlightenment, *Osho Times*, 32-33.

Quigley, D. (1999). What is Alchemical hypnotherapy? Alchemical Institute of Hypnosis. Retrieved on November 6, 2008, from http://www.alchemyinstitute.com/articles.htm

Shapiro, S.I., Lee, G.W., & Gross, P.L. (2002). The essence of transpersonal psychology: Contemporary views. *The International Journal of Transpersonal Studies*, 21, 19-32.

Simpson, E. (1977). Humanistic psychology: An attempt to define human nature. *Humanistic Psychology—New Frontiers, 67-68.*

Tart, C. (1970). Self-report scales on hypnotic depth. *International Journal of Clinical and Experimental Hypnosis*, 18, 105-125.

Tart, C. (1970). Transpersonal potentialities of deep hypnosis. *The Journal of Transpersonal Psychology*, 2, 27-40.

Tart, C. (1999). State of the art in transpersonal psychology. In C. Lee, (Ed.), *The Transpersonal Research*. Mountain View, CA: Sino-American Institute.

Vyas, B., & Vyas, R. (2006). *Indian Handbook of Clinical Hypnosis*. Kolkata: New Central Book Agency.

Weiss, B. (1988). *Many Lives, Many Masters*. New York: Simon and Schuster.

7

Transpersonal Hypnosis
Discovering the Wellspring Within

REENA BISWAS

Introduction

The playful, innocent, make-believe scenarios of a child's world often transforms into trances which gradually become necessary for survival in this world. Trances help focus attention in order to navigate one's journey through life. Some of these trances may be beneficial, enabling the individual to achieve important goals. However, they can also be negative and dysfunctional, giving rise to problems which become barriers to a happy, fully functional life. Habitual patterns of thoughts, feelings and behaviour gradually shape the individual's life, to the point where each day is lived in a trance fabricated by the ego-mind. Often, such dysfunctional trances create problems, not only in the individual's life, but also for others who are a part of this world.

Transpersonal hypnosis is an ancient, yet modern view of the mind. It is a simple but profound healing practice that not only facilitates spiritual development, but also addresses behavioural issues in order to effect deep, long lasting positive change. It is an exquisite synthesis of Eastern and Western philosophy and psychology, researching and exploring ways to destroy the negative trance created by the ego-mind, and heal the pain it causes. The aim is to discover the wellspring within, which allows each one of us to live with authenticity, integrity and joy, from the core of our being.

Clinical hypnosis has struggled for a long time to establish its credibility, particularly in the conventional medical community. It has finally achieved a degree of success in establishing itself as a highly effective adjunctive therapeutic modality in a clinical setting. This degree of success has been hard earned, and, perhaps its success, in some parts of the world, is yet unknown or is still in its infancy. There remains much scope for exploring the benefits of clinical hypnosis. However, another element— the transpersonal perspective—has had to take a back seat while the benefits of clinical hypnosis were being researched. There is no conflict between the two. Transpersonal hypnosis explores the spiritual dimension and benefits the participant at another, more profound level, which in turn, has the potential to benefit the person as a whole. At present, we are witnessing an increased interest in transpersonal psychology and transpersonal psychotherapy. This is an excellent time for transpersonal hypnotherapy to take its rightful place and establish its credentials in our exploration of the mind-body-spirit continuum. Transpersonal hypnosis integrates a range of research interests, particularly from psychology and psychiatry, as well as a number of spiritual traditions.

The objective of this chapter is to look at a few disparate techniques and schools of thought, with a common denominator—using one's energy and calling upon higher energy, when appropriate—to heal, not superficially, but at a profound level. This viewpoint explores the potential of the multidimensional nature of human consciousness. In the context of transpersonal hypnotherapy, the method used to tap into the spectrum of consciousness for therapeutic purposes, is hypnosis.

The Role of Hypnosis in Energy Healing

Franz Anton Mesmer's highly controversial technique, referred to as Animal Magnetism, included application of magnets and sweeping hand gestures along the length of the patient's body; and a number of patients were linked to each other by means of mirrors and mechanical equipment. The culmination of such sessions was a "healing crisis" which was a highly dramatic event, resulting in the disappearance of symptoms. He claimed he was working with an invisible substance he referred to as the "fluidium." His work was a highly dramatic event, resulting in the disappearance of symptoms. His work was much maligned and dismissed as quackery by the medical community. However, it appears from records that James Esdaile, a British surgeon, used a version of Mesmer's technique to perform a number of major surgeries in India during the 1840s. The procedure involved numerous passes of the operator's hand along the length of the patient's body without any verbal instruction, which, after several hours, produced a deep precursor of the Therapeutic Touch, which is taught and practiced today.

Mesmer's version of working with the human energy field involved shifts aimed specifically at the energy field by passing of the hands along the length of the body, without verbal communication. It would appear that hypnosis aims to create shifts in the energy field verbally. The science of biomagnetism has shown, using sophisticated equipment, that biological activity is basically electrical in nature, and that moving electrical currents induce a corresponding magnetic field that extends out beyond the human body. When there is a shift in this energy field, there is a corresponding change in the body. These findings merit further objective scientific exploration in order for us to understand the true nature of human consciousness as this research continues.

The basic premise of energy healing is that the human body is more than just the physical body. Scientists say that human beings are composed of several layers of varying density. In the Yogic tradition, there exists various layers of vibrational structures, like a series of sheaths, going from the food sheath, on to the energy or breath sheath, followed by the sheath of emotions, a layer of thoughts, and ultimately a sheath of pure spiritual essence. Chinese medicine works with the *pranic* sheath, manipulating the *prana* or *chi*, using acupuncture needles in order to facilitate smooth flow of energy through the meridians, also recognized by the Yogic tradition as *nadis*. Within this network of energy flow system, are certain key distribution centres, referred to as *chakras*. In recent years, researchers in the West have discovered a resemblance between the location of these subjective energy centres or *chakras*, and the anatomic structures known as endocrine glands.

In the words of Leskowitz (2000), energy healing can be described as "a process in which the healer brings about sympathetic resonance between his own finely tuned body/mind energetic system and that of the patient. The healer himself becomes the instrument of healing. And one of the most important steps that can enhance this resonant energy exchange between two people is the state of focussed attentiveness we call hypnosis."

The therapeutic application of hypnosis is at its most exquisitely profound state when the therapist and the client have both entered a state of deep absorption. This cannot be achieved when the therapist merely reads out a script, and have not taken into account the symptoms of the presenting problem. A truly deep, profound healing state is nurtured in an environment where the therapist allows himself or herself to become totally absorbed in the therapeutic relationship; where rapport is complete and profound, and where the therapist is able to receive subtle non-verbal feedback from the client, without closely observing muscle tone, facial features and depth of breathing. Several authors, including Jung (1966) and Tart (1976), have recorded and described amazing intuitive insights experienced by hypnotherapists revealing specific information about the client. In each case, the information was not revealed via by any of the five physical senses. In the author's experience, when she is able to tune in to her own subtle energy processes, it becomes easier to establish a deep rapport with the client, which facilitates detection of subtle changes occurring in the client's energy processes.

Recently, I was reading through the notes of a client in preparation of her appointment. She was in the midst of an acrimonious divorce, which was made worse by the fact that she had two children, aged seven and five. She was struggling to come to terms with the impending separation, and could not find a way to look at a future without her husband. Just before the arrival of the client, I had a brief mental vision of a beautiful butterfly flying joyously. During that session, the client announced that she could finally see "the light at the end of the tunnel"; that she was mentally and emotionally prepared for her new life without her husband. She was "ready for freedom", as she viewed her future. The brief vision of the butterfly had given me a glimpse of her current state of mind even before she had arrived at my office. I have deep respect for these flashes of empathic connection.

For transpersonal hypnosis to be a truly remarkable therapeutic tool, the state of mind of the therapist is a vital ingredient. There is no room for a perceived sense of superiority on the part of the therapist because of his specialist knowledge. The therapist must recognize and respect the client's own inner wisdom and the fact that he has deep inner resources which can set him up on the path toward healing. Once the therapist consciously cultivates an attitude of compassion and empathy, the true magic of transpersonal hypnosis can begin to unfold, both for the therapist and the client.

The concept of a human energy field is fundamental to many ancient traditions, including Celtic, Taoist, Buddhist, Yogic, Sufi, early Egyptian and Greek, Native American, and Christian. When a therapist gleans information via a source other than the five physical senses, the term used is *intuition*. Perhaps intuition can be described as an interaction between the energy fields of the client and the therapist. Once the therapist becomes aware of this interaction, it can facilitate the healing process by setting their intention to project healing, compassion, empathy, and acceptance of the situation. As the gap between science and spirituality narrows, the role of spirituality in healing is gaining credibility with scientists and researchers. Dossey (1993) notes that the attitude of the physicians has been shown in double blind experiments to have a therapeutic effect in the medical setting. This is encouraging news for those physicians unhappy in their work because they initially set out to be healers, but find themselves to have become technicians instead, bowing to the demands of modern medicine.

Hypnosis also works effectively with Yoga. Hypnosis and Hatha Yoga, for instance, are, respectively, a primarily mental and more physical way of probing into the subconscious realm. Used in conjunction, the two systems can complement each other, enabling the participant to reframe old patterns of self-defeating thoughts and actions. Both methods aid relaxation, focussing attention, and adopting the stance of an observer or witness to one's experience, without being judgmental, and learning valuable lessons in the process. The transpersonal element common to both processes allows a glimpse into the realms of the super conscious not visible in a state of ordinary consciousness.

Transpersonal hypnotherapy calls for a maturity in outlook, an open mind, and a non-judgmental viewpoint. Awareness of the interaction between the energy fields brings with it the responsibility to be honest and humble because, at an unconscious level, the client may have an insight into our inner truths.

Transpersonal Hypnosis and the Ericksonian Approach

Trances can play a positive role in that they allow us to focus clearly in the pursuit of a goal. However, they can often be negative and dysfunctional, resulting in illness and unhappiness. Wolinsky (2000) cites the following example from the *Upanishads* about the Self:

> *There are ten men walking through the woods. They come upon a river, which they must cross. Because the current is so strong, they are afraid that some of them might be washed away. So they decide to hold hands and lock arms as they cross. This way, no one will get lost. They reach the other side and just to be sure, they decide to count to verify that everyone has made it.*
>
> *The first man counts 1, 2, 3 , 4, 5, 6, 7, 8, 9. "Somebody is missing!" he shouts in alarm. The next person in the line*

> *begins to count: 1, 2, 3, 4, 5, 6, 7, 8, 9! "Oh, no! Somebody is missing! Who did we lose?" Each person, in turn, counts the lot of them and comes up with only 9 people. Finally a sage comes by and, hearing the nature of their complaint, realizes their mistake. He counts them one by one and reaches 10. "You are the tenth one," the sage says to each.*

In the context of a therapy session, the therapist needs to communicate with the "self" behind the trance because that is the true self, the creative self; only this true self can change the negative trance created by the ego-mind and thus disperse the symptoms. A symptom manifests itself when the inner resources are not being utilized. The individual's attention is shrunk in order to focus on the problem. Erickson's unique approach was to utilize this constriction of attention to sharply focus the patient's concentration on the present problem and to evoke unconscious resources. He then utilizes these unconscious resources to effect problem resolution. This can be viewed from another angle, as Wolinsky (2000) suggests. It is the trance state that creates the problem in the first place. This can be explained with an example of a panic attack. The symptomatic trance state in an anxiety or panic attack is a pseudo-orientation in time. Focus of attention shrinks to such an extent that the person feels completely cut off from the world. There is a shift from an *inter*personal trance to an *intra*personal trance. There is a feeling of helplessness (age regression). The person does not notice the payphone nearby (negative hallucination) and "forgets" that help is available (amnesia). The individual remains in a state of intense self-to-self trance, with its severely constricted focus of attention and the Deep Trance Phenomena of pseudo-orientation in time, age regression; negative hallucination and amnesia maintain their hold over the person. This state can be utilized, while the client is describing the anxiety attack, by changing the client's intrapersonal trance to an interpersonal trance with the therapist. The client remains focussed on the present while recounting the event, thus taking out the element of trauma. He or she then becomes an observer of the event. The client is dehypnotized from the original negative trance and becomes a witness to the panic attack without emotional involvement, and, therefore, free from pain and suffering.

The transpersonal state has been variously described as "therapeutic trance", the "no-trance state", or "meditation." This state transcends the personal; only when we leave this state do we identify with our limiting beliefs, thoughts and actions, and experience pain and unhappiness. Whilst in this transpersonal state, we are merely observers. There is, however, a difference. In therapeutic trance, the therapist utilizes the contents of the client's mind. They are reprogrammed, reframed, dissociated, and so on, in order to bring about an end to the problem. In meditation, there is no such intervention for therapeutic purposes. As soon as the individual assumes the transpersonal witness or observer's stance, the process of disidentification with the ego-mind begins. The same principle underlines the practice of mindfulness meditation where the practitioner simply observes the emotions and feelings as they come and go, one after the other, without involvement.

Past Life Regression

Many non-western cultures accept the concept that certain physical and psychological illnesses may have their roots in the psychic residues of events in previous lives. This view is summed up in the opening lines of the Buddhist text, the *Dhammapada*: "All that we are is the result of what we have thought." In the West, all traces of teachings relating to reincarnation had been obliterated by the Christian Church by the sixth century. It did not occupy any meaningful place in Orthodox Judaism, although there is a strong belief in the doctrine of reincarnation in the Kabbalah. In France, America and England, it was not until the nineteenth century that doctrines of *karma* and reincarnation made reappearance among a few spiritualist groups. Carl Jung investigated psychical phenomena, and coined the term *archetype* to denote split off fragmentary personalities encountered during the channelling of a young medium.

Past life regression is worthy of investigation in the context of transpersonal hypnosis insofar as accessing the true self is concerned. Elias (2006) is of the view that we are defined by our waking trances. These are the collection of learned behaviours, both functional and dysfunctional, with their origins in the past. Similar experiences accumulate and there comes a point when the unconscious mind "fixes the message, the learning, and the emotional dynamics around this class of experiences." This can be described as the *critical mass* experience—a point at which the person stops learning anything new from ongoing similar experiences, and ceases to look for new choices or alternatives. The outcome of such an experience is that the true, or core-self stays hidden under an exterior of a waking trance.

The aim of the hypnotherapist is to regress the client back to the point where the dysfunctional trance originated. The client is put in a trance state; the task of the therapist is to focus the client's awareness on it and evaluate it from an adult's perspective, being in the here and now. The inner wisdom of the client brings into view useful insights which ultimately result in beneficial change. Layer upon layer of long-established thought patterns, emotions and behaviour are stripped away, revealing the wellspring within. Perhaps for the first time, the client has the courage to peer over the confines of their existence and view the breath taking view beyond. In practical terms, if a client's persistent, unexplained back pain which has not responded to medication is healed through past life regression, he or she is given a new lease of life, as it were. Whether the individual is a believer or not, of the concept of past life, is of no consequence.

Spirit Releasement Therapy

Spirit Releasement Therapy (SRT) or Clinical Depossession, as it was originally known, was developed by Dr. William Baldwin (1993). A number of past life regression therapists are involved in this area of work. The word *spirit* in this context refers to a range of spirits or entities that can attach to or influence the human energy field. These entities are broadly classified as either deceased, earthbound, human spirits, or as other discarnate entities.

Spirit Releasement Therapy is utilized with patients diagnosed with a spirit attachment. This advance therapeutic technique can be classified as a form of transpersonal hypnotherapy as the patient usually enters an altered state of awareness via hypnosis. It is vital that the therapist undertaking this kind of work is a qualified mental health professional trained in psychotherapy, hypnosis and hypnotherapy, differential diagnosis, and in the application of this technique, in particular. Knowledge of spirituality and metaphysics is helpful. In addition, being spiritual can enable the therapist to understand the nature of this work, and can provide protection from spirit attachment.

The therapist must be able to discern whether or not the client is suitable for such therapy, since many individuals who may seek such treatment are not appropriate for it. This would include a patient with severe mental disorder. Symptoms can include hearing inner voices, sudden urges to act in uncharacteristic ways, personality changes, and onset of unusual behaviour. If the therapist is inadequately trained, he or she may naively embark on Spirit Releasement Therapy.

At present, further research needs to be undertaken to understand when SRT is appropriate. It is an important transpersonal, therapeutic technique, applying hypnosis, with a view to enabling an individual find a solution to a problem. As we gain better understanding of the technique, and the circumstances in which it is appropriate, there is further scope for transpersonal hypnosis to be employed with beneficial outcomes. SRT is poised to gain greater acceptance as the shift toward complementary and alternative medicine becomes more widely known and accepted by the conventional medical community and by society in general.

The Role of Transpersonal Hypnosis Across Diverse Cultures

There is growing interest in transpersonal psychology, and an entire school of psychology has grown around the findings of transpersonal psychologists, who define their field as the study of experiences in which the individual's sense of identity extends beyond the personal to encompass wider, broader, and deeper facets of human beings, life and the universe. Krippner (2000) defines Transpersonal Psychology as "the disciplined study of behaviours and experiences that appear to transcend those hypothetical constructs associated with individual identities and self-concepts, as well as their developmental antecedents, and the implications of these behaviours and experiences for education, training and psychotherapy".

Consciousness is another area of great interest in the study of the transpersonal dimension. Consciousness can be defined as the pattern of awareness, perception, cognition and affect defining or characterizing an individual at a particular point of time. For transpersonal therapists, alterations in consciousness is of particular interest because these altered states facilitate contact with the divine, the spiritual element, and insights into the true potential of the core that resides within a human being. It offers a brief glimpse into the immense potential of the wellspring within such altered states can be attained during meditation, group dancing, chanting, or drumming. It can also be accessed via hypnosis.

Recorded observations from diverse cultures, from different parts of the world bear witness to the fact that several versions of what is known as transpersonal hypnosis have been practiced for centuries, and are still practiced today. Records indicate that hypnotic-like procedures were used in ancient Egypt around 3766 B.C., while ancient Druids chanted over their clients until the desired result was obtained. Other studies indicate that herbs were used to enhance verbal suggestion by native healers in Central and South America.

According to Krippner (1993), a survey of the social science literature, as well as his personal observations in several traditional societies indicate that there are frequent elements of native healing procedures that can be termed hypnotic-like. Transpersonal, hypnotic-like procedures are often observed in the healing practices of native shamans, who may be described as socially approved practitioners, whose chief role is usually that of healer. Such practices and procedures have been observed amongst Japanese shamans, and North American Indian shamans. Another research records the practice of the Eskimos of Eastern Greenland thus: their "continuous rubbing of stones against each other may be seen as a simple way of inducing trance . . . . The monotony, loneliness, and repetitive rhythmic movement join with the desire to encounter a helping spirit. This combination is so powerful that it erases all mundane thoughts and distracting associations." Similarities have also been observed between the behaviour of Balinese healers and that of hypnotized subjects. In Bali, Indonesia, researchers have observed and recorded a large number of rituals and ceremonies that are transpersonal in nature and that utilize hypnotic-like procedures.

Expectation, which plays an important role in hypnosis, has also been recorded as being present in these cases. In the words of Kirsch (1990), "Hypnosis, like many culturally-based rituals, serves to shape and bolster relevant expectancies that reorganize consciousness and produce behavioural changes relevant to the goals of hypnotic subjects and shamanic clients." He goes on to observe that ideomotor signals that often characterize hypnosis resemble the postures, gestures, collapsing motions, and rhythmic movements that occur involuntarily during many native rituals.

Transpersonal experiences were a regular occurrence in early West African cultures where individuals were perceived to be closely connected with nature, the community, and their communal group. Strained or broken relationships were regarded as the chief cause of sickness. Traditional healers held the view that ecology and interpersonal relations affected people's health and wellbeing.

In conclusion, it can be said that transpersonal hypnosis is an ancient tradition, rooted in diverse cultures, that is attracting considerable interest and investigation at present. In some instances, hypnosis is perhaps not the most appropriate term for the transpersonal elements of certain cultures. There is much to learn from the different cultures of the world because, although we are superficially different, we are all linked together, as human beings. Keeping an open mind and a willingness to learn are the key ingredients.

REFERENCES

Baldwin, W. (1993). *Spirit Releasement Therapy: A Technique Manual* (2nd ed.). Los Angeles: The Human Potential Foundation Press.

Dossey, L. (1993). *Healing Words*. New York: Harper.

Elias, J. (2006). *Finding True Magic: Transpersonal Hypnosis and Hypnotherapy/NPL*. Seattle, W A: Five Wisdoms Press.

Jung, C.G. (1960). *The Practice of Psychotherapy* (Coll. Works). Princeton, NJ: Princeton University Press.

Krippner, S. (1993). Cross-cultural perspectives on hypnotic-like procedures used by native healing practitioners, in J.W. Rhue, S.J. Lynn, and I. Kirsch, (Eds.), *Handbook of Clinical Hypnosis* (691-717). Washington D.C.: American Psychological Association.

Krippner, S. (2000). Cross-cultural perspectives on transpersonal hypnosis. In E.D. Leskowitz (Ed.), *Transpersonal Hypnosis: Gateway to Body, Mind, and Spirit*. NY: CRC Press.

Krisch, I. (1990). *Changing Expectation: A Key to Effective Psychotherapy*. CA: Pacific Grove.

Leskowitz, E.D. (2000). Energy healing and hypnosis. In E.D. Leskowitz (Ed.), *Transpersonal Hypnosis: Gateway to Body, Mind, and Spirit*. NY: CRC Press.

Tart, C. (1976). *Learning to use Extrasensory Perception*. Chicago: University of Chicago Press.

Wolinsky, S. (2000). Trances people live: Healing approaches in quantum psychology. In E.D. Leskowitz (Ed), *Transpersonal Hypnosis: Gateway to Body, Mind, and Spirit*. NY: CRC Press.

8

Hypnosis and Christianity

SANIL MATHEW

> One man's religion is another man's superstition and one man's magic is another man's science.
>
> —*Arthur Shapiro*

Introduction

Hypnosis is a state of deep relaxation in which the subconscious mind is extraordinarily receptive to positive thoughts and suggestions. It is not something a hypnotist does to you, but it is something you give to yourself. Nobody can make you do something you do not want to do or have the desire to do. Through hypnosis, your behaviour can be modified to benefit you.

Dating back from 2600 BC to the present, different methods of hypnosis have been used. Wang Tai, the father of Chinese medicine, used medical procedures that were of hypnotic nature. There were many other people and scientists that used various forms of hypnosis, but the most influential of them all was Frank Anton Mesmer. He is remembered for the term "mesmerism" which is a process of inducing a trance through a series of passes he made with his hands and magnets. Working with a person's psychic and electromagnetic energies, he performed mesmerism on many people across the world, and taught his students of his techniques. Many of his students got greatly involved in the study of mesmerism and other types of psychological subjects. He was admired, and scientists followed his example and came up with their own ideas.

Another influential person in the field of hypnosis is James Braid (1943). He opposed mesmerism originally, but soon he became interested in the subject and began studying it. He said that cures were not due to psychic and electromagnetic energies, but due to suggestion. He developed the eye fixation technique of inducing relaxation which became to be known as hypnosis, after the Greek God of sleep *Hypnos*. He characterized hypnosis as deep concentration by a person in a single dominant idea. He realized that ideas could be implanted in the hypnotic state. He could not explain it, but he knew that it was the most amazing thing he had ever seen. He thought this phenomenon was a form of sleep, but when he realized his error, he wanted to change the name to "monoideism", or the influence of a single idea, but the rudimentary name hypnosis prevailed.

Position of Religious Organizations on Hypnosis

Most religious groups accept the proper and ethical use of hypnosis for helping people. Hypnosis is steadily gaining recognition in the world as the means to help people, be successful and experience abundance in their lives.

Jewish Faith: There has been no opposition to the use of hypnosis in the Jewish Faith when it is used for the benefit of mankind.

Eastern Faiths: Many of the far Eastern faiths such as Buddhism, Yoga, Shintoism, and others approve the use of hypnosis and they often use hypnosis techniques in their worship. The Christian Church also uses many hypnotic techniques in their worship. The use of eye fixation on the candles, cross, and pulpit; the bowing of the head in prayer; and the closing of eyes in prayer are some of them.

Moslem Religion: has no opposition to hypnosis that is cited in literature.

Roman Catholic Church : has issued statements approving the use of hypnosis. In 1847, a decree from the Sacred Congregation of the Holy office states,

"Having removed all misconception, foretelling of the future, explicit or implicit invocation of the devil, the use of animal magnetism (Hypnosis) is indeed merely an act of making use of physical media that are otherwise licit and hence it is not morally forbidden provided it does not tend toward an illicit end or toward anything depraved."

In 1956, The Pope Pius gave his approval of hypnosis. He stated that the use of hypnosis by health care professionals for diagnosis and treatment is permitted. In an address from the Vatican on hypnosis, in child birth, the Pope gave these guidelines:

(1) Hypnotism is a serious matter, and not something to be dabbled in.
(2) In its scientific use the precautions dictated by both science and morality are to be heeded.
(3) Under the aspect of anesthesia, it is governed by the same principles as other forms of anesthesia. This is saying that the rules of good medicine apply to the use of hypnosis.

Protestant Churches: Exceptions among Christian groups are Christian Science, Seventh-Day Adventist and some individuals of various churches. In recent years, the Seventh-Day Adventist have lessened their resistance to using relaxation and suggestion therapy. Though many in various churches opposed to hypnosis, use the principles of hypnosis (including Christian Science and Seven-Day Adventists) in their healing service, they denounce hypnosis. Barring exceptions, no other Protestant Church has any laws against the use of hypnotherapy.

Some Arguments against Hypnosis from Christian Perspective

One of the major arguments put forward by those who oppose hypnosis from a Christian perspective is:

Hypnosis has been used for thousands of years by

> *witchdoctors, spirit mediums, and shamans. Although a hypnotist may encourage only a light or medium trance, he cannot prevent a hypnotized subject from spontaneously plunging into the danger zone, which may include a sense of separation from the body, seeming clairvoyance, hallucination, mystical states similar to those described by Eastern mystics* (Bobgan & Bobgan, 1984).

Dr. Bunny Vreeland (2008), a Christian hypnotherapist based in California, counters this argument in the following words:

> *Hypnosis is a naturally occurring state, commonly experienced on a daily basis when we lose awareness of surrounding distractions. We all enter the hypnotic state just before we fall asleep at night, and again just before awakening in the morning. Other forms of hypnosis include day-dreaming, becoming engrossed in a book, movie, or sport. While in hypnosis, the subconscious mind will not allow a person to do or say anything against their moral or ethical beliefs. Hypnosis is neither a belief nor a religion. It is not even a matter of conviction. Used in therapy, it is simply another tool, further; hypnosis has no need to be defended. When properly used by a trained professional, it defends itself by the results obtained.*

According to Chaplin Dublin and others who are clerics as well as hypnotherapists, the greatest assurance which the Bible can present to a believer who is beginning to live the Abundant Life is the quote from the pen of the Apostle Paul according to the Clarified Bible in Philippians 4 : 13, "I can do what I ought to do for God will provide me the power." This one verse has given great strength to millions who quote it daily. Many follow the prescription of saying it three times a day. Under hypnosis, an individual can be assured that he is able to follow through with the good decisions which have been made, for God will provide the power.

In the context of medical hypnosis, patients are in safe hands. Practitioners have an ethical code, and it is important to note that hypnotists have no mind control powers. They cannot read the future, cannot cast spells or talk to the dead. There is also an irrefutable safeguard of hypnosis that keeps hypnotists from abusing the power. Any suggestion or idea not in accordance with the patient's beliefs, morals, wishes, principles, or desires will quickly and automatically be rejected. No one can make anyone do anything they do not wish to do through hypnosis. If the hypnotist gives a suggestion and the person absolutely does not want to accept that suggestion, then he will not do it. No one can be hypnotized against his will. As God's creatures, humans have the freedom and capacity to choose, decide and act.

Childhood Memories and Past Life and Former Identities

One popular use of hypnosis has been that of searching the memory by "going back into childhood." Some patients even describe experiencing what they believe to be their life in the womb and subsequent birth. This is impossible, however, because of the neurological, scientific fact that the myelin sheathing is too underdeveloped in the prenatal, natal, and early postnatal brain to store such memories. Still others describe some sort of disembodied state and then what they identify as past lives and former identities. How much of this is created by heightened suggestibility, unrestrained imagination, trance hallucination, or demonic intervention cannot be determined.

There are heated debates and arguments with regard to the memories retrieved using hypnosis. There are many who say that these are genuine and there are many who say that there is a very high possibility of memory being fabricated under hypnotic trance. Both the factions come up with their own evidences to support the proposition.

This issue is as yet not fully settled and it calls for more efforts on the part of the researchers in hypnosis to test if the memories are indeed genuine.

Age Regression

Age regression is another area in which many believers can have serious objections. Because, Christianity does not teach past life directly, therefore when hypnotherapy deals with past life regression, it can lead to stern concerns for many believers.

However, there are many who support this idea saying that no one, including Jesus, seemed to find anything absurd in the idea that the blind man could have performed some act before his birth to cause his blindness at birth.

Past life regression thus remains another controversial area of debate.

BIBLICAL INFERENCES

There are a number of instances in the Bible which many point out as examples of the instances of hypnosis. There, of course, can be disagreements with these instances being cited as examples of hypnosis. However, the major ones are illustrated for academic interest.

The "Surgery" on Adam

The Bible records several instances of hypnosis. The first one is in the book of Genesis, chapter 2, verses from 1 to 22: "So the Lord God caused a deep sleep to fall upon man, and while he slept, took one of his ribs and closed up in its place with flesh. And the rib which God took from man, he made woman and brought her to man." In this case, God probably used hypnosis as anesthesia, so Adam felt no pain when his rib was taken out.

The Hypnotic Experience of Joseph

The first of the synoptic gospels presents the classic description of an individual being hypnotized and while under hypnosis being given a post-hypnotic suggestion on which he immediately acts as soon as he awakens from his hypnotic trance. This account comes in the very first chapter of the first book of the New Testament.

In Matthew l : 24, the Greek word, "hypnos" is used. It is interesting to note that in Greek there are three different words of which two are translated into English as "sleep." They are "Katheudo" and "Koimaomai". The other is either transliterated—the sound in Greek is *"hypnos"* —or is translated as "sleep."

The account in Matthew reveals that a messenger from God went to visit Joseph after Joseph had discovered that Mary was to have a child. Joseph knew that he was not the father. The Greek word "aggelos" is either translated "angel" or "messenger." It does not always convey the meaning of a heavenly, winged creature. A messenger from God came to Joseph after Joseph had made it known that he would not follow through with his vow to marry Mary. The scripture indicates that all of this occurred in a dream. Joseph was told that it would be appropriate for him to follow through with his marriage plans because Mary had conceived by the Holy Spirit.

In verse 24, the Greek text indicates that when Joseph came out of hypnosis, he acted on what had been suggested under hypnosis. He took Mary and they went home as husband and wife. He had received positive insight through a hypnotic experience upon which he acted as soon as he regained full mental awareness. This is a classic example of post-hypnotic behaviour which had been agreed upon under hypnosis.

The Mount of Transfiguration

The experience of Jesus on the Mount of Transfiguration with Peter, James and John is recorded in all three of the synoptic gospels, but the one in Luke is most interesting— particularly since Luke is the only Gentile writer in the Bible and is also the only physician (Luke 9:28-33). There were no Jewish physicians. That function was fulfilled by the religious leaders or, in later years, gentile physicians were engaged. That is how Luke became involved in the Christian movement. He was enlisted by the Apostle Paul.

The biblical narrative in Matthew, Mark, and Luke is similar. Jesus took Peter, James, and John up on a mountain or high hill. The three disciples became sleepy and then they saw Moses and Elijah talking with Jesus and telling Him that he must go to Jerusalem and allow God's will to prevail.

The significant difference in the three accounts is that Luke uses the word "hypnosis" to describe the sleep of Peter, James, and John. Since Luke was a physician and hypnosis was a common experience of the first century, it is logical to accept that a hypnotic induction occurred. Since there were only four people who went up on the mountain top and three of them underwent hypnosis, it is a logical conclusion to draw that Jesus was the hypnotist.

It was used as a positive force to enable the disciples to be able to accept that which would later develop in Jerusalem. It was not only reinforced by the great teacher, Jesus, but by the most revered lawgiver and prophet, Moses and Elijah.

The Sleep of Lazarus

The Gospel of John records the vivid account of the misunderstanding of the death of Lazarus (John 2: 1-44). Mary and Martha sent word to Jesus that Lazarus was ill, yet Jesus did not immediately respond and Lazarus died. When Jesus was informed that Lazarus was dead, he declared that he would go and awaken him. The disciples misunderstood what Jesus was saying. They understood Jesus to say that he would awaken him from a hypnotic trance, but in reality Jesus had stated that he would bring him forth from the dead. The significant point to be made at this time is that hypnosis was understood and practiced during biblical times.

Paul as a Hypnotist

The author of Acts is the same as the writer of that gospel which bears his name: Luke. He was a great first-century writer who wrote from a physician's point of view. There are more of his lines in the New Testament than anyone else other than from the Apostle Paul. In Acts 20 : 7-12, Luke records incident in the life of Paul, the evangelist.

In Troas, Paul has met a number of believers who gathered for communion and worship. Paul is the preacher and he goes on and on. A young man sitting in an open window by the name of Eutychus finally drops off to sleep and falls out of the window, to the street below. Luke describes this incident by saying that Paul hypnotized Eutychus and after a while Eutychus lost his balance and fell. Paul went down to see what had happened. Many thought Eutychus was dead, but Paul said, "No." Paul awakened him out of hypnosis and together the group went back upstairs and spent the rest of the night enjoying food and conversation.

The Hypnotized Society

Apostle Paul uses the concept of hypnosis in a different way (Romans 13:18). He suggests that it is time for society to be aroused from a hypnotic slumber and become fully aware of its God-given potentials to live the Abundant Life. He indicates that no longer does one need to struggle with all the negative aspects of broken laws and demanding rules which cause sluggish behaviour like one under hypnosis. He urges the faithful to become fully alive and simply live a life of love of God, of others, and of self and all the laws would fulfil.

Hypnosis was thus very much a part of the first century. With a Judeo-Christian perspective, it was very common to them. It is described in Matthew, Luke, John, Acts, and Romans. It was known and practiced by those who wrote the majority of the New Testament. I have illustrated the major instances in the Bible that many point out as examples of hypnosis seen in the Bible. But they are subjective interpretations and there can be many who dissent with my observation.

In Acts of the Apostles, Gamaliel is described as a Pharisee and celebrated scholar of the Mosaic Law. Gamaliel is represented in Acts (5 : 34ff), as advising his fellow-members of the Sanhedrin not to put to death Saint Peter and the Apostles for preaching the Gospels. He said, "if this plan of this undertaking is of human origin, it will fail; but if it is of God, you will not be able to overthrow them—in that case you may even be found fighting against God!" The same can be said to hold true with regard to hypnosis too. As long as it helps in alleviating the suffering of the people it needs to be promoted and it will self-propel.

REFERENCES

Bobgan, M., & Bobgan, D. (1984). *The End of "Christian Psychology."* Santa Barbara: Bethany House Publishers.

Braid, J. (1843). *Neurypnology or the Rationale of Nervous Sleep considered in relation with Animal Magnetism Illustrated by Numerous Cases of its Successful Application in the Relief and Cure of Disease*. London: John Churchill.

Christianity and Hypnosis: Answers from an Academic and a Minister, Retrieved on 24 December, 2008, http://www.hypnosisnetwork.com/articles/index.php.

The Holy Bible. (1999). Revised standard version. Catholic edition for India.

Vreeland, B. (2008). *Hypnosis and Religion,* Retrieved on 27 December, 2008, http://www.articlecity.com/articles/religion/article_712.shtml.

9

Mind and Body
A System Approach

KEYUR VYAS

"It is the theory which decides what can be observed"
—*Albert Einstein*

Mind and body are very vast subjects and I agree with Hyland and Kirsch (1994) that "the mind-body problem has not been solved and may not be solved." Yet the efforts to understand it from varied view points, such as in the present chapter, will continue. I have taken basic elementary established practical examples from science and mathematics, and have tried to interpret mind-body relationship using analogies and/or illustrations.

Developing a system *model* of mind-body necessitates knowledge of individual components of mind-body and the relationships among those variables. There are number of different *psycho-philosophical positions* that could provide such data for organization and interpretation to fit into models. One of those positions is that everything can be *reduced* to a simple entity and if we want to know about multiple entities, we can study the entities one at a time and then aggregate our knowledge for an understanding of the whole. This is the foundation of Newtonian physics and the position that forms the foundation for much of the research in psychology. One assumption of this belief is that the interaction of entities can be studied by adding and subtracting them in multiple variations. For example, if we want to study the relationship of thinking and emotional development, we can study each separately and then we can study them together by first introducing one factor, then removing it and introducing another factor (Huitt, 2003). This method, as adopted in my approach here, uses standard scientific method to divide a big subject into small parts, analyze it, and then interconnect with other part forming a whole system.

I have used basic principles of mathematics and science to analyze simple facts of life. In the scientific world mathematical models are thought to "mirror" structural relations in nature, and among things, and to reveal e.g. causal connections. Also, in social fields there is evidence of "structures." There are several system theories such as, non-linear system dynamics, stochastic resonance, Chaos theory, limit set attractors etc. (Rossi, 1996, pp. 39, 131). A system model approach considers these theories as sub-sets. While suggesting analogies, I do not wish into debate whether "mind is matter" or not (Churchland, 1992), nor whether quantum mechanics is more amenable to an account of consciousness than is classical mechanics (Stapp, 1995). My illustrations are on simple basic system design principles.

Science is characterized by its use of highly mathematical methods and conceptualizations in conjunction with a quantitative description of the phenomena. The goal of science is to give as complete a description (mathematical model) as possible of the physical state of the world and its evolution. Such a goal is rather new in the history of mankind. While humans have always strived for ordering the world into systems, from Aristotelian physics to the *mantras* of Indian scriptures, the scope of modern science has expanded exponentially in its attempt to explain everything in terms of a few mathematically formulated laws. Now, as the fundamental laws of nature seem to be charted, the scientists are already rushing with their nets to catch the biggest fish of all, the human consciousness (Borg, 1995). The scope of this chapter, however, is limited to presenting mechanistic analogies to human system.

Let us now start with a small model, as in Fig. 9.1, which is capable of exhibiting self-stabilizing response to an external force event.

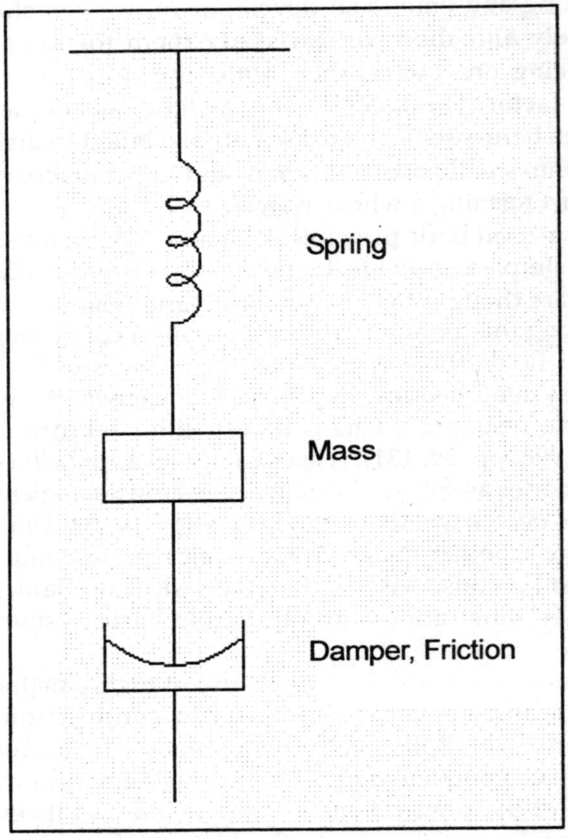

Fig. 9.1 : Spring and Weight

When Step force is applied, it moves. The response is graphically shown in Fig. 9.2

We find similar response patterns in human nature. Different people respond differently. But interesting is that they all learn by iteration. Initial response to emotional stimuli, say shocking or pleasant news, is extreme. With time the effect is dampened.

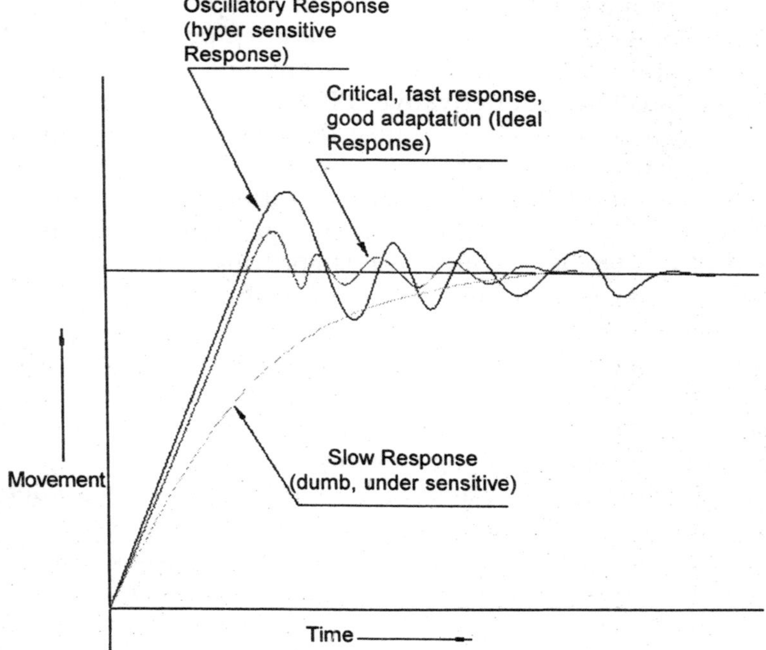

(*Source*: Nagrath and Gopal, 1989, p. 194)

Fig. 9.2 : Response in spring-weight

Let us now take analogy of feedback system from engineering in context to human beings. Any dynamic entity can be represented as a system like machine, PC, software, algorithm etc. A system modelling tools can also be used for modelling of more complex systems, like weather, traffic loading patterns in big city, biological system and ecological systems. It is noteworthy that these were also considered earlier out of mathematics reach and non-predictable. Such systems normally contain natural set of interdependent controllers. The engineering and applied mathematics subfield of "control theory" refers to the use of feedback loops to ensure that system outputs, such as product purity, for example, are maintained at set values. An air conditioner is a simple example of a feedback control system. It works on simple ON-OFF control.

As the set temperature is reached, the compressor shuts off. Most biological systems such as body temperature control system, immunological functions etc. are more complex proportional integral derivative (PID) controls; meaning, the inner controller uses not only the feedback difference (proportional control), but also the time history of the difference (integral control) and how fast that difference is changing (derivative control) to decide how strongly to respond. Faster control always comes with a cost. Higher dose of medicine for fast relief, for example, has side effects disturbing equilibrium of other biological functions.

Apparently, God is an engineer, and a very good one. The very same scheme of feedback control as described above and the network topology reflected in the diagram has been found in mammals' self regulating biological systems. The biological control system is a strict and rigorous analogy to second order PI control systems widely used in engineering applications. Fig. 9.2 and Fig. 9.3 illustrate the feedback principle. Figure 9.4 and 9.5 illustrate the systems in terms of transfer function.

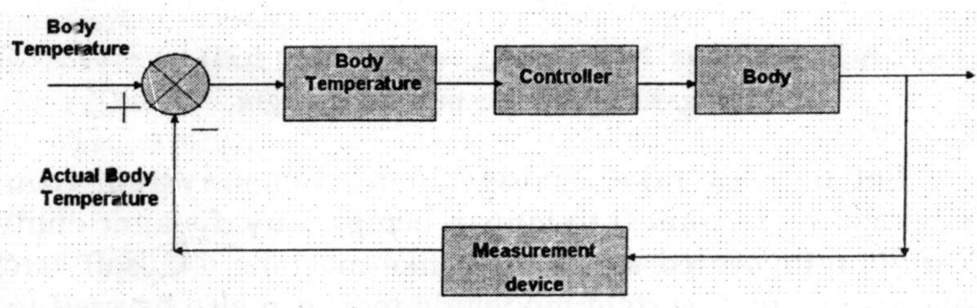

(*Source*: Valkenburg, 2002, p. 398)

Fig. 9.3 : Feedback System 1

Heart rate, blood flow, uric acid in body and hormone concentration in body are also controlled in similar feedback principle. A system may have many such self controlled parameters (Fig. 9.4). Fig. 9.3 is similar to process control loop in a reactor, where various parameters, such as temperature, pressure, flow etc. are having a feedback control loop.

Some of the controls are acquired as in Fig. 9.4.

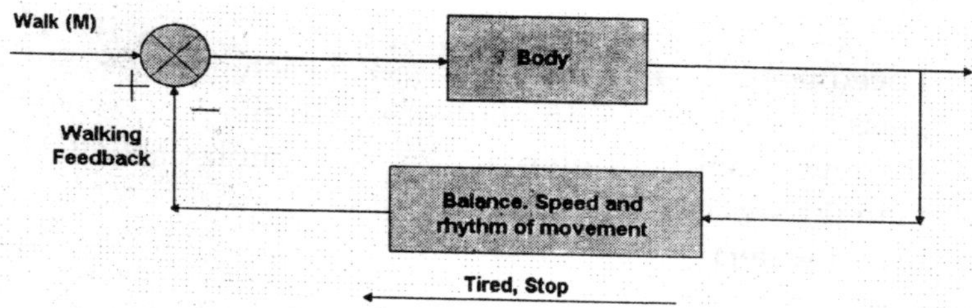

Fig. 9.4 : Feedback System 2 (acquired control)

Each such system has set point, feedback path, sensing method, and controlling element and command method (by chemical or by nervous system). When system set point and feedback path is right and controlling arrangement is below 100 per cent load, the things are normal. Abnormality is seen, when controlling arrangement has reached 0 per cent or 100 per cent load and cannot do more (called controller saturation). In case of stress response, we can presume a set point or feedback itself is changed from mind which can create high or low pressure, in spite of other things being okay.

So, disorder is not within algorithm part or how it is done, but it could be in controlling element saturation, or set point/ command generation part and/or in sensing device.

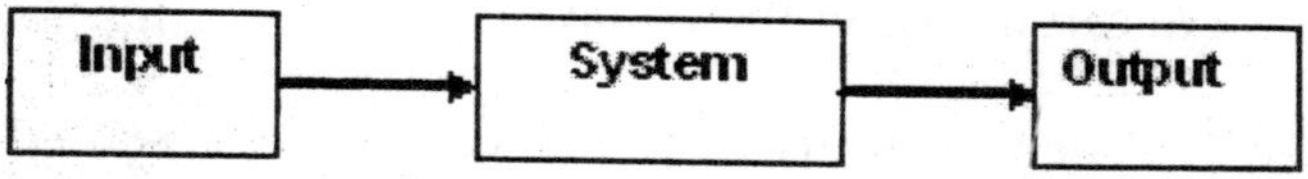

Input → System → Output

Fig. 9.5 : Input Output Relation

Each system is sub-part of larger universal system. System modelling job is to understand system by modelling in such a way that for given input, output (response) can be known.

In terms of mind-body relationship, it can be translated as

Sense → Interpret → Respond

Example :

I need water →	Find water →	Reach there → Fill
glass →	Grip of glass →	Drink
(I know, when	[Internal	[Complex activity]
I am thirsty,	Command]	
I need water)		

It is a simple interpretation function. It tells us, one command is capable of generating sequence of commands in distributed time frame. What we respond to or what we sense is on the basis of our transfer function. This is true, when event is directly affecting us.

So, if X is what we sense, Y is what we respond and H is the transfer function of that particular part, then we can represent it as:

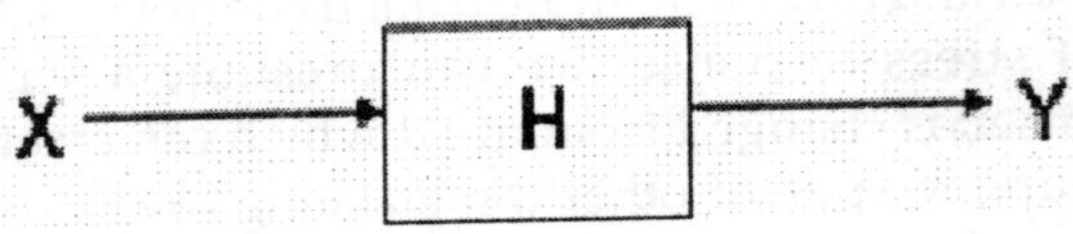

Fig. 9.6 : Transfer Function

So, $Y = H \times X$ (Nagrath & Gopal, 1989, p. 782)

We can interpret the equation as:

1. Each (output) response can be represented as some function of input.
2. Section of world from which we sense and on which we respond to is our world.
3. The function amply reflects—*Yatha Bhav, Tatha Bhavati*

Matrix functions, Laplace transform, and Fast Fourier transform are mathematical functions that help to derive transfer function in real time. Response dependency on to complex phenomena such as past experience, memory and judgment etc. can be included in these mathematical models.

We evaluate people in history by what they have done. For weather forecast earlier weather data is necessary along with current data for functioning of system. History is, therefore, important parameter in eliciting the response to any stimuli. Genetics tells us that each one of us carry human history in terms of genes and to some extent our behaviour has shades of responsive output from history.

When we work, we have certain expectations. In fact, expectations precede action. If Y' is desired and Y happens, then reworking happens. If reworking, too, fails or not possible, then stress results. It needs adaptability in transfer function to make desired output as Y'. Here adaptability may refer many psychobiological functions that may act upon the individual. It is an internal response to external stimuli. He will have to work on his transfer function, if he wants Y' as his result. The modified transfer function is shown in Fig. 9.7.

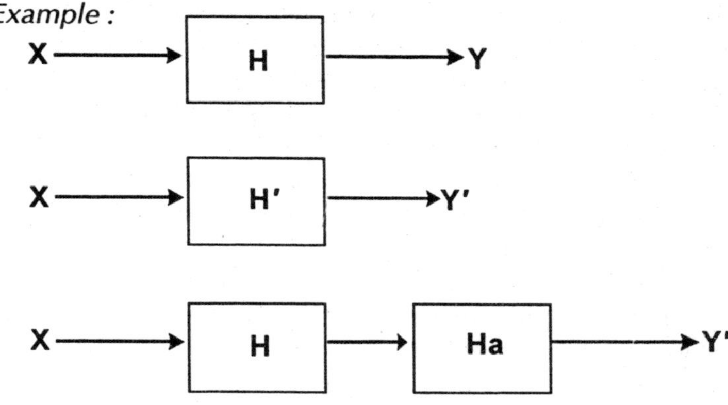

Fig. 9.7 : Transfer Function Network 1

Ha is an adaptability transfer function = $H'/H = H' \times H^{-1}$

As we know, the inverse of a function is possible only when we know the system quite well and for matrix mode, it is not trivial (Function is continuous and consistent!!). Working out H^{-1} means, philosophically, *Knowing Self Fully*.

Moving further, we need to incorporate inputs from spectrum of events from different subject matters and multiple outputs in same way. This we do by denoting *'w'* as frequency (0 – ∞) of spectrum as sub-script. So, our transfer function becomes as below (Fig 9.8). It can also be represented by multi-dimension matrix.

We need to make three basic parts of *H* (*w*) one which senses, one which responds and third constitutes remaining factors.

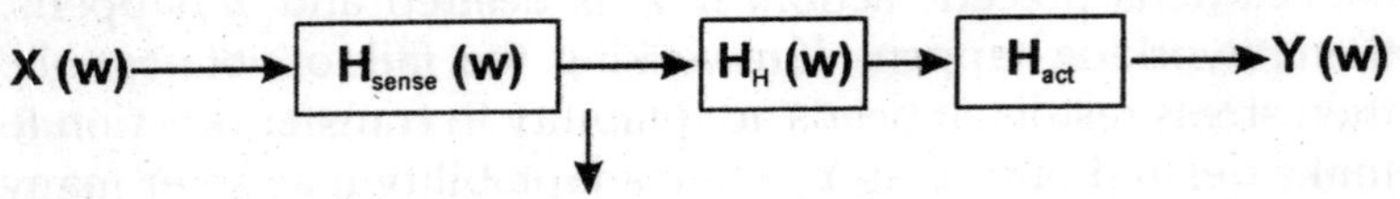

Fig. 9.8 : Transfer Function Network 2

X itself becomes *X'* and is modified with *H* sense *(w).*

We know that there is limit by which H_{sense} *(w)* can receive inputs in unit time and there is a limit by which H_{act} *(w)* can respond in unit time. What we sense has got limitations (e.g. eyes cannot see all spectrum of light, sound below and above certain decibels cannot be heard etc.). Moreover, what we perceive is also modified information. Same way, when we may want to respond very fast, say in race, our response takes its own time based on nature's law. Not appreciating it could be the cause of disappointment and depression. Also, inputs and outputs can be derived as soft and hard, external and internal. For example, a command given by a boss in the office is external hard input. Mind's internal activities without any external observations like, thoughts and desires may be categorized as a soft internal input, which can only be inferred. External inputs are normally written, audible, observable commands

Combining all these interacting inputs and outputs, larger picture can be drawn such as in Fig. 9.9. This model integrates a whole lot of variables such as command path, feedback path, perceiving part, data processing path, old memory linkages, action related limitations, controller saturation etc.

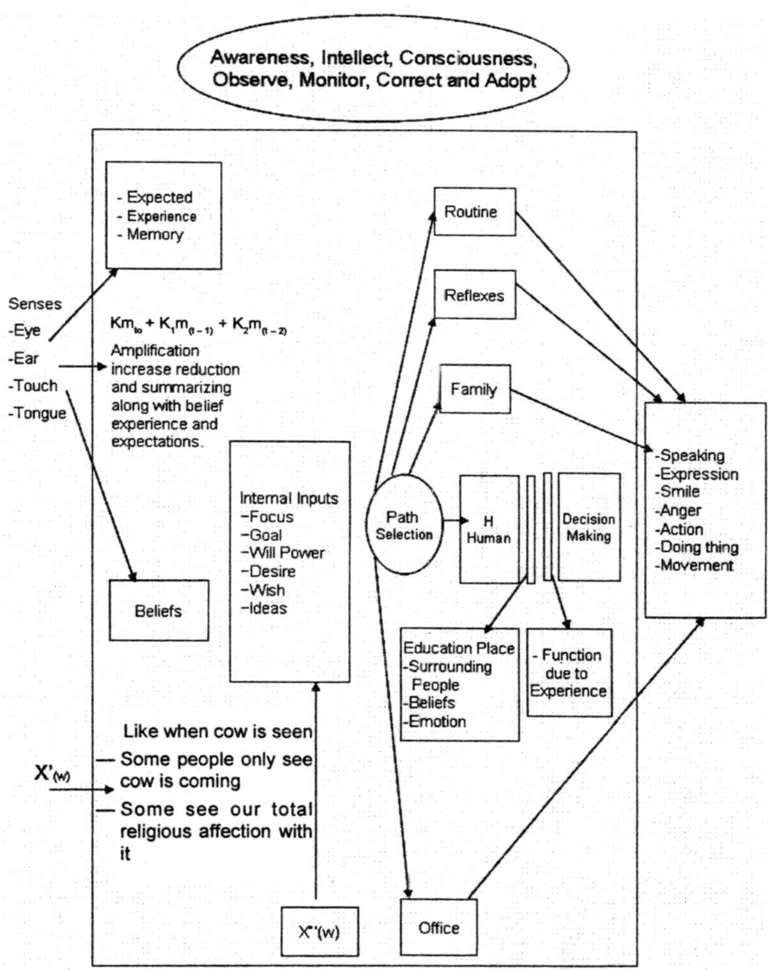

Fig. 9.9 : Human Functioning Network

We also find that few minds outperform despite apparent limitations. They overcome their shortcomings by possibly simplifying their transfer function in that function path for extraordinary response in human learning model (Fig. 9.10).

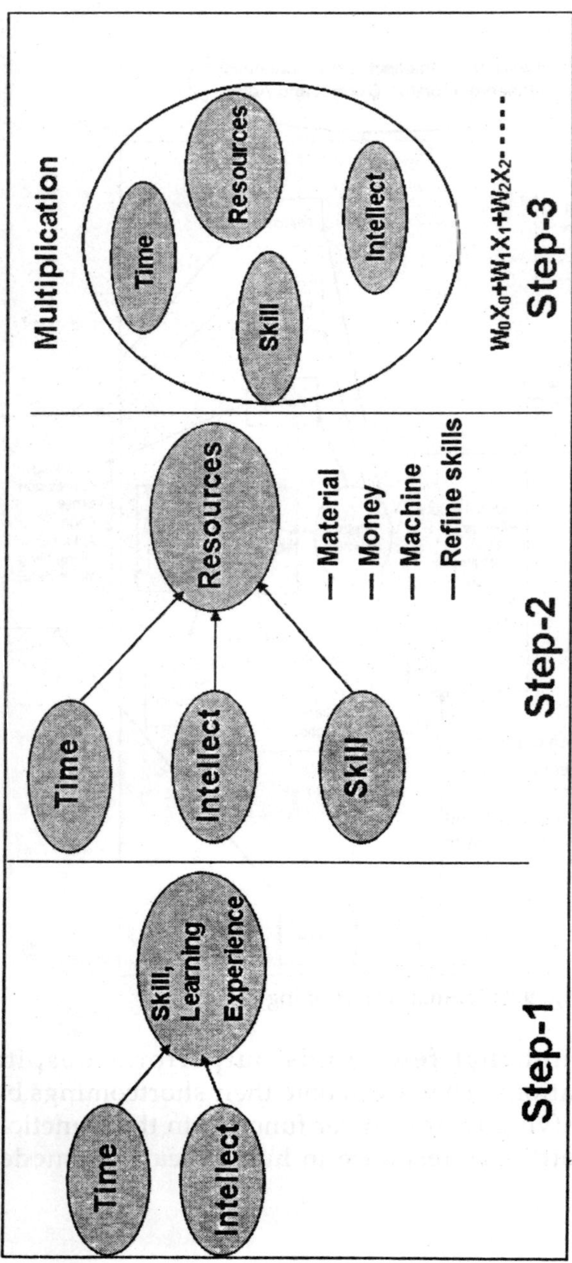

Fig. 9.10 : Human Learning Model

In multiplication W_0, W_1, W_2 are weighing or utilization factors and X_0 is Self, X_1, X_2 are other people contributing to same cause. This way time resource towards same cause (may be of X_0) is also multiplied. While discussing of interconnection among people, we can draw analogy with networks, but in non-continuous way as represented in Fig. 9.11.

A Simple Neural Network

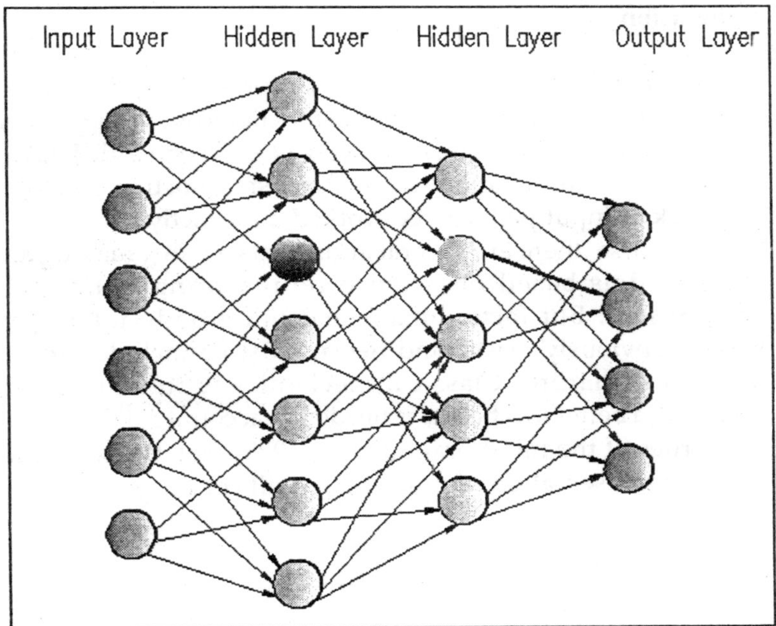

Fig. 9.11 : Neural Network

A dark neuron shown in above figure has higher output weighing factors than others; so powerful enough to communicate with other elements in dual directions in such a way that net output is largely influenced by that element. The same thing can be imagined in cybernetics, where one node (may be main server!) has higher influence over section of network segment. Same way, we find some people more influential in one set of society. They draw others' strength for their own success. In technical terms, such an element has capacity to eliminate its output response time limitation (due to physical limits) with the help of other elements by making them act on its clear distributed time output frame!! They can transform capacity, and create new adaptation functions. Many such subsystems interacting together resemble world functioning.

Conclusion

There are numerous possibilities of representing mind-body interactions as well as psychological functions by system models using tools like matrix transfer function, neural network, Laplace transform or Z transform. Adaptive transfer function, its role in feedback or input path can be worked out exactly.

Of course, there are several arguments against making any such models based on science representing mind-body relationship. But facts remain that mind-body interactive system obviously exists, and hence must be included in our account of nature. Classical mechanics is fundamentally deficient: a better mechanics is needed to account for the known properties of the mind/brain (Stapp, 1995). Yet, the search for proper representation of mind-body will continue.

REFERENCES

Borg, F. (1995). New directions in cognitive science, In P. Pylkkänen, & P. Pylkkö (Eds), *Proceedings of the International Symposium, Saariselkä, 4-9 August 1995, Lapland, Finland*. Helsinki: Finnish Artificial Intelligence Society.

Churchland, P.S. (1992) *Neurophilosophy: Toward a Unified Theory of the Mind/Brain*. Cambridge, MA: MIT Press.

Gopal, N. (1989). *Control System Engineering*. New Delhi: New Age International.

Huitt, W. (2003). A systems model of human behaviour. *Educational Psychology Interactive*. Valdosta, GA: Valdosta State University. Retrieved [Dec. 22, 2008] from http://chiron.valdosta.edu/whuitt/materials/sysmdlo.html.

Hyland, M.E., & Kirsch, I. (1994). Methodological complementarily and the mind-body problem. *PSYCOLOQUY* 5(16) metapsychology. 4.hyland.

Nagrath I.J., & Gopal, M. (1982). *Systems: Modelling and Analysis.* Delhi: Tata McGraw Hill.

Rossi, E.L. (1996). *Symptom Path to Enlightenment: The New Dynamics of Self Organization in Hypnotherapy.* California.: Palisades Gateway Publishing.

Stapp, H.P. (1995). Why classical mechanics cannot naturally accommodate consciousness but quantum mechanics can. *PSYCHE,* 2(5), Retrieved 12.12.2008 http://psyche.cs.monash.edu.au/v2/psyche-2-05-stapp.html.

Valkenburg, V. (2002). *Network Analysis.* New Delhi: Prentice Hall.

PART II
Therapeutic Perspectives : Some Case Studies

10

Psychodynamics of Unexplained Reproductive Failure

RAJNI VYAS, GEETA ADWANIKAR, LEENA HATHI,
BHASKAR VYAS AND RATUBHAI PARIKH

Introduction

Over the years, modern medicine has undergone a major paradigm shift from the Cartesian mechanistic view of the body as separate from the mind. This radical shift has occurred from better understanding of psychobiology of mind-body communication (Rossi, 1996; Rossi & Cheek, 1988). Psychosomatic medicine has found academic acceptance (Kaplan & Saddock, 1985). The molecular biological basis of emotions has been deciphered and subsequently, the conceptual division between the sciences of physiology, psychology, neuroscience, immunology and endocrinology has come to be a historical artifact (Pert, Ruff, Weber & Herkenham, 1985). Thoughts have been equated with floating particles in the blood stream (Reichlin, 1993) and there is a conceptual shift as to how the information is transmitted noncontiguously by information substances (Schmitt, 1984)). This would mean that for most thoughts and particularly for the thoughts with emotional contents, there is a corresponding physiological state that is encoded as memory by the body.

After the battery of investigations proven to be within normal limits, there still remains a group of enigmatic couples with unexplained infertility (Dastidar, 1999). During the last decade or so, there have been some reports linking stress to etiopathology of reproductive failure (Edelmann, 1986; Jeker, Micione, Ruspa, Zeeb, & Campna, 1988; Wright, Allard, Lecours, & Sabourin, 1989; Domar, Seibel, & Benson, 1990; Le Lirzin, Robin, & Geudon, 1990; Pines, 1990; Vartiainen, 1990; Lopes, 1991; Wasser, 1999). But a detailed psychodynamic probing to explore its role in the causation of unexplained reproductive failure is not reported so far. It is postulated that in the pathogenesis of unexplained reproductive failure, be it primary sterility or secondary failure to conceive, or failure to progress to full term, psychodynamic factors are causative. This chapter explores the etiology in the minds of such couples at the conscious, subconscious and unconscious psychic planes.

To say that woman by nature is emotional is a platitude. Femininity is synonymous with deep experiential feelings. When feelings connected with sexuality are concerned, man is also affected at all levels of consciousness. This has been the basis of our hypothesis that psychodynamic reverberations of negative emotional feelings result in stress, and the resultant state of chronic stress causes reproductive failure.

METHOD

Researchers have compiled data of 2,235 couples who came for consultation/treatment of reproductive failure during the 20 years of period from 1978 to 1998. Out of them, 1,325 couples either succeeded in conception by standard therapeutic norms, or had some organic cause or dropped out. They do not form the part of the study. Of the remaining 910 couples, rapport building was possible in 454 couples. They were taken for psychoanalytic evaluation and therapy.

The standard format for the investigation and treatment of infertility was applied to all the couples. It involved detailed history taking inclusive of job, career, educational status, economic background, sibling and their fertility status. Physical examination was conducted to exclude any obvious defect. Investigations included studies of semen, ovulation studies, patency of tubes, and modified Huhner's test (vide *infra*). The hormonal studies were carried out in 50 couples. Since the results of these studies were not significant, they were discontinued.

Formal psychoanalytical sessions by psychiatrist were not conducted but after establishing rapport, psychological probing was done by us. It was possible to elicit data in most couples at interviews. In 41 couples, exploration of unconscious was thought to be necessary to access the repressed material. They were then taken for hypnosis.

Hypnotherapeutic Strategies

Hypnotherapy was individually structured initially to build rapport and general stress relief. The suggestions for infertile couples were categorized as :

1. For couple,
2. For female partner, and
3. For male partner.

The initial strategy was indirect hypnosis. That meant engaging in a dialogue without formal induction so that the subject is so engaged as to go to a hypnoidal state that may progress to a trance. The dialogue is such that the subject ventilates with probing questions and, even catharsis may occur. Hypnoidal state was utilized to conducive acceptance of all methods of psychotherapy such as Supportive Therapy, Re-educative Therapy and Reconstructive Therapy that were thought to be useful to divert to creative activity. Stress relief helped stabilize autonomic nervous system, restoration of disturbed hormonal axis (reproductive hormones and stress hormones) and even reverse the auto immunology. Achievement of normal status was in the form of pregnancy.

Supportive therapy was given in the form of reassurance, prestige, persuasion, removal of guilt feeling by explaining normal pituitary-utero-ovarian axis, or normal emotional intelligence, tension control with technique of relaxation and ego strengthening.

Alienation of anxiety was brought about by change in value system and beliefs by using metaphor, similes and story telling. Provocative environmental irritants like educational, economical, vocational disparity, difference in family set-up were identified and adjustments suggested through indirect hypnosis so that there was externalization of interests.

Re-educative psychotherapy and insight generation was achieved through direct approach to the deranged physiological parameters like PCOD, PC TEST, missed abortion, demonstration of ovulation under sonography, explanation of spasm of tube, dysparunia etc.

Through rational emotive therapy illogical ideas and attitudes were brought to the notice of couple. The irrational links were revealed and couples were taught to rethink in rational way. At times even confrontational approach worked when the couples were plainly told that they were normal and they only would have to decide whether or not they wanted to have a baby.

Such approaches along with direct hypnosis carried the couple to reconstructive awareness of crucial unconscious conflict and its derivatives. This was further strengthened as a protection by imagery of super power or of their own belief system.

Direct Hypnotherapeutic Approach

Hypnotherapy involves targeting the autonomic nervous system (through relaxation and deep trance, metaphors applied are, for example, removal of road blocks while going on a joy ride; traffic propels in pulses), balancing the hormonal system (direct explanation of physiology; there is a composer of the orchestra as well as a band-master who conducts it in harmony) and immune responses (indirect hypnosis by way of demonstrating live sperms before; and in lysis after they are instilled in vagina). The therapy that is applied to the couple together is on the following lines.

Direct hypnosis was used in fifty couples. Couples were at times treated in groups and, if privacy was imperative, separately. While the suggestions were individually crafted, a common visualization technique that was loaded with significant metaphors and archetypal symbols was as under:

> *Two of them decide to go for a joy ride after taking a refreshing shower of cool water...comfortably and pleasantly dressed...riding on a scooter...enter a garden...garden of Eden...so beautiful...where the gods play...hand in hand...tall trees...beautiful flower beds...beds of green grass...velvet like green grass...beds...The birds are chirping...The sun is going down in the West...They see a garden with children playing...They pause...look! ...A mother is holding an infant in her arms...beautiful smile...Your partner takes out his mobile phone...that has a camera...takes a picture...both of you see...There is a picture of a mother that is you with a child...Both of you look into each other's eyes...leisurely saunter back...sun is setting in the West...ride on your vehicle...a bit of bumpy drive...enjoyable...reach home...There is a lock...you are fumbling with the key...your doctor, Dr. R. is just around...helps you, the lock just opens...You go to your bed room...You see at the foot end of the bed a nice picture...it is a mother with a baby... it is a mother with a baby...that your partner has flashed in the garden...It is You with your baby!...nobody around...only you and your partner...open door...open the windows...fresh flow of air...you make love...*

Huhner's test in modified form was performed in 295 cases in the office. The semen was collected after two days of abstinence as a masturbation specimen on the premises. The motile spermatozoa in the ejaculate were shown under the microscope to both the partners. Thereafter, with the insemination cannula, the semen was poured on the cervix and it drained by itself into the posterior fornix. Whatever changes occurred after half an hour of the deposition of the ejaculate was also shown and explained to the couple.

Results

Psychodynamic profile of these couples revealed deep-seated maladjustment/negative feelings. When conscious about them, they were helpless/unable to cope with them. Or, when they were not perceived by the couple, they were repressed to the subconscious/unconscious. The negative feelings arose from conflict, fear and intense desire or hyper anxiety (Table 10.1).

Table 10.1 : Psychological Profile of Patients

Sl. No.	*Patient's Psychological status*	*No of Patients*
1.	Conflict	224
2.	Fear	135
3.	Intense desire and hyperanxiety	95

The conflict situations covered a wide range of personal, interpersonal, social and cultural issues (Table 10.2).

Table 10.2 : Causation of Conflict

Sl. No.	*Reason of Conflict*	*No. of Patients*
1.	Educational disparity	49
2.	Economic disparity	37
3.	Cultural disparity-Intercaste marriage	34
4.	Professional disparity and discord of career expectations	35
5.	Joint family—family discord, dominant mother-in-law	35
6.	Second child not desired by the wife	10
7.	Second marriage	10
8.	Hostility either to the partner or to his/her family	14
	Total	**224**

The most common conflict situation arose from inability to cope with disparities like educational (49 couples), economic (37 couples), professional (35 couples) and cultural (34 couples) between the partners. A model profile of couple emerged from these groups. In cases, when the wife assumed a superior stance either on account of educational, social, intellectual, economic or other strata, she thought she had a climb down from a better city, a more aristocratic family or affluence. The lady felt let down. The husband in such a combination was gentle, kind, understanding and caring. He lacked assertiveness and was subdued. An alternate profile was that of male dominance countenanced by passive aggression from the woman. This combination produced a contradictory field of expectations and a negative feedback. Living in the joint family caused conflict situations in 35 couples. The mother-in-law in Indian cultural milieu has archetypal significance. The normative value for the ideal size of the family in India is fast changing in educated couples. In 10 couples, the female did not want yet another child. Discord arising out of the previous marriage caused tensions in 10 couples. Hostility on any other account either to the partner or his family was the cause of conflict in 14 couples.

Fears and apprehension arising from varied perceptions were the dominant psychodynamic force in 135 couples (Table 10.3).

Table 10.3 : Fears and Apprehensions among Patients

Sl. No.	*Type of fear/apprehension*	*No of Patients*
1.	Fear based on earlier abortion/s	35
2.	Fear of child-bearing, caring and rearing	30
3.	Fear based on family history of sterility	15
4.	Fear of pain	15
5.	Fear based on late age of marriage	10
6.	Fear based on earlier traumatic delivery/caesarian section	10
7.	Fear based on earlier ectopic pregnancy	5
8.	Fear of his/her illness, its effect on delivery and repercussion on the child	10
9.	Fear based on earlier birth of congenitally deformed child	5
	Total	**135**

Earlier abortions left a trauma and caused fear of subsequent pregnancy in 35 women. Fears regarding the childbearing, labour and child rearing were noted in 30 couples. If there was a history of sterility in the family, it was projected on self in 15 cases. Fear of pain was noted in 15 women. Late age of marriage causing apprehension about coping with the pregnancy and the baby were noted in 10 women. The previous obstetric history in the form of traumatic delivery (10 cases) and unfortunate incidence of an ectopic pregnancy (5 cases) were fundamental to apprehension. The health status of either or both was a cause of fear and worry in 10 cases. A previous birth of a congenitally deformed child provided a strong deterrent in 5 women.

Intense desire and high selectivity were counter-productive in 95 (Table 10.4) as per the psychodynamics of reverse effect (Kroger, 1963).

Table 10.4 : Cases of Patients with Intense Desires

Sl. No.	*Type of desire*	*No of patients*
1.	Hyperanxiety and agitation	45
2.	Only male child wanted	40
3.	High ideal for the child to be born	10
	Total	**95**

In 145 women modified Huhner's test showed immobility of sperms, extending to autolysis after half an hour of deposition. This forms the text of a separate paper that attempts to explain transduction of negative feelings to immunity. In couples taken for hypnosis, it proved therapeutic in 20 cases. This data is being compiled and shall be reported later in a separate publication.

Discussion

Fertilization of an ovum by a sperm is a molecular biochemical event, based on so many known and yet to be known biochemical factors. While the infertile couples are known to be under various levels of psychological stress arising from their infertile status, we postulate a different paradigm whereby the stress arising out of a difficult relationship is attributed as the cause of unexplained reproductive failure. We aim towards hinting at the mind-body continuum whereby molecular biological events are seen as arising also from the ideas, thoughts and emotions. The negative feelings undergo transduction to cause such molecular biochemical events that result in reproductive failure.

The emotions and ideation work through a three-tier mechanism comprising of the autonomic nervous system, hormonal mediation and immunology. First level of operation is the effect of the psyche on the autonomic nervous system. Ever since Selye demonstrated a fight or flight response to stress, the influence of the autonomic nervous system over the various organs of the body is well recognized. Frigidity, dysparunia, and spasm of the fallopian tubes are some of the manifestations. At the laparoscopic examination under general anesthesia, we have seen white string like tubes that will not allow any dye to flow through. Repetition of intravenous administration of atropine and taking the patient under deep anesthesia made the tubes to relax and open out.

The chronic stress has its effect on the function of the endocrine glands. It is usual for the menstrual cycle to be irregular during bereavement and such other emotional turmoil. It may also become anovulatory or there may be irregular ovulation. While single readings of the hormones were found normal in our studies, the hormone levels may fluctuate during acute exacerbation of stress to abnormal levels causing failure in fertilization and nidation. In male, impotence and low sperm count are frequently seen as a consequence to stress. The striking instance was that of a stock market broker, who following a crisis in the market not only became impotent but his sperm count also fell to a low of less than a million.

The third tier of operation is immunological. In coining the term, "cervical hostility" for the Huhner's test, the gynaecologist of yore has demonstrated her insight. The "hostile" factors in the cervical mucus have been identified as immunoglobulin IgG, IgA and rarely IgM. The prognostic value of their presence in the cervical mucus is established (Sood, Gupta, & Saha, 1987).

We have been treating infertility over a period of 40 years (1959-1999). During the early period of our practice (1959-1978), we were guided only by the standard therapeutic norms and were confused when we encountered unexplained reproductive failure. Every clinician matures in her practice: it is commonplace that the results improve over a period of time. This happens not only because of dexterity but also on account of the generation of insight. Following the changing paradigm of the body-mind relationship in 1979, we came to believe that psychodynamic factors may be causative in such cases and decided to investigate them. This chapter is the result of our own insight generation.

The process of insight generation applies particularly to the patients. We have employed various forms of psychotherapy (Khorana, 1999). It was client oriented to suit individual needs. The therapy comprised of various methods, like non-directive psychotherapy, rational emotive psychotherapy (Ellis, 1973), guided imagery as well as Ericksonian indirect and direct hypnotherapy (Erickson & Rossi, 1980). Hypnotherapy was particularly useful with difficult couples. All forms of psychotherapy bring about insight generation that reverses the abnormal psychocybernatics so as to normalize molecular biological events. Out of 454, 335 women conceived following some form of psychotherapy. This is being reported separately.

Our results indicate a significant role of psychodynamic stressors in the causation of so far "unexplained" reproductive failure. A recommendation is, therefore, made that investigation of the psychodynamic profile of the couples should be routinely done (Wright, Allard, Lecours, & Sabourin, 1989). We tend to agree with Le Lirzin *et al.* (1990) that the gynaecologist as the leader of the infertility team is in a better situation to establish rapport and take care of the psychotherapeutic aspects.

REFERENCES

Dastidar, S.G. (1999). Infertility and its management: Some unresolved issues. *JIMA, 97*, 734.

Domar, A.D., Seibel, M.M., & Benson, H. (1990). The mind/body programme for infertility: A new behavioural treatment approach for women with infertility. *Fertil. Steril.*, 53, 246-9.

Edelmann, R.J., & Connolly, K.J. (1986). Psychological aspects of infertility. *Brit. J. Med. Psychology*, 59, 209-219.

Ellis, A. (1973). My philosophy of psychotherapy. *J. Contempt. Psychol.*, 6, 13-18.

Erickson, M.H., & Rossi, E. (1980). *Innovative Hypnotherapy: Collected Papers of Milton H. Erickson on Hypnosis.* New York: Irvington.

Jeker, L., Micione, G., Ruspa, M., Zeeb, M., & Campana, A. (1988). Wish for a child and infertility: Study on 116 couples: Interview and psychodynamic hypothesis. *Intern. J. Fertil.*, 33, 411-22.

Kaplan, H.I., & Saddock, B.J. (1985). *Comprehensive Textbook of Psychiatry, IV.* (pp. 356-357, 400-401, 1124-1130). Baltimore: Williams and Wilkins.

Khorana, A.B. (1999). Psychotherapy. In J.N. Vyas (Ed). *Textbook of Postgraduate Psychiatry*, (pp. 817-831). New Delhi: Jaypee.

Kroger, W.S. (1963). *Clinical and Experimental Hypnosis* (p. 43). Philadelphia: J.B. Lippincott.

Le Lirzin, R., Robins, D., & Geudon, V. (1990). An overview of psychogenic sterility. *Reveu Francaise Gynecol. Obstet.*, 85, 307-312.

Lopes, P. (1991). Psychogenic sterility: A myth? *Revue Franca. Gynecol. Obstet.*, 6, 77-80.

Pert, C.B., Ruff, M.R., Weber, R.J., & Herkenham, M. (1985). Neuropeptides and their receptors: A psychosomatic network. *The Jour. of Immunol.*, 135, 820-826.

Pines, D. (1990). Emotional aspects of infertility and its remedies. *Intern. J. Psycho Analysis*, 71, 561-8.

Reichlin, S. (1993). Mechanisms of disease. *The New Eng. Jour. of Med.*, 329, 1246-1253.

Rossi, E.L. (1996). The psychobiology of mind-body communication: The complex self-organizing field of information transduction. *Biosystems.*, 38, 199-206.

Rossi, E.L., & Cheek, D. (1988). *Mind-Body Therapy: Ideodynamic Healing in Hypnosis* (pp. 71-91). New York: WW Norton.

Schmitt, F.D. (1984). Molecular regulators of brain function: A new view. *Neuroscience*, 13, 991-1001.

Shulman, S. (1988). Sperm antibody: Detection and significance in infertile couples in human reproduction. In R. Iizuka & K. Semm (Ed.), *Transactions of VI World Congress on Human Reproduction* (pp. 93-95). Japan: Elsevier.

Sood, M., Gupta, P., & Saha, K. (1987). Immunoglobulin profile of infertile couples. *J. Obstet. Gynecol. India*, 37, 331-334.

Vartiainen, H. (1990). Effects of psychosocial factors, especially work related stress, on fertility and pregnancy: A prospective study from the stage of planning to become pregnant. *Acta Obstet. Gynecol. Scand.*, 69, 677-678.

Wasser, S.K. (1999). Stress and reproductive failure: An evolutionary approach with application to premature labour. *Am. J. Obstet. Gynecol.*, 180, 272-2, 74.

Wright, J., Allard, M., Lecours, A., & Sabourin, S. (1989). Psychosocial distress and infertility: A review of controlled research. *Intern. J. Fertil.*, 34, 126-142.

11

Panch-Kosha Concept for the Application of Beck's Cognitive Approach

B. M. PALAN

Introduction

While thinking about personal problem or when one is agitated (angry, frightened, tense and like), the person generally thinks of "why" i.e., the person searches for the reason for her/his agitation (unhealthy feeling) or inappropriate behaviour. This creates external focus and person's thinking becomes subjective and irrational. Here, the person becomes a "thinking self" and would start blaming the situation or another individual for her/his problem. Dr. Aaron Beck (1985) suggested that one might think of "how" and not "why" in relation to one's unhealthy feeling. When a person thinks about how the unhealthy feeling (of anger or fear or tension) was created in her/his mind, the focus becomes internal and the person becomes an "observing self." One realizes that it is not the external event or situation but her/his own interpretation of the event that creates the agitation. While trying to understand the process of interpretation, the person will be able to get insight in her/his own irrational thinking pattern. And this insight may then be used for inducing rational thinking which can create healthy feeling.

This type of introspection (thinking of "how" with internal focus) requires rational and objective thinking mode; but when the person is already agitated, the mind is on irrational and subjective mode. Understanding the concept of *Panch-kosha* and utilizing the same makes it easier for the person to shift from subjective—irrational to objective—rational pattern of thinking.

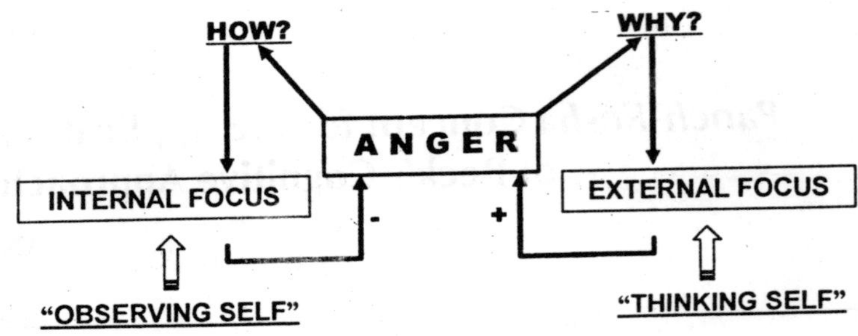

Fig. 11.1 : Shifting from "why" to "how"

The Concept of *Panch-kosha*

Vedanta philosophy explains that the omnipresent and omnipotent pure, absolute, eternal, blissful consciousness (the *Brahman*/Non-local Pure Potential) is manifested as the local, individual awareness—the "I-ness" or ego which always remains identified with (or operates from) one of the five *koshas* (imaginary sheaths). They are: *Annamaya kosha* (Food sheath), *Pranamaya kosha* (Vital sheath), *Manomaya kosha* (Mind sheath), *Vigyanamaya kosha* (Intellect sheath) and *Anandmaya kosha* (Bliss sheath). Originally the concept of *Panch-kosha* was utilized by the *shastras* or the *Guru* for explaining to the disciples the real nature of the 'self', the consciousness, the absolute reality by negation of each of the five *koshas*.

Annamaya Kosha (Food sheath): This includes the external physical body. When a person thinks (says or believes), "I am tall" or "I am beautiful or handsome", she/he is operating from her/his *Annamaya kosha*. She/he assumes that she/he is the body which actually is tall or beautiful or handsome.

Pranamaya Kosha (Vital sheath): This includes biological processes and their consequences (instincts or diseases). When a person senses that "I am thirsty" or "I am hungry" or "I am weak" or "I am suffering from diabetes", she/he is operating from her/his *Pranamaya kosha* (actually reduction in fluid volume or increase in electrolyte concentration in the body is causing activation of 'thirst centre', situated in the hypothalamus of brain, and it is sensed by the individual as thirst).

Manomaya Kosha (Mind sheath): This refers to the mind or thoughts and feelings. When a person says/perceives that "I am angry" or "I am sad" or "I am frightened", she/he is said to be operating from her/his *Manomaya kosha*. The anger or sadness or fear is a feeling created in her/his mind. But the person identifies with this emotion and gets totally indulged with the particular feeling.

Vigyanamaya Kosha (Intellect sheath): This refers to the knowledge. When a person says that "I know" or "I do not know" or when a person is using intellect or knowledge in performing any task, she/he is operating from the *Vigyanamaya kosha*.

Anandmaya Kosha (Bliss sheath): This refers to the presence of pleasure, joy or ecstasy in the mind. Generally an individual will identify with this *kosha* when she/he gets the object, person or situation which she/he desired to have or when she/he is able to get rid of an object, person or situation which she/he wanted to get rid of.

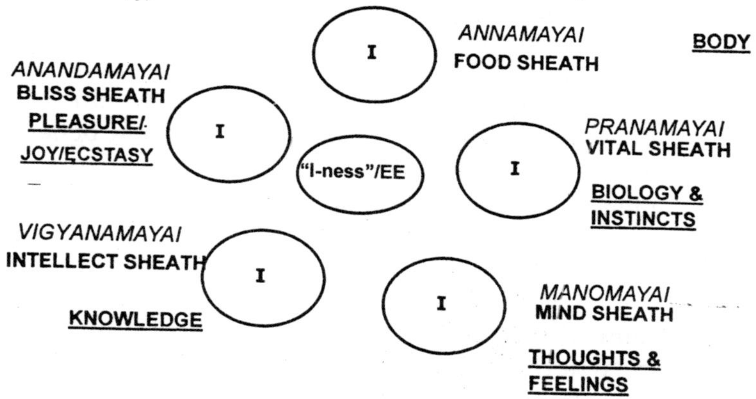

Fig. 11.2 : The Five *Koshas*

Identification with a *kosha* means ego energy (EE) is

invested (Federn, 1952) in that particular sheath—i.e., the person experiences her/himself having the qualities of that particular sheath, getting completely indulged with the contents of that sheath.

Use of the *Panch-Kosha* Concept for Introspection

When the ego energy is invested with one of the first three *koshas (Annamaya, Pranamaya or Manomaya)* and at that point of time if the contents of that particular sheath are unhealthy, the person will experience problem or agitation. With some background knowledge about the concept of *Panch-kosha,* when a person in agony enquires about the *kosha* from where she/he is operating at that moment, she/he is instantaneously and spontaneously shifting to *vigyanamaya kosha* and her/his mind picks up rational and objective mode of thinking. This makes it easier for the individual to shift from thinking of "why" to "how" and derive insight into her/his problem. Following are some examples to understand use of *Panch-kosha* concept for initiating the introspection.

Thinking about "how" will require the person to inquire about her/his undesirable thoughts at the back of inappropriate behaviour or unhealthy feeling and then to search for the irrational (disempowering) belief responsible for the undesirable thoughts. It is then easier for the person to think of a rational (empowering) belief which she/he would like to develop. One can then develop this new rational belief by repeatedly using auto-suggestions or sensory imagery conditioning in self-hypnotic state.

Example 1

An academically brilliant final year medical student was confused (whether or not to drop out from exam) and depressed as she was unable to concentrate in studies a month prior to her university exams. While discussing about the problem, she shared that she was concerned about not having any boy friend as she was obese and having dark complexion.

Her cognition was like, "why am I dark and obese?". . . "why God did not make me beautiful?"

She was explained the concept of *Panch-kosha* and was suggested to identify with her *vigyanmaya kosha*—be in contact with her rational, mature and objective knowledge that it is her body (the *annamaya kosha*) that is dark and obese. She is not her body only. At this juncture, it was more important for her to focus on studies and later, after her exams, she may take up some weight reduction programme. And, the beauty is not only in skin colour—her face and other body features were good. She was convinced that with optimization of body weight she would also look beautiful.

With some practice, she could adopt this new pattern of thinking and could focus on her studies to secure good grades in the exams.

Example 2

A young executive, aged 32 years, had severe anxiety as he was recently diagnosed to have hypertension and put on anti-hypertensive medication by his physician. His worries were, "why I got this ailment?", "I may develop some serious complications in future and die early" and "then who will take care of my family?"

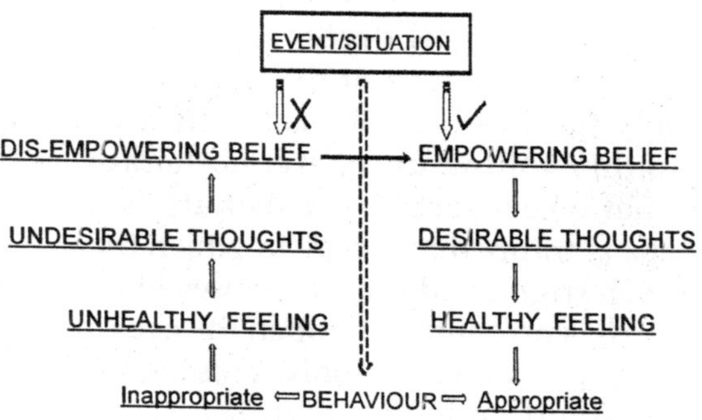

Fig. 11.3 : How to think about "How"?

After briefing the concept of *Panch-kosha* he was explained the role of life style changes and practice of relaxation, self-hypnosis and auto-suggestions in the management of hypertension. This is empowerment of the *Vigyanamaya kosha* with rational knowledge. He was then suggested to identify with this rational objective knowledge and understand that it is the biological process (the *Pranamaya kosha*) —the pressure of blood on his arterial walls that is deranged and he can do something to help his biology to be normal again.

The patient was relaxed instantaneously; he then took formal training in relaxation and self-hypnosis, and adopted healthy life style. He could gradually taper the dose of medicine and then gave up completely under the supervision and monitoring of his physician.

Example 3

A final year computer engineering student was under psychiatric care for her problem of obsessive compulsive disorder. She had several obsessions requiring her to repeat many activities (like, putting on her dress and putting it off or switching on and off the lights or coming out of her home and going in repeatedly before she can go out comfortably). Two years of medication reduced her anxiety to some extent but her need for repetitions did not improve.

After hypnotherapy and her own practice of self-hypnosis for about a year, she was on half the doses of medicines (compared to the original doses) and had only two to three bouts of repetitions instead of the original eight to ten bouts per day. Now she was working as a software engineer. In one of her monthly follow-up of hypnotherapy sessions, she described that whenever she gets her attack of repetition she feels as if she is trapped in a cage in which there is a tiger and she is so much frightened that she closes her eyes and runs in the cage. She has no courage to open the eyes and see whether it is a tiger or a small rabbit only. This description created a spark in my mind and I thought, she is telling that she is enclosed (identified) with her *manomaya kosha* where her 'tiger'—the fear is there and she is totally indulged with that feeling of fear (This was the time, 1992 when I was learning about *Panch-kosha* in a book, *"Vivek Chudamani"* by Shri Shankaracharya and also I was reading Aaran Beck's *"Cognitive Approach to Anxiety"*). And she became the first patient with whom I used the concept of *Panch-kosha* as discussed in this chapter.

I explained her that she is required to shift to her *vigyanamaya kosha* at the time of her attack of repetition and as it would be a different cage, she will be comfortable at once. The 'tiger' is in another cage. She may now be able to open the eyes and find out what that 'tiger' actually is. She was given the paper on which the diagram of the five sheaths was made while explaining the concept to her and instructed to keep it always handy. Whenever she gets her attack, for shifting from *manomaya* to *vigyanamaya kosha,* operationally she is supposed to take out this diagram, think and identify the *kosha* from where she is operating at that moment. In fact, the act of taking out the paper and thinking of the *kosha* from where she is operating will itself shift her to the *vigyanamaya kosha* (as she is connecting now with the knowledge). She will now require to think which *kosha* she was operating from a few seconds before.

In the subsequent meeting, after one month, she came with a very interesting insight. She had two bouts of that feeling of fear but upon looking at the diagram and thinking about "from where was she operating?", she did not require any repetition. She realized how all this started. She had a friend, with whom she would generally study. But at the beginning of second year, her friend developed friendship with a boy. She being from an orthodox family, considered her friend's this act as an immoral and thought of her as 'bad girl'. Since earlier they used to study together, now whenever she started her studies she would remember her friend—the 'bad girl'. She would then fear that because she remembered the 'bad girl', she would not remember or learn her lessons. She would then pray to God or to a holy person like Shri Ramkrishna Paramhamsa or so and then restart studies. But upon starting the studies, again the 'bad girl' would appear in her mind needing efforts to forget her. In this struggle, she started repeating the act of "starting and stopping" the studies. Then repetition appeared in other areas of her behaviour also. Her introspection gave her insight about the irrationality in her thinking. She then very confidently created rational thoughts, used them in self-hypnosis as autosuggestions and under supervision of her psychiatrist gave up medicines completely within two months.

The outcome of this patient's therapy encouraged me to think about and utilize the concept of *Panch-kosha* for exploration. I attribute the development of this technique to her. I found that the technique makes it easier for people to shift from "why" (subjective and irrational thinking pattern) to "how" (objective and rational mode of thinking) as suggested by Beck.

REFERENCES

Beck, A., Emery, G., & Greenberg, R. (1985). *Anxiety Disorders and Phobias: A Cognitive Perspective.* New York: Basic Books.

Federn, P. (1952). *Ego-psychology and the Psychoses.* New York: Basic Books.

12

Hypnotherapy as an Effective Management Tool to Improve Perinatal Outcome in Cases of Pregnancy with Oligohydramnios of Idiopathic Origin

MAITRI SHAH AND RAJNI VYAS

Introduction

Amniotic fluid is essential for normal, healthy development of baby and its amount increases with gestational age. Sometimes, amniotic fluid amount is less than the expected for that gestational age. This condition is known as oligohydramnios. Congenital fetal anomalies and maternal medical disease like PIH are two most common etiologies. However, many cases of oligohydramnios do not show any significant risk factor. Chronic placental insufficiency due to some unknown factor is responsible for reduction in amount of liquor and fetal growth restriction in such cases.

When oligohydramnios develops remote from term, it poses great challenges to obstetrician. As there is no definite treatment available to increase liquor amount, only options left are either to continue pregnancy with risk of significant fetal morbidity and even intrauterine death or to terminate pregnancy with risks associated with preterm birth.

As reported in literature, many mind-body methods including hypnotherapy that alter blood flow in body are useful to ameliorate many acute and chronic illnesses. In this study, we have tried hypnotherapy as a new management option in cases of oligohydramnios. Perinatal outcome was much better in this group compared to cases having traditional conservative management.

Objectives

1. To evaluate effect of hypnotherapy on pregnancy in cases of oligohydramnios.
2. To monitor perinatal outcome in such cases and to compare it with controls.

Methodology

Inclusion Criteria

Pregnant females between 30-34 weeks of pregnancy with diagnosis of oligohydramnios.

Diagnosis of oligohydramnios confirmed on ultrasound examination (AFI < 5).

Exclusion Criteria

1. Cases with diagnosis of PIH or any other medical disorder during this pregnancy.
2. Cases with diagnosis of gross congenital fetal anomalies.
3. Cases with history of leaking per vaginum leading to reduced liquor amount.

This was a longitudinal, prospective study where all pregnant females between 30-34 weeks of pregnancy with diagnosis of oligohydramnios were enrolled after taking informed consent. All these females were randomly divided into two groups. Experimental group (Group-1) cases were offered hypnotherapy (HT) as management option while the control group (Group-2) was followed up with traditional expectant management.

In both groups, gestational age and amount of liquor were confirmed by ultrasound examination at the time of enrolment in the study. Initially, 10 cases were enrolled in each group, but 2 cases in experimental group were lost to follow-up after initial HT session and were excluded from the study.

All these females were admitted in the Ward initially and pregnancy was monitored under close observation.

Hypnotherapy Intervention

The experimental group females were offered individual sessions of hypnotherapy. After taking detailed history, they were informed about what hypnosis is and how it helps as a therapy. During initial 2-3 sessions, they were made to practice breath-watching and progressive muscular relaxation. They were also taught self-hypnosis and were asked to practice it twice daily.

After each session, feedback was taken and counselling was done accordingly.

One of the cases had severe financial constrain and was worried whether she would be able to work and earn for the family with this pregnancy? This was constantly generating a fear and conflict about continuation of the pregnancy. She was given assurance that she is going to be fit and healthy to work during pregnancy and during trance, she was made to visualize God giving her a gift in the form of a baby. She was also suggested that "since this is God's gift, He is going to manage it. Your role as a mother is to nurture it during these nine months and God is going to help you for this".

Each case came out with one or the other subconscious conflicts after initial few sessions. Next session was planned accordingly to resolve their subconscious conflicts—major being fear of pregnancy complication, this pregnancy being unplanned or unwanted due to familial or social reasons etc.

Most of the cases received twice weekly sessions including guided imagery where they were made to visualize growth of the baby inside the uterus by putting a hand over the tummy, were made to talk with their babies ("look at your baby . . . . it is smiling at you . . . . it is listening to you . . . . feel cozy touch of your baby who is solely dependent on you for its nutrition and growth . . . . whatever you eat, whatever you think is reaching the baby" . . . .). They were also asked to reassure their babies. Suggestion was, "I am going to take care of you throughout pregnancy." Lastly, mothers were given suggestions to remain calm and cool so that they can give comfort to their babies.

For some of them, age progression was done where they were made to visualize their entire family along with this baby. They were made to feel happiness and security in the surrounding environment.

During this, specific suggestions related to increase in amount of liquor either directly or with use of metaphor ("water is needed everywhere for the life to continue". . . .) were given.

Role of mother in nurturing the fetus was constantly emphasized to them either with direct or indirect hypnosis throughout pregnancy. Use of pleasant imagery, e.g. scene of a garden during sunrise, where they made to visualize a small seed getting converted into a small plant was also used for few of them.

A few breathing and relaxation exercises were also taught to them to practice during labour.

Traditional Management

The control group females were constantly monitored in the ward for fetal well-being. Rest and adequate hydration to the mother was ensured.

Both group cases were given dose of steroid to increase fetal lung maturity as per protocol. Fetal wellbeing was monitored with DFMC (daily fetal movement count), CTG (cardiotocography) twice daily and ultrasound every week or whenever required. They were discharged from the Ward after ensuring fetal wellbeing and adequate rise in liquor. Follow-up was done in OPD till onset of labour. Few cases however remained in the hospital till delivery.

Non-reassuring fetal heart patterns or further decrease in the amount of liquor was taken as an indication for induction of labour. Labour was monitored in all cases as per the standard protocol and cesarean section was carried out whenever indicated. All neonates were examined and were cared by pediatrician.

Perinatal outcome and mode of delivery were evaluated and compared in both groups.

Results and Discussion

The study, as indicated in Tables 12.1, 12.2 and 12.3, shows that most cases in hypnotherapy group were able to pull on pregnancy till term without any complication while all 10 cases in group-2 had delivered preterm babies and two of them died in utero. In HT group, 75 per cent of deliveries were spontaneous vaginal deliveries while 50 per cent of deliveries in group-2 ended up in LSCS. Group-1 cases were also able to achieve good birth-weight of babies as compared to control group. Thus, hypnotherapy group was able to achieve better perinatal outcome in cases of oligohydramnios of idiopathic origin.

Table 12.1 : Gestational Age at the time of inclusion in the study

Gestational age in weeks	*Experimental Group*	*Control Group*
30-31	4	3
32-34	6	7

Table 12.2 : Mode of Delivery

	Experimental Group	*Control Group*
Spontaneous ND	6	3
Induced ND	0	2
Induced LSCS	2	5

Hypnosis has been used in obstetrics for more than a century with little empirical evaluation of the effects of this type of intervention on labour and delivery (Harmon, Hynan & Tyre, 1990). However, various studies over the years have shown importance and effectiveness of hypnotherapy in conditions like nausea-vomiting of pregnancy, pruritus and backache associated with pregnancy. Usefulness of hypnosis in preparation of childbirth and on improvement of birth outcome is also reported (Zimmer, Peretz, Eyal & Fuchs, 1988). Hypnotherapy has also been evaluated to pull on pregnancy in cases of preterm labour (Brown & Hammond, 2001).

Table 12.3 : Perinatal Outcome

	Experimental Group	*Control Group*
Fetal maturity		
FT	07	0
PT	01	10
Birth weight		
<=2kg	0	06
>2kg	08	02
Fetal outcome		
IUFD	0	02
Live delivery	07	05
Died after birth	01	01

In our study, most of the cases were having unplanned or unwanted pregnancies. Almost all cases revealed social, financial or any other type of pressure causing negative emotions during existing pregnancy. These were probable stressors causing reduction in placental blood flow leading to compromised fetal growth and reduction in amount of liquor.

Hypnotherapy serves as an opportunity for such cases to see their subconscious blocks and to identify their own negative emotions preventing healthy outcome. They can find out their own ways to overcome such obstacles with counselling done by experts after each session. Furthermore, maternal relaxation achieved through hypnotherapy is directly useful in improving placental circulation and thereby improving fetal growth and amount of liquor.

Thus, it appears that a simple intervention using hypnotherapy has far-reaching advantages for cases of oligohydramnios of idiopathic origin and further research in this direction can really serve as a ray of hope.

REFERENCES

Brown, D.C., & Hammond, D.C. (2001). Evidence-based clinical hypnosis for obstetrics, labour and delivery and preterm labour. *Journal of Family Practice,* 5.

Harmon, T.M.; Hynan, M.; & Tyre, T.E. (1990). Improved obstetric outcomes using hypnotic analgesia and skill mastery combined with childbirth education. *Journal of Consulting and Clinical Psychology,* 58, 525-530.

Rossi, E., & Cheek D.B. (1988). *Mind-body Therapy: Biodynamic Healing in Hypnosis*. New York: W.W. Norton & Co., Inc.

Waxman, D. (1989). *Hartland's Medical and Dental Hypnosis*. London: Bailliere Tindall.

Zimmer, E.Z., Peretz, B.A., Eyal, E., & Fuchs, K. (1988). The influence of maternal hypnosis on fetal movements in anxious pregnant women. *Eur. J. Obstet. Gynecol. Reprod. Biol.,* 27(2), 133-137.

13

Approach to Skin Patients through Hypnotherapy

A Ray of Hope for the Real Sufferers

SEJAL THAKKAR AND RAJNI VYAS

Introduction

If people are desperate, they will try anything. If they are angry, their anger can make them unreasonable. If they are depressed, nothing will seem to matter anyway. Unfortunately, these are symptoms of chronic skin diseases that are hardest to treat. Disorders of skin carry with them a disproportionately heavy psychological punishment (Messeri & Montagna, 1984). The desperation and depression of the patients with skin problems motivated us to help them through hypnotherapy. We have utilized it in some of the dermatologic conditions where stress was thought to be either culprit or the outcome of the disease.

As our body's largest and most visible organ, the skin incorporates all major support systems including blood, muscle and innervations as well as its role in immune competence, psycho-emotions, ultraviolet radiation sensing and endocrine functions etc. It reacts to both the stimuli from inside as well as outside. Being mirror of the mind, it reflects the internal state, especially emotional turbulence. It works as a site for the discharge of distress.

The relationship between the mind and the skin are usually more complex than understood, but development of the cutaneous system and CNS from the common origin in the embryonic stage reflects their interactions in certain disease processes. Brain and immune system are connected bidirectionally by ANS and neuro-endocrine outflow mediated by neuropeptides. Neuropeptides can activate number of cells like keratinocytes, Langerhans cells, mast cells, epithelial cells, granulocytes, eosinophils, macrophages and fibroblasts in skin. Release of CGRP (calcitonin gene related peptide), VIP, Neuropeptide *Y*, and substance *P* in skin hold the link between psychological stress and flaring of inflammatory skin disease.

Some of the disorders exacerbated by stress are like acne vulgaris, psoriasis, eczema, hyperhidrosis etc.; while the disorders with disfigurement/disability leading to stress are vitiligo (autoimmune condition), alopecia areata (autoimmune condition), pemphigus vulgaris (autoimmune condition), cystic acne, leprosy etc.

The Case Studies

Hypnotherapy was adopted for several skin disorders. Patients were drawn from various groups of skin disorders and were offered hypnotherapy following the standard strategy. Stress factors were observed in all patients. Anxiety regarding the resolvance of the skin problem was common to all. They were explained regarding the disease, the therapy and the role of mind in maintaining healthy biological processes. The relationship of conscious mind and subconscious mind and the role of subconscious mind in disease causation and healing process on the basis of belief system were explained. By their own willingness, they were given the formal sessions. Suggestions were created differently in each patient based on understanding level of the patient and involved psychological ailments in particular patient. The sessions were planned weekly. Before each session, feedback was taken and next session was planned accordingly.

Sessions were planned with the sequence of Breath Watching and PMR (to offer relaxation), Ego strengthening (considering mental nutrition) and Mind cleaning (which had a wonderful effect as reported by patients). The sessions were incorporated with positive visualization and guided imagery for their healthy skin and role of their own mind in getting it. Self-hypnosis was encouraged in all which was assisted by recorded sessions.

Table 13.1 : Number of Patients with Different Skin Disorders

Diagnosis	*No. of cases*
Acne Vulgaris	04
Psoriasis Vulgaris	03
Pemphigus Vulgaris	02
Eczema	03
Urticaria	02
Miscellaneous (Hyperhidrosis, Lichen Planus, Scleroderma, Allergic Vasculitis)	06
Total	**20**

Acne

Acne vulgaris is the most common skin problem affecting adolescent age group which may have its impact on body image. Acne, a skin lesion, is one side of the story but the emotional turmoil is the other side. Many acne patients experience shame, embarrassment, anxiety, lack of confidence, low self-esteem, poor self-image and impaired social contact (Javet & Ryan, 1985). These factors worsen their stress and eventually the lesions. So, the vicious cycle goes on. When the acne heals, it may leave behind scarring and pigmentation which again may lead to above mentioned distress. The spots of acne are magnified in any mirror. And so, it is the patient rather than the spots that must be treated.

In this study, amongst all dermatological problems, acne patients responded best. Four patients of acne were given hypnotherapy, initially in combination with medical management and later only hypnotherapy. These patients were given hypnotherapy in the form of initial breath watching and PMR sessions followed by therapeutic sessions utilizing the concept of mind cleaning. Mind cleaning was done with the imagery of having their own room (keeping in mind the need of adolescent—having their own space and identity) fulfilling the requirements having all the comfort and leisure. This room was very quiet and pleasant. It was cleaned so nicely from corner to corner including all the furniture and fresh flowers were giving nice fragrance too. So all unhealthy feelings were cleaned in the form of dust present in the room; and now patients were having very healthy and clear skin. One patient dropped out but remaining three responded very well. They continue to practice self-hypnosis and there is no recurrence as noted in follow-up after nine months of hypnotherapy.

All of them reported high self-confidence and self-esteem, and scored high in their exams (all of them being college students).

Psoriasis

Psoriasis is a common, chronic, disfiguring, inflammatory and proliferative condition of the skin, in which both genetic and environmental influences have a critical role. Patient with psoriasis may experience significant psychological and social disability in addition to the physical burden of the disease. Disability experienced by a psoriatic patient is comparable to other chronic illnesses like heart disease, diabetes, cancer and depression. Stress is also a proposed aggravator of the disease process in psoriasis. It is also possible that psychological stress may be associated with a diminished capacity to cope with regular treatment, and that this may lead to deterioration, especially in severe cases (Fortune *et al.*, 1998). Oversensitivity, aggressiveness and suppressed feelings of resentment and anger sometimes underlie the disorder (Gaston *et al.*, 1987). Psychological stress is known to aggravate the condition by altering cellular constituents of the immune system.

Three patients were given hypnotherapy. After the initial sessions of breath watching and PMR, ego enhancement was done by Hartland's suggestions. They were appreciated for performing their activities efficiently. In their pleasant imagery, they were taken in the garden with friends where it was a nice cold (touch sensation) breeze and a beautiful sunset (visual). They were asked to imagine: "Chirping birds are going home and *'kalrav'* of children playing in the ground seem so sweet (auditory sensation). Now you hear sound of *'ghantarav'* which is coming from the nearby temple. You feel thankful to God for such a wonderful world and to express it you enter the temple . . . . There is lovely fragrance of the *agarbatti* (olfactory sensation) and smoke is coming from it. Now, you pray to God to make you as beautiful as He has made many others . . . . Now, you are feeling that all your skin lesions are going into the air with the smoke of the *agarbatti* . . . . Slowly, all the skin roughness is dissolving in the air. The skin is now as beautiful as that of the fresh flower in the garden."

Mind cleaning session was also given with the imagery of being in their own room and cleaning it thoroughly. Initial response was very good in two patients and moderate in one patient who dropped out after two sessions. Two patients had resolved the lesions after four sessions and stopped the therapy abruptly. They, however, came back with the recurrence after six months again. Further sessions to explore the underlying distress and to cope up with it are currently underway.

Pemphigus

It is an auto-immune blistering disorder in which antibodies are produced against cellular component of their own keratinocytes. Patients of pemphigus present with generalized fluid filled lesions which ruptures and leaves erosions. Stress may be an aggravating factor (Brenner & Bar-Nathen, 1984).

Two patients were given hypnotherapy in which suggestions were planned for faster healing and to accept their own cells (to revert the auto-immune reaction).

First case was of 19 years old girl who suffered with the pemphigus for last two years. She was given sessions using guided imagery for healing and accepting her own self along with ego strengthening. She responded very well within four sessions and did not have recurrence.

Second case was of 43 years old female having skin lesions on her whole body and oral cavity for last six years. She had exacerbations off and on, but twice she had severe attacks; first, at the time of her mother-in-law's death, and second, on her father's death. She was introduced to hypnotherapy which helps in changing the immune response and ultimately healing and control of the disease. Initially she was little bit reluctant and apprehensive to have any such therapy as she had misconception with the word *"vashikaran"* and she repeatedly asked *"mane knai thashe nahin ne?"* All her doubts were discussed and cleared. After she was satisfied and consented, ego strengthening suggestions were given as per the Hartland's ego enhancement verbatim.

Pleasant imagery was given to go in the garden where she is surrounded by a number of flowers which are with varied colours and fragrance. She was asked to imagine: "you are in a beautiful garden, and enjoying the nature's beauty .... fragrance and colours. You are enjoying this period, feeling that perfume of the flowers and soft touch of the petals .... With blessings of the God Sun in this soft morning .... now you are feeling that your skin is also getting as soft and smooth as that of flowers. The soft rays of sun are helping you to heal your body lesions .... You are very happy to see your new smooth, soft and supple skin like a new baby, after such a long time on your body .... You are now enjoying this moment .... every moment."

Mind cleaning session was given with imagery of going into deep water of the ocean where multiple pebbles of healthy programmes as well as unhealthy programmes were visualized. Unhealthy ones were thrown away. One of the pebbles representing the divine power of the subconscious mind was identified and activated to get recovery.

After the session, she was much more confident of herself and had a good image of herself—happy, healthy and fresh. She has responded well in terms of healing of lesions, but she still gets new lesions. We are now planning to try age-regression on her to go to the roots of the problem.

Eczema

Literal meaning of eczema is "boiling out." It is an inflammatory disease characterized by itching and oozing from the lesion. It is not a fatal disease but can be crippling physically as well as emotionally. It has profound impact on health and quality of life. Repeated skin trauma by scratching is the single most amplifying factor that leads to chronicity. Breaking itch-scratch cycle is very crucial. Behavioural modification to avoid scratching motivates patients for skin self-care rather than self-destruction. It helps to prevent relapses in the healing phase of chronic eczema. These behavioural changes can be very well achieved through hypnotherapy.

Three cases were given the therapy with suggestions of gradual freedom from itching and resolvance of the lesions. They responded well after four sessions and discontinued the therapy. Two of them had recurrence within three months. Further exploration is required to get the thorough benefit.

One of them being with Atopic Eczema, was just fed up with her persistent, severe itching. Sometimes it was distracting her from the work also. She was highly frustrated as she frequently remarked, *"aa shun roj roj davao lagavya karavani*?; Should I ever get relief from this condition?; Will there be any day when I will be free from all these lesions?"

Pleasant imagery was given to go in the waterfall where she was enjoying with her group: "There is a big waterfall with a beautiful sound emanating from the fall. There are several other smaller falls also coming out from the same mountain. She is going slowly near to one of the falls . . . . and she is feeling nice soothing coldness of that water. She is sitting on the stone and enjoying that soothing touch with water. After some time she is just walking around and sees some pool of water surrounded by a natural arrangement of stones . . . . She is going there, washing her hands and feet there and takes *aachaman* of that water with a great faith. She is feeling free of her skin problem with that holy water."

Urticaria

Urticaria presents with wheal formation associated with itching. There may be varied etiology but in about one-third of cases of chronic urticaria, psychological factors seem to play a contributory role (Whitlock, 1976). Itching may be more intense during stress period (Fjellner & Arnetz, 1985).

Two patients were given hypnotherapy and responded well to get the itching control. The imagery was given of an ice application over the affected area to get cool sensation and reduce the itching. Initially, suggestions were given to reduce the intensity of the symptoms gradually to a comfortable level so that they could do their job at their work places without getting disturbed even though they have urticaria.

Allergic Vasculitis

This is a case of allergic vasculitis (biopsy proven). The person was having recurrence of the lesions since five years. She was frustrated with the recurrent skin problem. She was very desperate when she approached us. Her parents wanted her to get married. But she was worried about her skin problem. As such she showed a great faith in us, she needed someone with her during therapy as she was little apprehensive of the notion of hypnosis.

She was asked to come along with her mother in follow up and to plan her session. Pleasant imagery of going to the river bank was given: "It is a nice beautiful morning and sun is just about to rise. She is enjoying the fine, fresh air and the warmth of the sun as she feels with her father . . . . There is a nice temple some distance away . . . . She is going into that temple, praying to God and taking *prasad* . . . . After coming out of temple, she sits on the steps by keeping her feet into the water. Surprisingly, she is feeling so cool and comfortable . . . . Her both the feet seem absolutely alright . . . . Her skin is as beautiful as it was some years back . . . . She is feeling thankful to God . . . . She is taking some water in her right hand, taking *'aachaman'* and rest of it putting it on her head by imagining that this holy water is going into her body and is altering her immune response and all her allergic manifestations are vanishing."

Mind cleaning session was given with the imagery of her own room cleaning. She responded very well within five sessions of the hypnotherapy and had no recurrence of disorder.

Discussion

An emotionally distressed patient is more likely to consult with physical symptoms than to complain about psychological or social problems (Murphy, 1989). These type of patients are often passed to medical, surgical or dermatology clinics.

The most efficient treatment of dermatological diseases is achieved with combined evaluation of emotional factors (Sneddon & Sneddon, 1983). Prevention of psychiatric morbidity and enhancement of coping skills will help to have better control over such chronic disfiguring and disabling conditions. The mechanisms by which hypnosis produces improvement in skin disease symptom and lesion are not fully understood but have been hypothesized to work via regulation of blood flow and other autonomic functions not usually under conscious control (Tausk, 1998).

These areas of overlap among psychology, psychiatry and dermatology are important. A competent dermatologist should be able to pick up emotional and psychological clues and cues to treat the patient as a whole. Here, hypnotherapy can be a very good tool to achieve symptomatic relief, long lasting improvement and prevent the disease progress in various dermatological conditions. Advantages of medical hypnotherapy for skin diseases include the ability to obtain a response where other treatment modalities have failed; the ability to reduce relapses; and the ability of patients to self-treat and gain a sense of control when taught self-hypnosis.

REFERENCES

Brenner, S., & Bar-Nathen, E.A. (1984). Pemphigus vulgaris triggered by emotional stress. *J. Am. Acad. Dermatol.*, 11, 524-525.

Crosby, I.A. (1995). My skin is only the top layer of the problem. *Arch Dermatol*, 131, 783-785.

Fjellner, B., & Arnetz, B.B. (1985). Psychological predictors of pruritus during mental stress. *Acta Derm Venereol*, 65, 504-508.

Fortune, D.G., Richards, H.L., Main, C.J., & Griffiths, C.E.M. (1998). What patients with psoriasis believe about their condition? *J. Am. Acad. Dermatol*, 39, 196-201.

Gaston, L., Lasonade, M., Bernier-Buzzanga, J. *et al.* (1987). Psoriasis and stress: A prospective study. *J. Am. Acad. Dermatol*, 17, 82-86.

Javett, S., & Ryan, T. (1985). Skin disease and handicap: An analysis of the impact of skin conditions. *Soc. Sci. Med.*, 20, 425-429.

Messeri, P., & Montagna, W. (1984). Ethologic implications of the skin and its disturbances. In E. Pancosei (Ed), *Psychosomatic Dermatology Clinics in Dermatology* 2, 27-36.

Murphy, M. (1989). Somatization: Embodying the Problem. *Br. Med. J.*, 298, 1331-1332.

Sneddon, J., & Sneddon, I. (1983). Acne excoriee: A protective device. *Clin. Exp. Dermatol*, 8, 65-68.

Tausk, F.A. (1998). Alternative medicine: Is it all in your mind? *Arch Dermatol*, 134, 1422-1425.

Whitlock, F.A. (1976). *Psychological Aspects of Skin Disease* (Chapter 9). London: Saunders.

14

Mind-Programming as a Tool to enhance Socio-Cognitive Abilities

A Study of School-Going Adolescents

URMI NANDA BISWAS, PRIYANKA KACKER AND B. M. PALAN

Introduction

Hypnotherapy has been extensively used in school age children and adolescents to improve their overall academic performance by enhancing and altering the functioning of cognitive faculties. The use of hypnosis to bolster a child's symptom management, ability to solve problems, or self-esteem, has been suggested by Valente (1990). Substantial clinical literature demonstrates that hypnosis effectively reduces anxiety, enhances coping, and has been used successfully to treat behaviour disorders, school phobias, and sleep disorders (Anbar & Slothower, 2006; Aviv, 2006). Hypnosis can effectively reduce a child's anxiety and has few side effects when used competently. Stress can interfere with the ability to focus and remember information; students need to manage their stress and remain calm. Although memorization tricks are useful, stress and lack of focus are the key reasons why people are afflicted with memory problems and do not respond for a longer time to such techniques. Hypnotherapy memory improvement techniques help students to manage the stress and focus on information. Many students suffer from test anxiety which they can overcome by learning and practicing self-hypnosis (Densky, 2008).

Most research in this field has been effective in controlling examination anxiety and enhancing examination performance. In a study done by Gruzelier, Smith, Nagy and Henderson (2001), the authors report the effects of self-hypnosis training on immune function and mood in medical students at exam time. Hypnosis involved relaxation and imagery directed at improved immune function and increased energy, alertness and concentration. Hypotheses were made about activated and withdrawn personality differences. Eight high and eight low hypnotically susceptible participants were given 10 sessions of hypnosis, one live and nine tape-recorded, and were compared with control subjects. Life-style, activated *vs.* withdrawn temperament, arousal and anxiety questionnaires were administered. Energy ratings were higher after hypnosis, and increased calmness with hypnosis correlated with an increase in CD4 counts (the immunity parameter). The sizeable influences on cell-mediated immunity achieved by a relatively brief, low cost psychological intervention in the face of a compelling, but routine, stress of examination in young, healthy adults have suggested the use of hypnotherapy to enhance academic performance as well as immunity.

Wachelka and Katz (1999) used a randomized pretest-posttest control group design to examine the effectiveness of a cognitive-behavioural treatment for reducing test anxiety and improving academic self-esteem in a cohort of high school and college students with learning disabilities (LD). All of the students participated voluntarily. Before the study began, they complained of test anxiety and showed an elevated score on the Test Anxiety Inventory (TAI). Eleven students completed the 8-week long treatment, which consisted of progressive muscle relaxation, guided imagery, self-instruction training, as well as training in study and test-taking skills. Compared to the control group, the treated group showed significant reductions in test anxiety on the TAI, as well as improvement in study skills and academic self-esteem as measured by the Survey of Study Habits and Attitudes, and the school scale of the Coopersmith Self-Esteem Inventory. These results extend the generality of similar studies on reducing test anxiety and improving academic self-esteem in younger students. They also suggest that relief from test anxiety can be expected fairly quickly when cognitive-behavioural methods are used.

Kanji, White and Ernst (2006) tried to determine the effectiveness of autogenic training in reducing anxiety in nursing students. Autogenic training is a relaxation technique consisting of six mental exercises and is aimed at relieving tension, anger and stress. In a randomized controlled trial with 93 nursing students aged 19-49 years, the treatment group received eight weekly sessions of autogenic training, the attention control group received eight weekly sessions of laughter therapy, and the time control group received no intervention. Result reported statistically significant greater reduction of State and Trait Anxiety in the autogenic training group than in both the control groups immediately after treatment. The authors concluded that autogenic training has at least a short-term effect in alleviating stress in nursing students. In a similar study, Charlesworth, Murphy and Beutler (1981), assessed the effectiveness of a 10-session, 5-week, group-administered stress management programme for nursing students. The stress management programme included sessions on progressive relaxation, deep muscle relaxation, autogenic training, visual imagery and modified systematic desensitization. A pre-post comparison of state and trait anxiety measures revealed that the stress management group effectively reduced trait anxiety, while the control group's trait anxiety levels remained relatively unchanged. The experimental group showed a reduction in state (test-taking) anxiety from mid-semester to final examinations, while the control group showed a slight increase from mid semester to final examination

Palan and Chandwani (1989) divided fifty-six volunteer medical students in three groups balanced for a number of subjects, performance at last examination, and hypnotizability. The hypnosis and waking groups attended eight group sessions once a week with general ego-strengthening and specific suggestions for study habits, with a ninth session of age progression and mental rehearsal. Subjects in these two groups practiced self-suggestions (in self-hypnosis or waking respectively) daily for the study period of 9 weeks. The control group experienced sessions of passive relaxation induced by light reading for the same period of time. The hypnosis group improved significantly in coping with examination stress, but there was no significant change in performance on examinations by any of the groups.

Research done to examine the effect of hypnotherapy on memory has presented mixed findings to confirm the hypermnesic effects of hypnosis. Fligstein, Barabasz, Barabasz, Trevisan and Warner (1998) in a study to understand how hypnosis enhances recall memory under forced and non-forced conditions, reported that those exposed to hypnosis and to a forced recall procedure were significantly more confident of their responses to correct items than those exposed to a non-forced recall procedure or a waking condition. Participants exposed to hypnosis and forced recall procedures recalled more correct items than those exposed to a waking condition. The findings support the hypermnesic effects of hypnosis when participants are required to provide a fixed number of responses. Relationships between recall of low and high imagery paired-associate words and hypnotic susceptibility, and the influence of hypnosis on recall as moderated by hypnotic level were examined by Crawford and Allen (1996). The study reported that hypnotic level was not a moderator of performance during hypnosis. Low hypnotizables recalled more words in the within-subjects design. Visualization ability was a poor moderator of imagery-mediated learning. Two experiments by Dinges, Whitehouse, Orne, Powell, Orne and Erdelyi (1992) investigated whether hypnosis enhances memory retrieval *per se* or merely increases a person's willingness to report recollections. Both experiments assessed immediate and delayed (i.e., 1 week) recall for pictorial stimuli. The findings provide no evidence for alleged hypermnesic properties of hypnosis.

De Vos and Louw (2006) studied the effect of hypnotic training programmes on the academic performance of students. They used two types of interventions, e.g., one of the experimental groups was exposed to active alert hypnosis and the other to relaxation hypnosis. One control group was exposed to progressive relaxation, while the other did not receive any intervention. The participants' April grades were used as a pre-test, while their June grades served as a post-test. The two hypnotic training programmes had a significant effect on the academic achievement of the participants, which was not found in the control groups. Regarding the efficacy of the two programmes, however, no significant difference was found. In another study with similar objective, study of group hypnosis and Jacobson's muscle relaxation techniques evaluated change in academic examination grades of undergraduate students in educational psychology. A group of 30 students who were hypnotized were compared, over 15 weeks, with a class of 22 students given muscle relaxation instruction. Although initially scores were similar, the former group had significantly higher mean scores on the final examination than the latter (Schreiber and Schreiber, 1998).

However, most of these studies have considered college students as the sample, and very few studies have attempted to study the effect of clinical hypnotherapy on the cognitive abilities of school-going adolescents. Adolescence being a period of emotional turmoil, these students are more vulnerable to stress and anxiety, which in turn may affect their academic performance. On the back drop of the earlier research discussed, the present study was designed to study the effect of mind-programming package which consists of hypnotherapeutic techniques and relaxation techniques on the students who were preparing for either their High School Certificate (H.S.C.) examination or Secondary School Certificate (S.S.C.) examination. The objectives of the study were to :

1. Investigate the influence of mind programming, through hypnotherapeutic techniques, on concentration, memory, confidence and anxiety level in students who are preparing for their final school level examinations.
2. Examine the influence of duration of intervention.

METHODOLOGY

Subjects

Short term intervention (20 hours) was administered on a group (Group 1) of 25 S.S.C. and H.S.C. students who had enrolled themselves for a stress management and mind programming workshop. While another group (Group 2) of 36 S.S.C. and H.S.C. students were enrolled for a long term (45 hours) stress management and mind programming training. But at the end of 7 months intervention, we could get completed data sets from only 14 students in the post-test. Both the groups were mixed groups of boys and girls, hailed from almost similar socio-economic status. They were studying in the schools in and around Vadodara, Gujarat (India).

Short Term Intervention

All the students were asked to write about their problem areas. Total 20 hours of workshop was conducted (five days, four hours each). They were trained to practice Breath Watching, Muscular Relaxation, Guided Imagery, Self-hypnosis with general ego enhancement and specific study skills related suggestions, Mini-nap, Sensory Imagery Conditioning and Dynamic Imagery. Pre- and post-training testing was done on Self-Confidence Inventory, Digit-symbol substitution test and letter cancellation test (for measuring concentration), State and Trait Anxiety Inventory (STAI) and PGMI test to measure influence on different aspects of memory. Follow-up testing was done after one month but as only five students turned up for the same we did not consider the data of follow-up for discussion.

Long Term Intervention

All the students were asked to write about their problem areas and create appropriate goals on the basis of the same. Total 45 hours of training was conducted (30 weekly sessions of one and a half hours each). They were also trained to practice Breath

Watching, Muscular Relaxation, Guided Imagery, Self-hypnosis with general ego enhancement and specific study skills related suggestions, Mini-nap, Sensory Imagery Conditioning and Dynamic Imagery. In this long term programme, the students could practice the same techniques with investigator's guidance several times and also they had one session on diet habits by an expert in diet and nutrition and one session by an adolescent pediatrician on sex and sex linked disorders. Pre- and post-training testing was done on Self-Confidence Inventory, Digit-symbol substitution test and letter cancellation test (for measuring concentration), State and Trait Anxiety Inventory (STAI) and PGMI test to measure influence on different aspects of memory. Pre-training data were collected from all the 36 students who registered for this programme but at the end of seven months, as the pre-board preliminary exams started, many students stopped coming for the sessions and so post-training data could be collected from 14 subjects.

The students were asked to practice self-hypnosis during the five programme days as well as one month of follow-up period in Group 1 and during the remaining week days for the total period of 7 months intervention in Group 2.

DETAILS OF INTERVENTION

Intervention techniques, in context of students, are presented here for the benefit of readers.

1. Study Skills related Auto-Suggestions

Auto-suggestions for this technique are devised by Dr. Palan.

"Now, as I am relaxed deeply and thoroughly, I would like to think about the matters of concern related to my studies. I will have the thoughts and images of my auto-suggestions only, flowing through my mind smoothly like a dream."

"These suggestions will have great influence upon the way in which I am thinking, the way in which I am feeling and behaving during my normal waking state, all the time consistently."

Physical Health

"With each passing day, I am becoming physically more fit . . . . more strong . . . . more alert and energetic. I feel good appetite at the right time and I take right amount of good and nourishing food necessary for my health. I am developing good control over my sleep . . . . I take optimum hours of sleep . . . . very deep and sound sleep which makes me fresh and fine . . . . healthy and fit in my body and mind."

Relaxed Mind

"Day by day my mind is becoming more relaxed, calm and composed. I am enjoying peaceful and balanced state of my mind. I am becoming more and more settled emotionally, having better control over my emotions . . . . my feelings . . . . and my mood."

Self-confidence

"As each day is passing, I am becoming more and more dependent upon my own ideas . . . . my own judgments . . . . and my own efforts. I am aware of my limitations and weaknesses also. I do take advise and guidance from elders . . . . my teachers and seniors, as and when required. At the same time, I am aware of my own potentials . . . . my own strengths. I am developing more and more confidence in my own abilities to think and give a mature response to the situation. I am becoming a self-confident individual."

Motivation for Study

"I have realized and I do understand the importance of studying sincerely the curriculum which I am undergoing now. The study is going to make my career. Better learning and clear understanding of the topics and subjects which I learn now, will make my performance in the professional work in the future more effective. This will, in turn, give me better opportunities to earn name, fame and wealth."

Interest in Study

"My interest and liking for studies are increasing day by day. I am developing liking for all the subjects which I am studying now. I am developing ability to work . . . . read and study for longer and longer period of time with a feeling of freshness and alertness in my body. While studying, I am having a sense of pleasure . . . . feeling of joy. Studying is becoming an enjoyable event for me. This improves the speed of my reading and also understanding of the subject. So, day by day, my reading is improving in quantity as well as in quality."

Concentration

"As each day is passing, my concentration in the study is increasing. I am paying maximum . . . . my total . . . . undivided attention to the study, wherever I am studying; i.e., while attending lectures in the classroom, while reading in the library or while preparing my subjects at home. I am studying each topic with deep concentration . . . . while studying I am getting completely absorbed . . . . thoroughly engrossed in the topic."

Understanding

"My interest and concentration in the study lead to better understanding of the topics . . . . quick grasping of the subject. Day by day, I understand clearly whatever I study."

Registration and Retention of Memory

"My mind is registering clearly and perfectly whatever I study. My eagerness to learn and understand new things; and my feelings of pleasure and satisfaction of gaining knowledge are increasing as each day is passing. The memories associated with such positive feelings are registered deeply in my mind and are retained for a very long period of time . . . . as long as I need to remember the same."

Recall of Memory

"The recall of the memories stored in my mind is becoming much easier for me now. I am able to recall and reproduce the right matter at the appropriate time, precisely whenever it is required. During recall of memory, there is a very smooth . . . . coordinated . . . . and integrated chain of thoughts developing in my mind. Uninterrupted flow of thoughts is running through my mind while reproducing the topics learnt."

Converting Threat into Challenge

"While preparing for my exams, I am using adequate time to ensure success . . . . and also I am taking sufficient rest pauses to rejuvenate my energy. I am remaining very alert and efficient throughout the working hours of my day. While appearing for the exam, my mind is learning to remain more relaxed . . . . calm . . . . and composed. The examination is a situation of challenge for me (and not of a threat) generating a feeling of self-confidence in me. Day by day, I am developing confidence in my preparations and my ability to perform 'at my level best' in the exam. Facing any examination, theory, practical or oral, objective or descriptive, is becoming much easier for me now."

Summary of All Suggestions

"I am having thorough understanding and knowledge of the subjects which I am learning with interest and concentration. The knowledge is registered clearly and retained in my mind as long as it is required. As and when required, I am able to recall and represent my knowledge easily and instantaneously. I am, rather, enjoying the easy recall and systematic reproduction of memories stored in my mind . . . . precisely at the right moment. Thus, with each passing day, I am becoming better and better in my studies."

2. Mini Nap

This is a technique for giving good rest to the body and mind in a brief period of time which Dr. Palan, one of the authors, learnt from Beata Jenks and suitably adopted for school children. It is a very useful technique when one is tired and feeling sleepy but one does not want to sleep or one cannot afford to sleep due to any reason.

Steps of the Technique

1. Put aside your work and sit comfortably on a chair. Close your eyes.
2. Attend to the process of your breathing. Continue sensing the process of your normal, natural breathing for about a minute.
3. Then start associating thoughts, as indicated below, with every breath which you are letting out :
   - First breath out .... "One minute is passing and I am sleeping."
   - Second breath out .... "I am sleeping for the last two minutes."
   - Third breath out .... "Four minutes have passed; I am sleeping for the last four minutes."
   - Fourth breath out .... "I am enjoying good sleep for the last eight minutes."
   - Fifth breath out .... "Quarter of an hour has passed; I am enjoying deep sleep."
   - Sixth breath out .... "I am sleeping for the last half an hour. It is beautiful sound sleep."
   - Seventh breath out .... "I am enjoying very deep and sound health sleep for the last one hour."
   - Eighth breath out .... **"I enjoyed a very refreshing and wonderful sleep for two hours. Now I am feeling fresh and fine in my body and mind. I am sensing the waves of alertness and energy throughout my body. I am feeling like waking-up now."**

4. Then slowly open your eyes. Take a couple of deep

refreshing breaths. Stretch your body and be absolutely wide awake to start your work.

Further Hints on Mini Nap

1. Some people may like to prolong the rest for some more time by doubling the time mentally, at every second or third breath instead of every breath.
2. If your mind gets diverted to some other thoughts while doing mini nap, consider your diversion to be a dream.
3. One cannot replace the natural sleep altogether by repeatedly doing mini nap. But one can reduce the requirement of sleep to a significant extent.
4. Mini nap is an useful technique for avoiding 'jet-lag' while travelling long distance by air. One may practice mini nap, during the journey, at the interval of every one and a half to two hours.

3. Sensory Imagery Conditioning

This is one of the most powerful behaviour modification techniques used for working with situation based problems. When one wants to make desirable changes in one's usual set pattern of thinking, feeling and behaviour, one can use this technique. Conditioning means habit formation. Here, one is going to form a new, desirable habit of thinking, feeling and behaviour through creating specific, sensation-rich images.

Steps of the Technique

Following are the three steps of this technique. Learn them and then, while using the technique, you may use your own creativity to produce relevant images. Feel free to be flexible.

Step 1

Under the self-hypnotic state, imagine yourself in your Inner Mental Tranquillity room, sitting comfortably on a sofa. Watch a movie on the T.V. screen. It is the recording on you while you were undergoing your problem situation. See, in this movie, that you are undergoing your usual, stereotyped negative experience. Watch yourself behaving in an inappropriate way. Beware of the unhealthy feeling expressed on the face of that person and also (if possible) the undesirable thoughts passing through the mind of that person. But then find the movie gradually fading away . . . . becoming black and white . . . . small and far off. The sound track is also not clear. Continue this for a minute or so only.

(Use this step only once when you are working on a problematic situation for the first time. Then in later sessions do only steps 2 and 3)

Step 2

Now switch off the T.V. Go near the CD player and take off the CD which is an older recording. You never want to see this again, so destroy that CD and throw it away. Put a newly recorded CD in its place. Come back and sit comfortably on the sofa. Put on the new movie. See yourself undergoing the same experience once again, but now your behaviour has become appropriate (exactly as you wished). Sense the healthy feelings and positive, desirable thoughts generated in your mind on the screen. Let there be some close-ups. Make the picture bright and colourful with a very clear sound track. Continue watching this movie for about 3 to 5 minutes.

Step 3

While step 2 is in progress, remember in your mind the following two post-hypnotic suggestions :

(a) "Day by day I am going to see this healthy image of myself more and more clearly . . . . vividly . . . . during my self-hypnosis sessions."

(b) "Here I am creating the internal reality which is becoming an external reality for me, gradually and naturally. So, in my normal waking state of consciousness, day by day, I am becoming this new person. I am getting positive and desirable thoughts and healthy feelings under such circumstances. My behaviour and actions are becoming more and more appropriate as each day is passing."

4. Dynamic Image of Arrow and a Bow

This technique is very useful for improving concentration and also for bringing consistency in our efforts.

Imagine that you have a bow and an arrow in your hands. Feel your feet and legs solidly in contact with the earth. Hold the bow with one hand and the notched arrow along with the string of the bow with another hand. Stretch the string and experience the muscles of your arms contracting as the bow is bending. Now, see the target clearly in front of you and adjust the tip of the arrow pointing exactly to the centre of the target.

The bow is bent to its limit; the arrow is precisely aimed at the target. Sense, how much energy is stored in this static position. All you need to do is release the string for that energy to carry the arrow to your target.

Imagine yourself being that arrow, mounted on the bow . . . . ready to go. Now the arrow is released. See it in its flight, see yourself in your flight . . . . and feel its extraordinary one pointedness. Nothing exists for the arrow except the target—no doubts . . . . no distractions . . . . no deviation. Flying perfectly straight, the arrow hits the centre of the target and stops there . . . . quivering in its tail. Experience in yourself the *unwavering, one-pointed and concentrated power.*

Testing Tools

P.G.I. Memory Scale (Prasad and Wig, 1988): The test measures different aspects of memory, viz., remote memory, recent memory, mental balance, attention concentration, delayed recall, immediate recall, retention for similar pairs, retention for dissimilar pairs, visual retention and recognition. The scale consists of both performance tests and verbal measures.

Digit Symbol Substitution Test: It is a part of Weschler's Intelligence test (1981) to test the concentration.

Self Confidence Inventory (Basavanna, 1975): A 100 items inventory used for measuring the confidence in adolescents.

State-Trait Anxiety Inventory (Spielberger, Gorusch and Lushene, 1976): It is a self-report assessment device which includes separate measures of state and trait anxiety. According to the authors, state anxiety reflects a "transitory emotional state or condition of the human organism that is characterized by subjective, consciously perceived feelings of tension may fluctuate over time and can vary in intensity." In contrast, trait anxiety denotes "relatively stable individual differences in anxiety proneness . . . . " and refers to a general tendency to respond with anxiety to perceived threats in the environment.

Results and Discussion

The common problems indicated by both the groups were lack of concentration, lack of self-confidence, poor memory and anxiety.

Comparison of pre- and post-test scores on the variables under study in the Group 1 showed that short term intervention through mind-programming and hypnotherapy significantly improved immediate recall and reduced state and trait anxiety in the students. There was no significant difference between the pre- and post-test scores on other memory tasks, i.e. delayed recall recognition of similar and dissimilar word pairs, on attention and concentration or on self-confidence etc.

Table 14.1: Paired Sample 'T' tests for both Long-term and Short-term Intervention

Variable		*Long term intervention*			*Short term intervention*		
		Mean	*SD*	*t*	*Mean*	*SD*	*t*
Self-confidence	Pre	54.35	20.87		50.34	21.31	
	Post	77.71	22.04	–5.91**	5.2	39.91	0.02
Concentration	Pre	561.44	172.98		557.87	161.96	
	Post	838.03	178.99	–4.48**	578.67	449.82	–0.26
Concentration error	Pre	3.74	3.39		3.74	3.33	
	Post	5.15	4.22	–1.29	3.07	4.07	0.89
Remote memory	Pre	3.53	2.12		2.26	2.41	
	Post	3.82	2.19	–1.77	2	2.49	1.04
Recent Memory	Pre	3.71	2.14		2.31	2.43	
	Post	3.76	2.17	–0.57	1.97	2.46	1.58
Mental balance	Pre	6.24	3.85		3.97	4.29	
	Post	6.35	3.81	–0.31	3.34	4.23	1.45
Attention concentration	Pre	7.24	5.04		4.6	5.34	
	Post	9.53	5.66	–2.55**	5	6.3	–0.6
Delayed recall	Pre	4.59	2.83		2.86	3.13	
	Post	6.41	3.81	–5.45**	3.34	4.21	–1.38
Immediate recall	Pre	4	3.24		2.31	3.1	
	Post	6.53	3.81	–4.13**	3.43	4.29	–2.87**
Retention similar pairs	Pre	3.65	2.15		2.34	2.47	
	Post	3.82	2.19	–1.38	2	2.49	1.36
Retention dissimilar pairs	Pre	8.47	5.36		4.91	5.73	
	Post	10.94	6.45	–3.75**	5.74	7.22	–1.54
Visual retention	Pre	9.82	5.64		6.26	6.54	
	Post	9.94	5.68	–1	5.2	6.46	1.68
Recognition	Pre	5.59	3.39		3.54	3.83	
	Post	6.71	3.89	–3.27**	3.54	4.43	0
State anxiety	Pre	31.24	18.71		20.17	21.51	
	Post	19.71	11.71	5.61**	10.66	13.58	4.2**
Trait anxiety	Pre	31.71	19.44		20.49	22.02	
	Post	21.18	12.53	4.42**	11.4	14.46	3.93**

Note: * $p < 0.05$, ** $p < 0.01$

As the students were appearing for their board examination, most of them had reported high anxiety as a reason for registering for the five days workshop. Thus, the examination anxiety which must have reflected through the state anxiety was found to be effectively reduced through this programme. Similar findings have been reported in an experimental study reported by Charlesworth, Murphy, Beutler (1981). A pre-post comparison of state and trait anxiety measures revealed that the stress management group effectively reduced trait anxiety, while the control group's trait anxiety levels remained relatively unchanged. The experimental group showed a reduction in state (test-taking) anxiety from mid-semester to final examinations, while the control groups showed a slight increase from mid semester to final examination.

Long term intervention for mind programming was found to be effective in enhancing most of the socio-cognitive skills. The performance scores on digit-symbol substitution, and letter cancellation test reveals that, hypnotherapeutic techniques were effective in enhancing the attention and concentration of the students. Both immediate and delayed recall improved significantly in this group. Earlier research conducted to study hypermnesic property of hypnotherapy reports contradictory findings. Two experiments by Dinges *et al.* (1992) investigated whether hypnosis enhances memory retrieval *per se* or merely increases a person's willingness to report recollections. Both experiments assessed immediate and delayed (i.e., 1 week) recall for pictorial stimuli. The findings provide no evidence for alleged hypermnesic properties of hypnosis. Flingstein, Barabasz, Barabasz, Trevisan, & Warner (1998) in a study to understand how hypnosis enhances recall memory under forced and non-forced conditions, reported that those exposed to hypnosis and to a forced recall procedure were significantly more confident of their responses to correct items than those exposed to a non-forced recall procedure or a waking condition. Participants exposed to hypnosis and forced recall procedures recalled more correct items than those exposed to a waking condition. The findings support the hypermnesic effects of hypnosis when participants are required to provide a fixed number of responses. In the present study also, the respondents were supposed to recall a given number of stimuli provided.

Retention of dissimilar pair of words also improved in this group. Post-test scores on recognition test differed significantly from the pre-test scores which means mind-programming through hypnotherapy also improved skills for recognition. On the whole, long term hypnotherapeutic intervention improved skills for most of the memory tasks like recall, recognition and retention. Visual retention and retention of similar pair of words were not improved in post-test scores.

Self-esteem and self-efficacy have been found to have significant effect on academic performance and career efficacy (Bandura *et al.,* 2001). Wachelka, and Katz (1999) reported results of their study which extends the generality of similar studies on reducing test anxiety and improving academic self-esteem in younger students. The findings of the present research also reports that, 30 weeks intervention of hypnotherapy resulted in significant increase in the self-confidence of the students.

The pre- and post-test scores on state and trait anxiety differed significantly in long-term intervention group. Earlier studies with hypnotherapeutic intervention of 5 and more weeks duration have reported similar results (Charlesworth, Murphy and Beutler, 1981; Kanji, White, and Ernst, 2006).

The comparative presentation of the results of short and long term hypnotherapeutic intervention for mind-programming and its effect on the socio-cognitive skills have been presented through bar-graphs in Figs. 14.1 to 14.9.

Conclusion

The findings as a whole suggest that, long term intervention for mind-programming using hypnotherapeutic techniques can be adopted as an effective therapy to enhance the socio-cognitive skills and to reduce the trait and state anxiety in

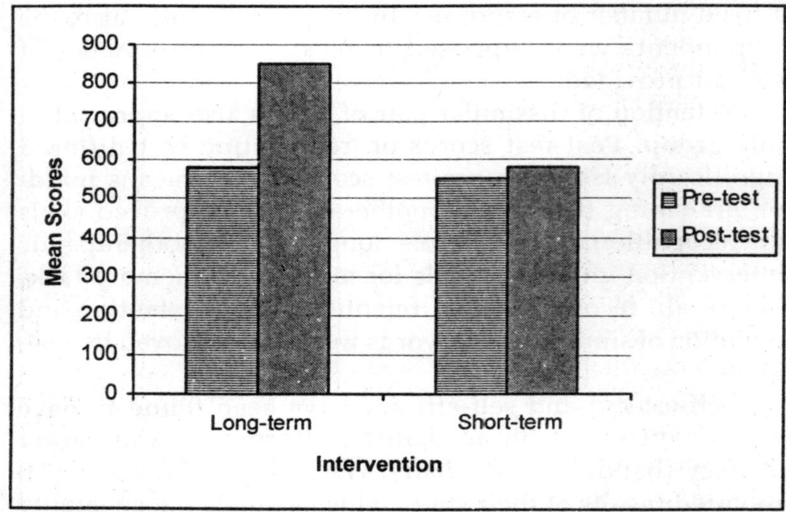

Fig. 14.1 : Pre- and Post-test Mean Scores for Concentration (Letters) for Long-term and Short-term Intervention.

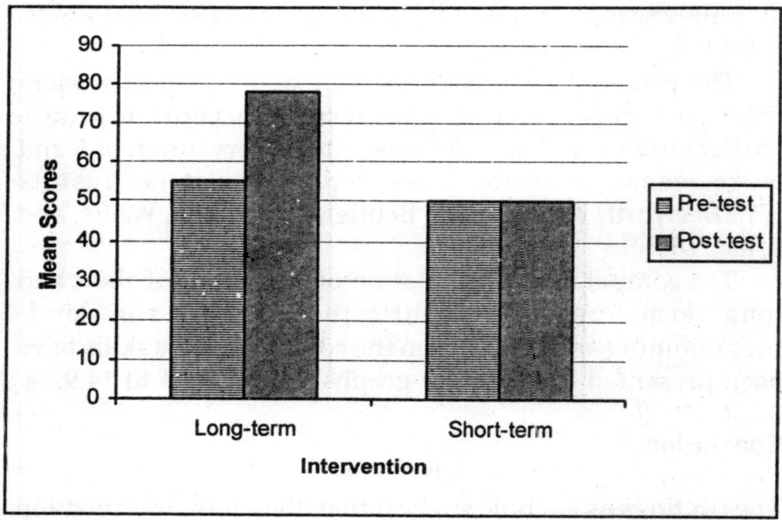

Fig. 14.2 : Pre- and Post-test Mean Scores for SCI for Long-term and Short-term Intervention

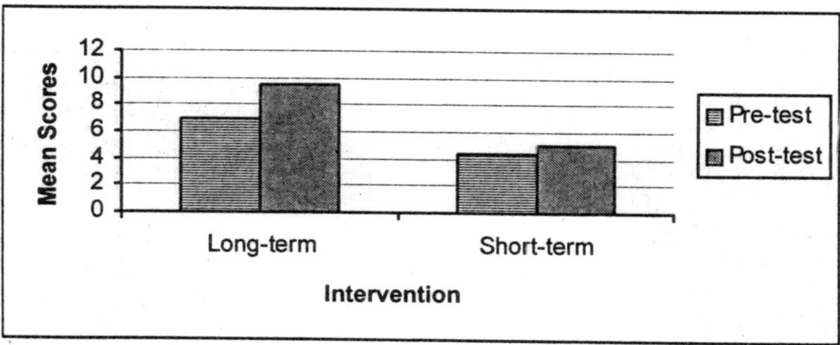

Fig. 14.3 : Pre- and Post-test Mean Scores of Concentration Attention for Long-term and Short-term Intervention

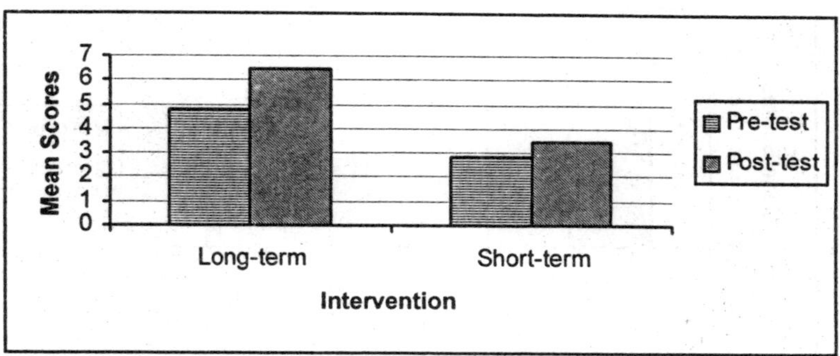

Fig. 14.4 : Pre- and Post-test Mean Scores of Delayed Recall for Long-term and Short-term Intervention

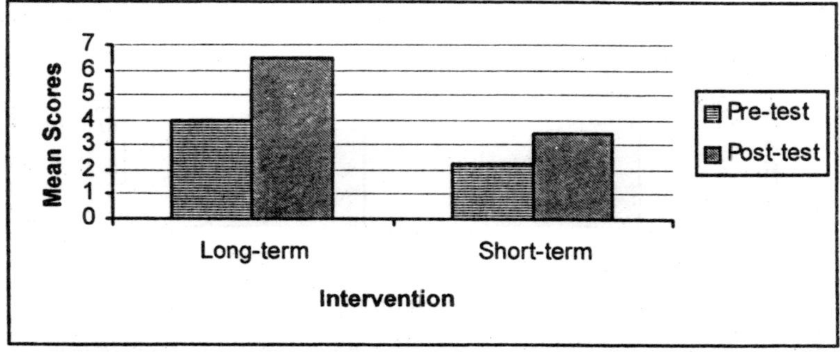

Fig. 14.5 : Pre- and Post-test Mean Scores of Immediate Recall for Long-term and Short-term Intervention

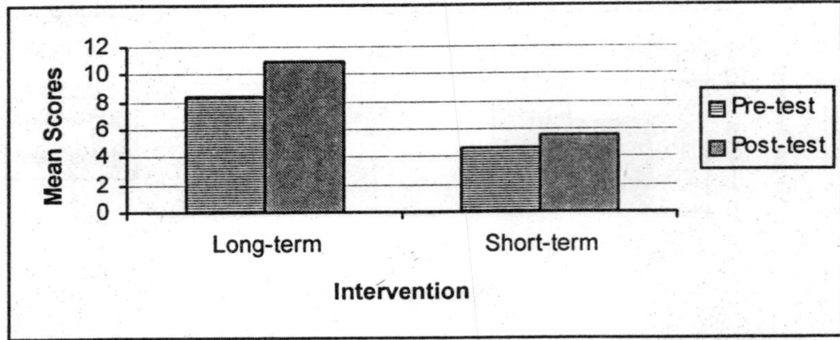

Fig. 14.6 : Pre- and Post-test Mean Scores of Visual Retention D for Long-term and Short-term Intervention

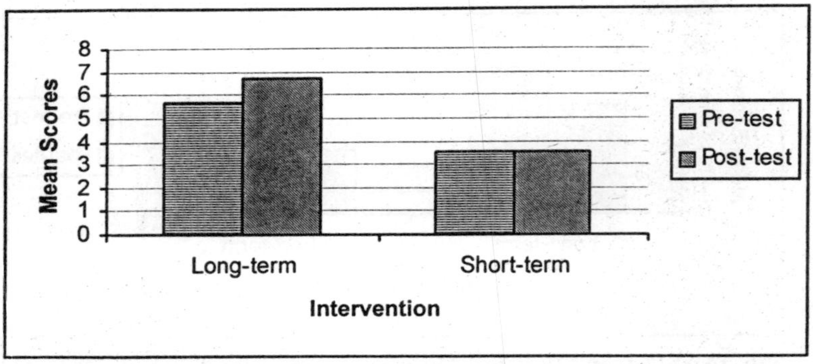

Fig. 14.7 : Pre- and Post-test Mean Scores of Recognition for Long-term and Short-term Intervention

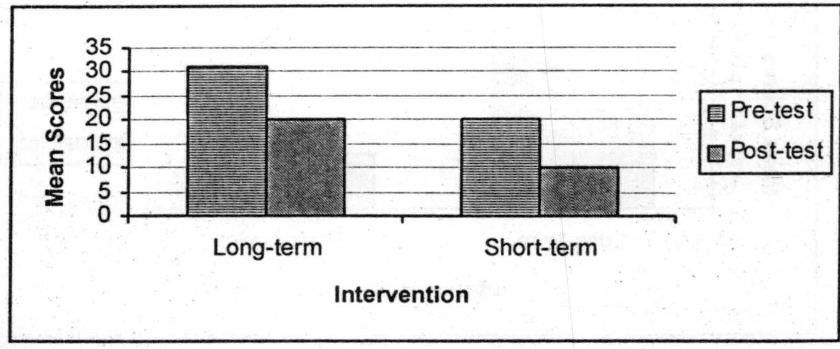

Fig. 14.8 : Pre- and Post- test Mean Scores of State Anxiety for Long-term and Short-term Intervention

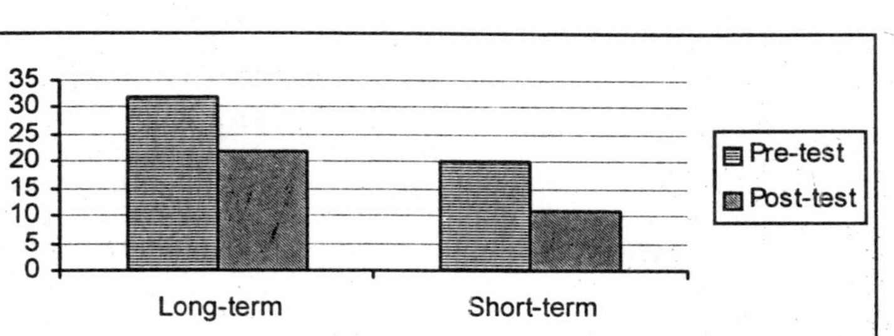

Fig. 14.9 : Pre- and Post-test Mean Scores of Trait Anxiety for Long-term and Short-term Intervention

adolescents. Moreover, it implies that by improving cognitive skills and parameters like recall, retention, recognition, attention, concentration, and self-confidence, the academic performance of the students can be enhanced. Irrespective of the duration of intervention, hypnotherapy has been effective in reducing both state and trait anxiety.

REFERENCES

Anbar, R.D., & Slothower, M.P. (2006). Hypnosis for treatment of insomnia in school-age children: A retrospective chart review. *BMC Pediatric*: 16, 6-23.

Aviv, A. (2006). Tele-hypnosis in the treatment of adolescent school refusal. *American Journal of Clinical Hypnosis*, 49, 1, 31-40.

Bandura, A., Barbaranelli, C., Capara, G., & Pastorelli, C. (2001). Self-efficacy beliefs as shapers of children's aspirations and career trajectories. *Child Development*, 72(1), 186-206.

Basavanna, M. (1975). *Self-confidence Inventory*. Varanasi; Rupa Psychological Centre.

Charlesworth, E.A., Murphy, S., & Beutler, L.E. (1981). Stress management skill for nursing students. *Journal of Clinical Psychology*, 37, 2, 284-290.

Crawford, H.J., & Allen, S.N. (1983). Enhanced visual memory during hypnosis as mediated by hypnotic responsiveness and cognitive strategies. *Journal of Experimental Psychology Gen*, 112, 4, 662-685.

Crawford, H.J., & Allen, S.N. (1996). Paired-associate learning and recall of high and low imagery words: Moderating effects of hypnosis, hypnotic susceptibility level, and visualization abilities. *American Journal of Psychology*, 109, 3, 353-372.

De Vos, H.M. & Louw, D.A. (2006). The effect of hypnotic training programmes on the academic performance of students. *American Journal of Clinical Hypnosis:* 49(2), 101-112.

Densky, A.B. (2008). Clinical Hypnosis. http://www.buzzle.com/articles/improve-your-mental-recall-with-self-hypnosis. Retrieved on 2/21/2008.

Dinges, D.F., Whitehouse, W.G., Orne, E.C., Powell, J.W., Orne, M.T., & Erdelyi, M.H. (1992). Evaluating hypnotic memory enhancement (hypermnesia and reminiscence) using multitrial forced recall. *Journal of Experimental Psychology, Learning, Memory, and Cognition,* 18, 5, 1139-1147.

Fligstein, D., Barabasz, A., Barabasz, M., Trevisan, M.S., & Warner, D. (1998). Hypnosis enhances recall memory: A test of forced and non-forced conditions. *American Journal of Clinical Hypnosis,* 40, 4, 297-305.

Gruzelier, J., Smith, F., Nagy, A., & Henderson, D. (2001). Cellular and humoral immunity, mood and exam stress: The influences of self-hypnosis and personality predictors. *International Journal of Psychophysiology,* 42, 1, 55-71.

Kanji, N., White, A., & Ernst, E. (2006). Autogenic training to reduce anxiety in nursing students: Randomized controlled trial. *Journal of Advance Nursing,* 53, 6, 729-735.

Palan, B.M., & Chandwani, S. (1989). Coping with examination stress through hypnosis: An experimental study. *American Journal of Clinical Hypnosis,* 31, 3, 173-180.

Prasad, D., & Wig, N.N. (1988). *P.G.I. Memory Scale.* Agra: National Psychological Corporation.

Schreiber, E.H., & Schreiber, K.N. (1998). Use of hypnosis and Jacobson's relaxation techniques for improving academic achievement of college students. *Perceptual and Motor Skills,* 86, 1, 85-86.

Spielberger, C.D., Gorusch, R.L., & Lushene, R.E. (1976). *State, Trait Anxiety Inventory.* New York: Consulting Psychologists Press.

Valente, S.M. (1990). Clinical hypnosis with school-age children. *Archive of Psychiatric Nursing,* 4, 2, 131-136.

Wachelka, D., & Katz, R.C. (1999). Reducing test anxiety and improving academic self-esteem in high school and college students with learning disabilities. *Journal of Behaviour Therapy and Experimental Psychiatry,* 30(3), 191-198.

Wark, D.M. (1996). Teaching college students better learning skills using self-hypnosis. *American Journal of Clinical Hypnosis.* 38, 4, 277-287.

15

Role of Hypnotherapy in Management of Generalized Anxiety Disorder

RITU NANDA AND BHUPINDER SINGH

Introduction

Hypnosis has a long history dating most knowingly back to the 1700s. The first recognizable practitioner of hypnosis was Franz Anton Mesmer, an Austrian physician of the eighteenth century who used the power of suggestions to cure illnesses. His technique was called 'mesmerism.' The term "Hypnosis" came from a Scottish physician James Braid (1840) who used the Greek word for sleep to create the term ('Hypnos' means 'sleep' in Greek). It soon came to replace the word 'mesmerism.'

Hypnosis is a complex mental phenomenon involving a state of heightened focal concentration and receptivity to the suggestions of another person. It is also called an altered state of consciousness (Tart, 1975). It is a dissociated state and an induced state of relaxation in which the person is open to suggestions. It can be understood as attentive, receptive focal concentration with diminished peripheral awareness. This intense concentration can be actively initiated and structured to achieve agreed upon goals.

Purpose of the Research

Hypnotherapy has cured or alleviated an enormous range of illnesses and ailments. Research proves hypnosis and auto suggestions can have organic, physiological effects. Hypnosis works on the body via the mind (Waterfield, 2002). With appropriate therapeutic design, this variant of imagination can be activated, identified, measured, controlled and used for specific therapeutic purposes.

The present era is an age of anxiety. Anxiety disorders affect approximately 15 per cent of the population. Anxiety is a state of hyper arousal experienced as both emotional and psychosomatic discomfort. Generalized Anxiety Disorder (GAD) is an excessive and pervasive worry accompanied by a variety of somatic symptoms like muscle tension, irritability, insomnia, restlessness and marked distress in the patient (DSM-IV).

Hypnosis can be a helpful adjunctive tool for treating anxiety disorders. It helps patients control their physical reactions to anxiety provoking stimuli, thus dissociating somatic response from psychological distress. This enables them to restructure their point of view and achieve a sense of mastery. Relaxation can be achieved easily with hypnosis, helping patients control their anxiety.

Objectives

The present study proposed to investigate the role of hypnotherapy in the management of female patients diagnosed with Generalized Anxiety Disorder (GAD).

Methodology

The sample consisted of 40 female patients diagnosed as suffering from Generalized Anxiety Disorder (GAD), on the basis of DSM-IV criteria. They were selected from various hospitals in Bhopal. All subjects were in the age group of 25-45 years, and belonged to broadly similar socio-economic and cultural backgrounds and educational levels. They were educated up to or above graduate level. Patients showing moderate or high hypnotic susceptibility and willing to undergo treatment using hypnotherapy were included in the study.

Tools

Hamilton Rating Scale for Anxiety was used as a tool to ascertain the physical and psychological status of the patient. The *HAM-A* was developed in the late 1950s to assess anxiety symptoms, both somatic and cognitive. There are 14 items each of which is rated 0 to 4 on an unanchored severity scale, with the total score ranging from 0 to 56. The HAM-A has been used extensively to monitor treatment response in studies of Generalized Anxiety Disorder.

The Cornell Medical Index known as *C.M.I. Health Questionnaire,* is translated by N. N. Wig, Professor of Psychiatry, All India Institute of Medical Sciences, New Delhi; Dwarka Pershad, Lecturer in Clinical Psychology; and S.K. Verma, Assistant Professor in Clinical Psychology, Post Graduate Institute of Medical Education and Research, Chandigarh.

The C.M.I. is a four-page sheet. The term 'Health Questionnaire' explains the nature and purpose of the form to the patient. It contains 195 questions in informal language, so worded as to be understood by persons with a reading knowledge. Technical terms are avoided. After each question a 'Yes' and a 'No' appears; the patient answers the questions by circling one. In every instance, a 'Yes' answer indicates that the patient claims to have the symptom. Each 'Yes' answered item is counted and considered as score.

Questions are grouped in sections. A to L section is called physical distress section (pages 1 to 3 of the test). And M to R section is called emotional or psychological distress section (page 4 of the test). All the sections from A to R are considered as total distress.

The translated version was correlated against original English form. Correlations between the scores on English and Hindi ranged between 0.77 and 0.87.

The Hypnotic Induction Profile (Spiegel & Spiegel, 1970): The Hypnotic Induction Profile is a clinical scale to measure hypnotizability. It is brief and aesthetically acceptable in the clinical setting. It has a moderate positive co-relation with the longer laboratory based Stanford Hypnotic Susceptibility Scale.

The Hypnotic Induction Profile (HIP) was developed by Herbert Spiegel for clinical use. Like any clinical instrument, it is designed to be individually administered. The main advantage claimed for it is its speed of administration. It expresses Hypnotic susceptibility on a 5-point scale and requires only about 5 minutes to administer. Like all of the foregoing instruments, this one is based on the induction of a hypnotic state, but the induction procedure never uses the word hypnosis, trance or sleep, and in this sense it is an indirect procedure that might be useful with a patient fearful of being hypnotized.

A person is asked to roll his or her eyes upward. The degree to which the iris and cornea are seen is measured. The less of this part of the eye observed, the more hypnotically susceptible a person is. Scoring criteria are based on the amount of roll produced in a subject requested to roll his eyes upward and then slowly close his lids, arm levitation, posthypnotic response, amnesia, and subjective reports.

Procedure and Research Design

Baseline data of sample was obtained with the help of tools before hypnotic intervention (Pre-therapy Assessment). Mid-therapy assessments were conducted after one month of hypnotherapeutic intervention. Post-therapy assessments were conducted after the completion of hypnotherapy. Data were analyzed using t-test.

Components of the Therapeutic Programme

Pre-Hypnotic Stage*—This included a detailed interview with the participants.*

Hypnotic Intervention*—This included five phases :*

1. *Preparation* which involved having the patients sit or lie down and get comfortable.
2. *Induction* guided the patients from normal awareness to a state of enhanced relaxation. It involved breath watching and progressive muscular relaxation.

3. The *Deepening* phase guided the patients from a very relaxed state into the fully "hypnotized" state, where conscious thinking was minimized. This state was achieved by suggesting to the patients that they were climbing down a beautiful staircase which had 10 steps. At every step, they felt more and more relaxed and they were entering into a deeper and deeper state of relaxation.

4. *Suggestions*—In the hypnotic state the patients were given suggestions like "You are relaxed and at ease. You are at peace with yourself, the world and everyone. You peacefully accept things you cannot change and change the things you want to and can change. You experience life peacefully and tranquilly. You are physically relaxed and emotionally at peace and feel in balance and in harmony. You are self-confident, self-reliant, filled with independence and determination. You have great inner courage. Your positive thinking creates a positive life for you. You can do whatever you set your mind to. You let go of the past and you free yourself. You are optimistic and enthusiastic. You look forward to challenges and know you are a winner."

5. *Awakening*—In this phase the patients were guided out of the hypnotic state and brought back to a state of awareness with the conscious mind fully re-engaged. This was achieved by counting upwards from 1-5 with awakening suggestions.

Post-Hypnotic Stage*—This included post-hypnotic counselling and review to plan future sessions.*

Plan of Interventional Programme—

Duration	: 2 months
Total Number of sessions	: 24 (3 per week)
Duration of each session	: 45 minutes to 1 hour

Results

Pre-therapy, Mid-therapy and Post-therapy scores on HAM-A and C.M.I. were compared for significant difference between means using t-test.

Results revealed significant decrease in anxiety symptoms after the mid-therapy and post-therapy period of hypnotic interventions. Results on Cornell Medical Index also revealed significant decrease in total distress, physical distress and emotional distress after the mid-therapy and post-therapy period of hypnotic interventions.

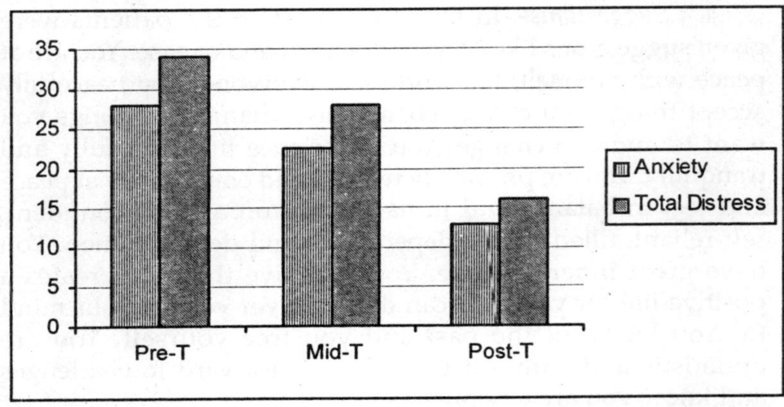

Fig. 15.1 : Pattern of Anxiety and Total Distress during Various Stages of Therapy

Conclusion

The present study examined role of hypnotherapy in the management of female patients diagnosed with GAD. A significant decrease in anxiety, physical distress and emotional distress was observed while comparing the pre-, mid- and post-therapy responses of the sample. Hypnotic interventions as an adjunct to pharmacotherapy were significantly effective in the management of GAD.

The effect of hypnotherapy, however, remains to be seen in the absence of pharmacotherapy as the participants of the study were not asked to discard the use of drugs which they were using. A comparative study of males and females may also be conducted to ascertain sex differences. Follow up research needs to be carried out to see the long term effects of hypnotherapy.

REFERENCES

American Psychiatric Association. (1994). *Diagnostic and Statistical Manual. IV,* Washington DC: Author.

Spiegel, H., & Spiegel, D. (1978). *Manual for Hypnotic Induction Profile.* New York: Basic Books.

Tart, C. (1975). *States of Consciousness.* New York: E.P. Dutton.

Waterfield, R. (2002). *Hidden Depths—The Story of Hypnosis.* pp. 36-37. Basingstoke: Macmillan.

Weitzenhoffer, A.M., & Hilgard, E.R. (1967). *Revised Stanford Profile Scales of Hypnotic Susceptibility Scale: Forms I and II.* California: Consulting Psychologists Press.

16

Hypnotherapy for Hypertension in Retired Life

A Case Study

BHAVANA JADAV

Introduction

Retirement is the "transition phase" which brings so many changes in one's life. Physical changes are due to ageing related effects. Psychological effects are result of sudden change from active life to the passive one. There is change in social and professional status as the power of the employment and status are no more with an individual. Most important effect is on financial status of an individual due to stoppage of regular salary which leads to compulsive change in life style. All these factors play a cumulative role and make an individual more prone to life style diseases, some of which may be psychosomatic in nature. Hypertension is one of such diseases that is most common among this prone group of retired individuals.

It is in bio-psychosocial concept of psychosomatic illness that hypnosis finds its niche. To the extent that it can influence the mind-body interaction, hypnosis can be utilized for the purpose of teaching the patient general relaxation, somatic and visceral, for working out conflicts and for modifying certain personality dynamics which may have aggravating influences on psychosomatic illness. The success of hypnotherapy has less to do with the type of psychosomatic illness present than it does with the particular patient involved.

Case History

The client (59 years, male) is a retired government engineer having pension as the only source of income. In the last year of his job he was transferred out of station and had to commute daily. In the same duration he was preparing for his elder son's study abroad and was stressed for managing finance for it. Ultimately, he took education loan and sent his son for study. But with this continued stress and hectic schedule of job, he developed sustained rise of BP for which he consulted physician and was put on anti-hypertensive medicine. It was always stressful for him to manage to pay instalment of loan in time. His BP started fluctuating more and he developed a complaint of on and off chest pain for which he was also admitted to the emergency cardiac unit. His sleep and appetite were normal.

The patient was prescribed Tablet Aten (50) 1 OD and Tablet Sorbitrate (5) SL SOS.

The patient did not have any addiction and was getting a good social support from his caring wife and two children as well as a good friend circle.

Hypnotherapy

Goals

(i) Reduce anxiety and tension related to the financial crisis,
(ii) Strengthen ego of client,
(iii) Solve problem of BP fluctuation and chest pain,
(iv) Train client for self-hypnosis,
(v) Explain client the physiological mechanism of development, of hypertension especially at this age, and
(vi) Modify life style of client.

Details of Hypnotherapy Sessions

During the first session, after taking the history, the client was prepared mentally for hypnotherapy and trance was induced by 'eye fixation and verbal suggestion' technique. The second session was devoted for reducing tension and anxiety through 'breath watching' coupled with positive suggestions. The next two sessions were utilized for ego strengthening and therapeutic work through visual imagery of clouds and rains with direct verbal suggestions for optimization of blood pressure. Self-hypnosis training was given during the fifth session. During the sixth session the client was given explanation about psycho-physiology of development of blood pressure and he was advised about life style modification including proper food, sleep, regularity in taking medicine and practicing relaxation techniques. During the last two sessions ego strengthening and life style modification suggestions were reinforced under trance and the client was advised to practice self-hypnosis regularly.

Each session was of 60-90 minutes duration and the total eight therapy sessions were completed spread over three months.

Results and Discussion

The client had light to moderate level of trance in all the therapy sessions and ideomotor signal was positive whenever elicited.

The client was very cooperative and highly motivated to solve his problems. He was observed relaxed after breath watching with verbal suggestions and in next session after practicing the same exercise daily at home, he looked less anxious and more stable. After the ego strengthening suggestions, client was observed better in general. During the session of imagery, client looked highly relaxed when he visualized the raining of clouds of unwanted emotions.

A reduction of about 8 to 10 mm of Hg was measured in systolic BP after every therapy session. Regular BP measurement showed little fluctuations and more stability after the fourth and fifth therapeutic sessions. In follow-up session client reported having not a single episode of chest pain in last 15 days. In the last session, client reported that self-hypnosis helped him to solve his other minor problems also. He was taking medicine regularly and his anxiety had decreased remarkably.

Hypnotherapy could help clients with hypertension in retirement age as there are so many factors that make retired people prone to the disease in this phase of life. Psychological factors and stress induced BP rise and fluctuations can be managed well but other factors also affect the outcome of therapy e.g., personality of client, motivation level and faith in therapist, hypnotizability, support system and other associated medical and psychological conditions. The case report suggests prospective future of role of hypnotherapy in life style diseases in retirement life. This needs further trials with more number of clients and with variety of other diseases of same category.

REFERENCES

Crasilneck, H.B., & Hall, J.A. (1985). *Clinical Hypnosis: Principles and Applications.* New York: Grune & Stratton.

Kroger, W.S., & Fezler, W.D. (1976). *Hypnosis and Behaviour Modification: Imagery Conditioning.* Philadelphia: J.B. Lippincott.

Riaz, A. *Hypnotherapy for High Blood Pressure.* Retrieved on November 12, 2008 from http://www.highbloodpressuremed.com/hypnotherapy-for-high-blood-pressure.html.

Sunnen, G.V. (nd). Hypnosis in psychosomatic medicine. Retrieved on December 16, 2008 from http://www.triroc.com/sunnen/topics/psychosomatic.htm.

Waxman, D. (1989). *Hartland's Medical and Dental Hypnosis.* London: Bailliere Tindall.

Wester, W.C. (1987). *Clinical Hypnosis: A Case of Management Approach.* Ohio: Behavioural Science Centre.

17

Use of Hypnosis in Coping with Basic Needs of Terminally Ill Patients

SURESH L. SADHWANI AND RUTA VYAS

Introduction

Cancer is the second leading killer of man and a source of innumerable morbidities, both physical and mental. The relationship of cancer and stress has been known since the time of Galen in the second century, and the cancer patient is one who poses challenges that clearly cross the mind-body gap. The physical toll cancer takes on a patient is striking to anyone who has witnessed the emaciated state of an advanced cancer patient. But, patients themselves will often mention the emotional devastation of the illness as its worst symptom. Recent research in hypnosis has, however, given a hope as it offers avenues to deal with both sides of this horrible illness (Reeves *et al.*, 1983; Jacknow *et al.*, 1994; Feldman & Salzberg, 1990).

Hypnosis finds applications at several levels of cancer care. First, it is useful as a means of dealing with the symptoms of the disease itself, pain and symptoms referable to specific organ systems, and general symptoms, i.e., fatigue, malaise, irritability and insomnia. Another significant focus has been management of untoward side effects of chemotherapy and radiation: nausea and vomiting (Morrow *et al.*, 1998; Feldman & Salzberg, 1990). Second, use of hypnosis is for addressing distressing psychological features which are associated with cancer such as depression and anxiety (Kirsch, 1990). Thirdly, many cancer patients view their diagnosis as a death sentence and are forced to grapple with profound existential issues. Hypnosis has a place in helping with this difficult situation. Lastly, somewhat controversial, hypnosis has been aimed at modifying the course of the disease process itself (Decker *et al.*, 1992).

Pain is the most feared symptom of cancer. Through hypnosis, by utilizing various options, alone or in combination with lower doses of medication, allow the patient more comfort, and still remain in a functional state to attend to many things that a person on death's door would like to be able to reconcile. A 10-year follow up of 86 cancer patients covered by specific panel of National Institute of Health, USA, showed that those who received self-hypnosis training along with group therapy had 50 per cent less pain than those who only had routine medical care (Spiegel, 1983).

Other symptoms of cancer therapy like nausea and vomiting can be addressed by hypnosis. Prevalence data from variety of sources show that approximately 25 per cent of patients receiving chemotherapy develop anticipatory nausea and vomiting by the time of fourth treatment. Gary Morrow and Dobkin (1988) in their paper mentioned that progressive relaxation and systematic desensitization appears effective in controlling both anticipatory and post-treatment nausea and vomiting. Lynch (1999) found in his work that hypnosis was an invaluable tool in cancer treatment. His work confirms the earlier work of Dr. Spiegel (1983) who found that hypnotic techniques were able to nearly double the duration of survival in patients with metastatic breast cancer.

Existential psychological theory and existential psychotherapy have not been directly cited in literature of hypnosis with cancer patients, though several authors have reported efficacious results when the focus of hypnotherapy has centered on principles of existential psychological theory. Leviton (1977) developed a hypnotic procedure called hypnotic death rehearsal that was designed to address and resolve the sequel attributable to the existential principle of death anxiety.

Rosenberg (1983) employed revivification of post accomplishments in the lives of cancer patients as a vehicle with which to approach and resolve existential sense of meaningless.

There is, thus, enough research evidence to use hypnotherapy as a supplement intervention for cancer patients.

Method

Two middle aged patients of either sex constituted the study subjects. First patient was a female of 50 years of age. She was given hypnotherapy post operatively after diagnosis of cancer and subsequent to chemotherapy. Total 6 sessions were given during this period. The preoperative symptoms included pain, abdominal discomfort and fatigue. The other symptoms were of severe anxiety, helplessness, mild depression, body pain, anorexia, nausea, vomiting, skin exfoliation and hair loss.

First session consisted of simple breath-watching and PMR (Progressive Muscular Relaxation) in order to condition the mind and body for relaxation and to give her the experience of trance.

Second session consisted of breath-watching, PMR followed by some ego-strengthening suggestions and pleasant imagery to further condition the client.

Third session consisted of induction of trance by eye fixation and mind distraction method and followed by ego strengthening, direct suggestions for symptomatic improvement and post-hypnotic suggestions for prevention of further symptoms related to chemotherapy and radiotherapy.

Fourth session included induction by eye fixation and mind distraction method and suggestions allowing the client to address her own existential issues. Here, the client was given suggestions to imagine that: "She is invited to an art exhibition. As she goes there, she looks carefully at a painting that seems very attractive to her and draws her attention. She examines the painting carefully and notices after careful observation that some parts in the painting are missing or are incomplete. She takes the painting with her and completes it the way she would like to."

In the imagery she is filling up gaps and making it more meaningful for her own self (The client was fond of art pieces and, therefore, this imagery was used).

Fifth session included induction by recapitulation method (Ericksonian Approach)—you recapitulate earlier years of your school learning, where you were taught how to spell and write letter 'A', how difficult it was then and how easy it is now to speak—suggesting thereby through association that trance induction is a learning process and becomes easier as time goes by. After this, metaphors of ongoing war sequences (War sequence was described, suggesting that there was a war between the alien "cancer" cells and the immune system of the client, and cancer cells were dying from each and every part of the body, the immune system was winning and overcoming the cancer cells, lot of energy is generated and finally the patient is feeling calm, cool and comfortable having achieved success) were given to address the issue of stopping the process of cancer metastasis followed by post-hypnotic suggestions (having won the war, the subject was feeling comfortable, and this relaxation will remain with the subject, the immune system will continue to monitor the activity of aliens in the body) for symptomatic improvement.

In the sixth session, breath watching and recapitulation method were combined for trance induction. Deepening was done by staircase method (You are on a high rise building and are slowly getting down the stairs of each floor and as you get down, you are going deeper and further deeper, and as you touch the ground floor, you have still gone deeper). Then pleasant imagery utilizing archetypal symbol (subject was believing in Lord Ganesha, and had lot of pictures and idols in the house, so a religious ceremony was described as being organized in her house, and the subject was sitting in front of the idol of the God, where the white light was emerging from the God's right hand and it entered the subject through her third eye on the forehead. This light-force was healing and curing her body by killing the aliens in the body) was utilized to give therapeutic suggestions for the disease to slow down and symptom reduction. Post-hypnotic suggestions were given for better sleep, appetite, bowel control, and pain reduction.

Before start of all the six sessions adequate history and feedback was taken. In all the six sessions trance was terminated using permissive approach (as and when you feel comfortable, open your eyes and make yourself totally alert, and active, full of energy and vigour).

Second patient was a 45-year old male and was seen immediately after diagnosis of cancer and subsequently after surgery and then during chemotherapy. Symptoms included fatigue, weakness, hopelessness, helplessness, mood fluctuations, anxiety related to disease and familial matters.

In all, four sessions were given to this client. First session consisted of breath watching and PMR for relaxation and conditioning the mind and body for future sessions.

Second session included induction by breath watching and PMR. Ego strengthening was done and then pleasant imagery was utilized to give suggestions for preparing the patient for surgery and chemo/radio therapy (Imagery of a beach was described and was suggested to feel comfort, enjoyment, relaxation and serenity; these experiences would remain with him as and when he would undergo therapy for cancer, feeling relaxed, and comfortable). Post-hypnotic suggestions for anxiety reduction and self control were given (You will remain calm and always feel strong and under self control to overcome your problem, as and when they occur during and after therapy).

Third session was given immediately after surgery. Eye fixation and mind distraction was used for induction. After adequate deepening, ego strengthening was done and then therapeutic suggestions were given for symptomatic improvement to control side effects of surgery (Direct suggestions were given—you are becoming free from pain, discomfort; nausea and vomiting will not occur, your body will be able to overcome all the stresses caused by the therapy and will lead to healing and recovery). Post-hypnotic suggestions were given for reduction of anxiety and depressive symptoms.

Fourth session was given after two cycles of chemotherapy.

Ericksonian confusional approach was utilized for induction (conscious mind was depotentiated by verbally using jargon of words and sentences, partly relevant to the subject, and then suddenly telling the patient to go into trance, and the subject clearly understanding this suggestion, readily follows it, to facilitate induction). Metaphor of war sequence (as described in the earlier subject) was given, followed by suggestions for reduction of side effects related to chemotherapy. Post-hypnotic suggestions were given for continuation of chemotherapy and improvement of general wellbeing.

During all four sessions trance was terminated by permissive techniques.

Observations and Discussion

Sessions were planned according to the main symptoms of the patient. Simple breath watching and progressive muscular relaxation (PMR) was helpful in achieving relief from anxiety and mild depression, anorexia, weakness and mood elevation. Techniques like ego-strengthening, pleasant imagery and direct suggestions for symptomatic relief helped in achieving further reduction in symptoms like pain, nausea, vomiting, diarrhoea and also psychological symptoms like anxiety, mild depression and mood fluctuations. Deep trance states were achieved using Ericksonian techniques combined with ego-strengthening, metaphors and other hypnotic approaches. These states helped in overcoming 'denial', side effects due to chemotherapy/ radiotherapy and in directing suggestions to combat the pathophysiology of cancer.

Overall four sessions were given to help the patients in symptomatic relief, to overcome the side effects of therapies and to try to accept realistic outcome. Two more sessions were given addressing the existential issues and attempting to modify the course of illness.

Finally, one of the subjects has achieved remission and is in follow up stage while the other subject succumbed to illness.

Cancer is a multisystem illness involving all levels of the organism from the cellular to the psychological. The relationship of cancer and stress is becoming more relevant now than ever and in addition to the physical toll on the patient, the emotional devastation of illness is the worst symptom. Hypnosis offers avenues to deal with both sides of the illness.

In this study, classical and Ericksonian techniques (1967) were used for induction. Various hypnotic approaches like guided imagery, metaphors, sensory alteration and dissociation were utilized in mitigating symptoms of pain, psychological symptoms like anxiety, irritability, frustration and post chemotherapy and radiotherapy symptoms; mainly, nausea, diarrhoea and vomiting.

Death is inseparable part of disease such as cancer. The sudden shock of cancer has devastating psychological effects, leaving many things unsaid and undone. Hypnosis can help a person look more objectively at death, become more accepting and comfortable with it, and by lifting the veil of denial, that so often accompanies the topic in our culture, allow the patient to die with dignity in a way that he or she chooses. In present case, we noted that clients could accept the reality with less discomfort and were more objective after the hypnotherapy.

Present study also addressed existential issues like lack of meaning in life and loss of control over events happening in one's life. Suggestions facilitate a process wherein the client himself/herself searches for a meaning and attempts for regaining control over events that occur in life or is at least able to accept facts that otherwise seem unacceptable.

Conclusion

The present study showed that hypnosis can empower the individual with the energy and the concentration necessary to have better control of his life and to achieve a higher degree of satisfaction with whatever time he may have left in life. It also allows patient to control some of the pain associated with the disease and provides him to slow down or arrest the disease process and thereby provide him to live the remaining life with a higher degree of physical, emotional and spiritual abundance. The observations are in line with other researches on use of hypnosis for cancer patients (Cangello, 1962; Newton, 1982).

There are certain limitations of this study. The sample size was small and control samples were not taken for comparison. Larger samples are needed to confirm the findings. Issue of modification of disease process through hypnosis has been briefly mentioned here because of its current interest and for the fact that it raises interesting issues for research.

REFERENCES

Cangello, V.W. (1962). Hypnosis for the patient with cancer. *American Journal of Clinical Hypnosis, 4*, 215-226.

Decker, T. W., Cline-Elsen, J., & Gallagher, M. (1992). Relaxation therapy as an adjunct in radiation oncology. *J. Clin. Psychol.*, 48, 388-393.

Erickson, M.H. (1967). Hypnosis in painful terminal illness, in J. Haley (Ed), *Advanced Techniques of Hypnosis and Therapy: Selected Papers of Milton Erickson*. New York: Crune & Stratton.

Feldman, C.S., & Salzberg, H.C. (1990). The role of imagery in the hypnotic treatment of adverse reactions to cancer therapy. *J. S. C. Med. Assoc.*, 86, 303-306.

Jacknow, D.S., Tschann, J.M., Link, M.P., & Boyce, W.T. (1994). Hypnosis in the prevention of chemotherapy-related nausea and vomiting in children: A prospective study. *J. Dev. Behav. Pediatr.*, 15, 258-264.

Kirsch, I., Montgomery, G., & Sapirstein, G. (1995). Hypnosis as an adjunct to cognitive-behavioural psychotherapy: A meta-analysis. *J. Consult. Clin. Psychol.*, 63, 214-220.

Leviton, D. (1977). The scope of death education. *Death Education*, 1, 41-56.

Lynch, D.F. (1999). Empowering the patient: Hypnosis in the management of cancer, surgical disease and chronic pain. *American Journal of Clinical Hypnosis*, 42 (2): 122-130.

Morrow, G.R., Roscoe, J.A., Hynes, H.E., Flynn, P.J., Pierce, H.I., & Burish, T. (1998). Progress in reducing anticipatory nausea and vomiting: A study of community practice. *Support Care Cancer*, 6, 46-50.

Newton, B. (1982). The use of hypnosis in the treatment of cancer patients. *American Journal of Clinical Hypnosis*, 25, 92-104.

Reeves, J.L., Redd, W.H., Minagawa, R.Y., & Storm, C.K. (1983). Hypnosis in the control of pain during hyperthermia treatment of cancer. In J.J. Bonica, U. Lindbland, & A. Iggo. (Eds), *Advances in Pain Research* (pp. 857-861). New York: Raven Press.

Rosenberg, S.A. (1983). Adoptive immunotherapy of cancer: Accomplishments and prospects. *Cancer Treat Rep.* 68(1), 233-255.

Spiegel, D. (1983). The use of hypnosis in controlling cancer pain. *CA Cancer J. Clin*, 35(4), 221-231.

18

Use of Empty-Chair Technique with Hypnosis on Survivor of Child Molestation

A Case Study

AAROHI PARIMU KHAR

Introduction

The society is dealing with several burning issues, some of which are fast becoming areas of urgent concern. Child sexual abuse (CSA) is one such issue. WHO defines *CSA as the involvement of a child in the sexual activity that he/she does not fully comprehend, is unable to give informed consent to, or that violates the laws or social taboos of society. CSA is evidenced by the activity between a child and an adult or another child who by age or development is in a relationship of responsibility, trust or power, the activity being intended to gratify or satisfy the needs of the other person.*

The forms, in which sexual abuse of children occurs, range from a one time attempt of molestation to incest at home spanning several years. The impact of sexual abuse in childhood is primarily psychological in nature, causing cognitive, emotional and sexual malfunctioning.

CSA may be committed within the family or outside family in schools, day care centres, hostels, remand homes, crèches etc. Various studies have been conducted to study the incidence of CSA, its causes and its consequences. According to a study by Sakshi Violence Intervention Centre, New Delhi in 1997, 63 per cent experienced CSA at the hands of family members. In another study by TISS, published in 1999, 58 out of 150 minor girls surveyed in Mumbai had been abused by a family member or a friend of the family. The Ministry of Women and Child Development, Government of India, in 2007 published data claiming a huge 42 per cent prevalence rate of CSA in India.

The causes of CSA can be understood in the light of four factors; one, abuser's sexuality and sexual development, this includes pedophilia; second, absence of internal inhibitors of the abuser—the moral values may be weak. The third is absence of external inhibitors such as parental supervision, and fourth is child's own resistance towards the adult, which is usually manipulated by abuser by the use of threat or renaming the abuse as love (Budin and Johnson, 1989; Conte *et al.*, 1989).

On being victimized the psychological impact children suffer include, lack of trust of the world, feeling different from the peers, anger and hostility towards others. Their self-esteem lowers and feelings of inferiority may set in. They may also experience guilt and tend to feel that something must be wrong with them for the abuse to happen. They may even fear retaliation from the abuser.

Jointly all these push the child towards secrecy and nondisclosure. The nondisclosure and often the trauma associate with the abuse banish the events into the realm of the unconscious. Unconscious material is usually well guarded from awareness; it does, however, become accessible to awareness under certain conditions like intoxication, dreams and hypnotic trance.

Hypnosis is among the first few techniques to be used to diagnose disorders with hidden causes. Hypnosis is a powerful technique to explore the subconscious and the unconscious and bring forth experiences that may be directing faulty or defensive behaviour. Hypnosis, therefore, is used for therapeutic purposes in various forms like auto suggestion, metaphoric suggestions, direct suggestions and hypnodrama, etc.

Many other therapeutic techniques can be used to deal with adult survivors of CSA. These techniques are (i) Narrative therapy, (ii) Somatic trauma therapy, (iii) Cognitive-behavioural therapy, (iv) Psychodynamic therapy, (v) Transactional analysis, (vi) Attachment theory, (vii) Neuro-linguistic programming, and (viii) Hypnodrama and Gestalt therapy.

In this chapter, researcher would like to talk about the techniques that she utilized out of the numerous techniques available. She has combined the use of hypnosis and Gestalt technique. Gestalt therapy stresses on the development of client's self-awareness and personal responsibility. It takes into account the whole person, including thoughts, feelings, behaviour, body sensations and dreams, focussing on integration. One of the techniques used by Gestalt therapists is the "Empty-Chair technique." This was developed and popularized by Fredrick "Fritz" Pearls. Researchers have validated the use of empty-chair technique for completing unfinished relationship issues (Greenberg and Foster, 1996).

McMain *et al.* (1996) related changes in self-other schemas to psychotherapy outcome. In the present case, researcher utilized the empty-chair technique on the client with the hope that the client would be able to unearth what was disturbing her.

The Case

During the tenure as a student of PG Diploma in Clinical and Applied Hypnosis, the researcher came across a client who had been to many psychotherapeutic experts but in vain. She needed to get rid of her oversensitivity to physical touch. She reportedly would get extremely disturbed mentally on anybody (same or opposite sex) touching her anywhere (not necessarily sensitive areas).

Case History

The client was a girl of 20 years of age doing graduation in arts at third year level and lived away from home in the university hostel. She shared her hostel room with her identical twin. Her twin was also doing graduation, but in different subject. The client was a good student with above average grades and was liked by peers. She was friendly, approachable and extrovert in social interactions. She did not show any history of mental illness prior to present problem, nor was any family history of any ailment reported.

Main complaints:

1. Feeling disturbed when touched by anyone including her sister.
2. Remaining occupied mentally with the imagined impression of the touch for hours after it happened.
3. Feeling dirty and wanting to clean away, rub away the touch.

Onset: Since past one month.

The main complaints of being occupied against will with thoughts of impression of touch on parts of the body which was touched, feelings of dirt, and desire to clean away the touch indicated high chances of sexual abuse.

Therapeutic Sessions

1. The first session was devoted to history taking. First half of the session was devoted to rapport formation. An attempt was then made to understand the symptoms in terms of behaviour, thoughts and feelings that accompanied it during history taking.
2. Second session was focussed on understanding the possible cause(s). An open ended interview was conducted for the same. No obvious cause appeared to be consciously forthcoming but the information that she was not deeply attached to her parents and she feared darkness and loneliness, made me think that client may not be consciously aware of the cause.
   Since unconscious processes can become accessible under hypnotic trance and the cause may have laid hidden in the unconscious, the therapist felt it was

appropriate to use hypnosis for uncovering the hidden cause. The therapist suggested hypnotherapy to the client, which the client agreed to try.

3. Third session begun with explaining what hypnotherapy was and what were its advantages. Whatever misconceptions existed about hypnotherapy were clarified. She was also helped to understand that the researcher was a well wisher and would keep all the interactions confidential within the file. All her other fears and doubts were also cleared.

   The first step towards hypnotherapy began with relaxation using the "Progressive Muscular Relaxation" (PMR) technique. After relaxation was achieved till satisfaction of the researcher, positive pleasant imagery was suggested. Then, suggestion to go to a place which the client considered safest was given. To the surprise of the researcher the client reported flashes of scenes which she herself described as feeling of being in her mother's womb. She gave vivid description of the liquid floating around, its colour etc. To the author, this suggested that, one, the client did not find any other place in the world as "safest"; and two, she was capable of and ready for age regression.

4. The next session focussed on further probe. After the state of relaxation was achieved, suggestion to scan the happenings of the past, by going back to the childhood experiences was given. The client was asked to raise the index finger to indicate that the said suggestion was translating into imagery of the past events. The client raised the index finger. No verbalization on part of the client took place during the trance.

   After the session ended the client related an event of the past which according to her could be related or close to the cause of her present condition. She recollected that at the age of 6 or 7 she had been a victim of continuous molestation by her father's friend who was staying with them. The molestation lasted 5 to 6 days and finally ended when she witnessed the molester making advances at her twin. She reported the event to her parents who immediately responded by ousting their guest.

On exploring her feelings regarding the episode, she remembered experiencing rage and uncontrollable urge to hurt the molester physically. She reported feeling helpless at the hands of the perpetrator and wanted someone to discover his misdeeds, so that she could be rescued. She could not, however, muster the courage to tell her parents of her plight, till she realized that her twin could also be victimized. The session turned into a cathartic one where the client cried and sobbed as she told her the story.

This experience gave a strong clue of the possible cause of her condition. Her narration was constantly punctuated with some very basic questions like "Why did it happen?", "Did it have anything to do with my behaviour?", "Would he tolerate it if his daughters were victimized the same way?"

Since hypnosis had worked well and she had shown high suggestibility, the therapist planned to use hypnotherapy as a tool for healing her hurt and angry feelings. The therapist also felt that the unsettled scores needed to be settled by the client with the perpetrator. Her feelings of anger and rage needed to be thrown out on the perpetrator.

To meet the above goals the therapist planned to use one of the Gestalt techniques called "The Empty-Chair" technique. The Empty-Chair technique has been found to be a useful tool to complete unfinished business by Greenberg and Fosters (1996) and McMain *et al.* (1995). Paivio and Greenberg (2001) found that high engagers in imagined confrontations in empty-chair work achieved significantly greater resolution of issues with abusive and neglectful others and reduced discomfort on current abuse-related target complaints.

The above studies show the utility of empty-chair work in dealing with victims of abuse who want to settle their grievances with others.

5. The next session was arranged to combine empty-chair work in a state of hypnotic trance, much like an attempt at hypnodrama without an audience.
During the session, the client immediately slipped into a trance after PMR. She was then asked to imagine that her molester was sitting in the chair in front of her. She was told to settle her scores and try to find answers that she always wanted.
What followed was spectacular. She started talking to the imagined person, initially calmly, asking for answers to questions like why me? How could you?
Gradually, she became more and more agitated, her pitch kept rising and anger kept getting more and more intense. Suddenly, she stood up from her chair and started screaming abuses at him. She went in fury towards the empty chair and started hitting violently. She kicked with her legs and hit with both hands and kept screaming her questions, without waiting for answers. She imagined him running for cover, followed him to the window of the clinic (which was on first floor). She saw him climbing on the sill of the window and with full strength she pushed him out of the window.
She did not stop at that and kept screaming abuses over the window to the imaginary person, oblivious of others who were watching her from under the window. She continued to scream on the perpetrator who, she later reported, was hurt by the fall and trying to limp away. After sufficiently abusing, till she could see him no more, she came back and sat on her chair. With a sigh of relief and expression of completion, she closed her eyes. The therapist then started counting backwards from five suggesting that at the count of one, she would open her eyes and will be fully awake.
After the session ended, the therapist discussed the happenings with the client. She was aware of what had transpired and was very happy and satisfied with the happenings. She explained again how she had hurt him sufficiently and that he bled when she pushed him

down. He looked scared after the fall, and when she screamed abuses at him from the first floor window.

6. Next session the client reported feeling absolutely fine, she said she had not felt anything when she was touched by her sister or any other friend. The therapist enquired regarding her feelings when a male companion touched her, she reported not noting if anyone had in fact touched her.

Two more follow-up sessions took place in which she reported not having those thoughts and feeling of impression of the hand bothering her any more. In the last session, she came with her male friend who expressed his happiness at her more normal responses to him. She reported that she had not got those disturbing thoughts again after that session of hypnotherapy combined with the empty-chair technique.

Discussion

This chapter intends to highlight the potential hold of, the combination of hypnotherapy and empty-chair technique, for dealing with victims of CSA especially when the victim very strongly wishes to give it back and settle scores. The author very strongly felt the client's need to hurt and take revenge. She particularly did not seem to be depressed with self-doubt and indulging in self-blame, she was enraged and felt exploited. She displayed her fury very clearly when she got the chance in the combined session.

Different victims may react to abuse in different ways, but this case shows that clients who feel victimized (and not that they have deserved it by somehow inviting the abuse—which many victims feel) this combination may help reduce the block they experience in life with sexual relations. The empty-chair technique helps to express feelings without being challenged in reality, which is very cathartic and when used in combination with hypnosis its effect multifolds as scores can be settled directly from the unconscious. The critical conscience also does not interfere. This allows true feelings to emerge and be expressed with minimum censor from the conscience. Hypnosis also allows it to be done in the way the Ego deems fit for the satisfaction of the Id. The basic driving forces of the Id include aggression, according to Freud and if aggression towards the perpetrator reduces the feelings of hurt and injustice, then hypnosis allows it without the interference of social inhibitions.

Conclusion

The case study presented above is an evidence of how hypnotherapy in combination with the empty-chair technique, leads to a release of the pent-up rage that a victim feels for the perpetrator of sexual abuse in childhood. This emotional release led the client to immediate relief from the symptoms that were bothering her. It also kept her symptom free for the next few weeks. Further follow-up, however, was not possible as the therapist shifted her base to another city.

REFERENCES

Budin, L.E., & Johnason, C.F. (1989). Sex abuse prevention programme: Offenders attitudes about their efficacy. *Child Abuse and Neglect*. 13, 77-87.

Conte, J.R., Wolf, S., & Smith, T. (1989). What sexual offenders tell us about prevention strategies. *Child Abuse and Neglect*, 13, 293-301.

Greenberg, L.S., & Foerster, F.S. (1996). Task analysis exemplified: The process of resolving unfinished business. *Journal of Consulting and Clinical Psychology*, 64, 439-446.

Kapur, A. (1998). *"I Am Witness To": A Profile of Sakshi Violence Intervention Centre in New Delhi, India.* Retrieved on Oct. 12, 2008 from http://www.ncbi.nlm.nih.gov/entrez/query.fcgi?cmd=Retrieve&db=PubMed& dopt=Citati on&list_uids=12294411.

McMain, S., Goldman, R., & Greenberg, L.S. (1996). Resolving unfinished business: A programme of study. In W. Dryden (Ed.), *Research in Counselling and Psychotherapy: Practical Applications* (pp. 211-232). London: Sage.

Paivio, S., & Greenberg, L.S. (2001). Resolving unfinished business: Experiential therapy using empty-chair dialogue. *Journal of Consulting and Clinical Psychology*, 63, 419-425.

19

Clinical Hypnotherapy in People Living with HIV/AIDS

A Study of Disease Progression and Coping Strategies

URMI NANDA BISWAS

Introduction

In India, the threat of HIV is looming large. It is estimated that India's adult HIV prevalence will peak at 1.9 per cent in 2019 (The Population Division of the Department of Economic and Social Affairs of the United Nations Secretariat, 2003), and that as a consequence, economic growth in India will slow down by almost a percentage point per year by 2019 (UNDP, 2006). People living with HIV and AIDS (PLWHA) can now have an almost normal life expectancy due to the highly effective pharmaceutical poly-therapies for the treatment of HIV and AIDS. However, the challenge for them is to live a physically and mentally healthy life while contributing to the economic development of the country. These challenges include avoiding and managing opportunistic infections and taking care of their mental health needs which promote psychosocial well-being. Considering the huge population affected by HIV, it is imperative to develop measures to enhance the quality of life, increase health behaviours and slow down the disease progression among people affected by HIV. Consequently, it could contribute to the sustenance of economic growth, valuable human resources, and positive national health. Research linking Psycho-Neuro-Immunology (PNI) and AIDS points out that biological mediators of psychological status can play an important role in mediating HIV disease progression (Kopnisky, Stoff, & Rausch, 2004; Nott, Vedhara, & Spickett, 1995; Solomon, Temoshok, O'leary, & Zich, 1987). Acquired Immune Deficiency Syndrome (AIDS), from being an untreatable fatal disease has almost gained a status of chronic illness like tuberculosis because of Highly Active Antiretroviral Therapy (HAAT). HAAT has not only increased the life-span of HIV positive individuals but also increased the potential of the individuals to lead an active life. Thus, it has also become important to find out alternative/adjunct therapies to provide better quality of life and well-being of the PLWHA. In last decade, effort has been made by researchers to test the efficacy of hypnotherapy in reducing pain, managing disease symptoms, promoting immune-competence as well as enhancing the immune parameters in people living with HIV/AIDS.

Role of Hypnosis, Relaxation, and Guided Imagery in Strengthening the Immune System

Hypnotherapeutic interventions have been administered successfully for different symptom management in HIV positive people (Langenfeld, Cipani, & Borchawdt, 2002). HIV positive men reported that the hypnotherapeutic intervention successfully helped in symptom management in the post-intervention and follow-up data (Rucklide and Saunders, 2002). Keicolt-Glaser (2004) found that students in the control group showed a 24 per cent decrease in T-lymphocyte proliferation compared to a 2 per cent increase in the hypnosis group. The more frequently students in the hypnosis group practiced their technique, the better their immune response was. In another study, Glaser and Keicolt-Glaser (2005) reported that during periods of stress, students had a decrease in NK cell activity. In an interesting study, Antoni, Cruess, Cruess, Kumar, Lutgendorf, Ironson, Dettmer, Williams, Klimas, Fletcher, and

Schneiderman (2000) tested the effects of a multimodal cognitive-behavioural stress management (CBSM) intervention on 24-hour urinary free cortisol levels and distressed mood in symptomatic HIV+ gay men. They found that men assigned to CBSM showed significantly lower post-treatment levels of self-reported depressed affect, anxiety, anger, and confusion than those in the wait-list control group. Among the 47 men providing urine samples, those assigned to CBSM revealed significantly less cortisol output as compared to controls. At the individual level, depressed mood decreases cortisol reductions over this period across the entire sample. These studies suggest that the actual functioning of immune system can be affected by hypnosis and relaxation techniques. In a recent research, Laidlaw, Kerstein, Bennett, Naito, Dwivedi, and Gruzelier (2004), related hypnotizability to changes in HIV immune blood markers after two psychological interventions. A course of four weekly 2-hour training sessions coupled with daily self-hypnosis practice was given to 13 participants with diagnosed HIV and for further participants a similar course was given in a Japanese healing method called Johrei (a total of 22 participants). All were naïve to anti-retroviral medication. The mean of two blood assays prior to intervention was compared to the results of the blood assay after the intervention. The results report that when highly hypnotizable subjects were compared to those of lower hypnotizability in a repeated measures analysis, their CD4+ t-lymphocyte counts were significantly higher. This was achieved by the highly hypnotizable subjects non-significantly raising their CD4+ counts while the CD4+ counts of the less hypnotizable subjects declined significantly. The differences in CD4+ T cell per cent of lymphocytes and the viral loads did not differ. This pilot study implied that hypnotizability may predict immunological response to psychological interventions in HIV.

However, the available published work on the application of hypnotherapy to enhance immune competence in PLWHA suggests that there are very few systematic controlled trial studies that have been carried out to examine the impact of hypnosis, relaxation, guided imagery, breathing exercises on clinical immune parameters in HIV+ individuals. The present research was undertaken based on a conceptual framework which suggested that, stress arising out of stigma attached to being HIV+ added to the disease progression. Research evidence cited above provided substantial reason towards strengthening the framework that there existed a strong mind-body connection and consequently, between stress and disease progression. Thus, hypnotherapeutic interventions leading to positive mood sets and controlling for stress would have a negative impacts on disease progression in HIV+ individuals.

The present research was intended to study :

1. Whether hypnotherapeutic intervention through relaxation, ego-enhancement, confidence building, positive thought induction, guided imagery and sensory imagery conditioning added by self-hypnosis would increase the CD4 count, and reduce the viral load in the experimental group.
2. Whether hypnotherapeutic intervention would improve the coping style in the PLWHA, suggesting their increased adaptation to their HIV positive status and related stress management.

Method

Sample

Participants for the study were selected through purposive sampling from Vadodara, India. They were contacted and recruited through Non Governmental Organizations (NGOs) in the area working with PLWHA. All participants were above 18 years of age, HIV+ patients having CD4 count above 250, and having plasma viral load less than 5,000. Individuals having any other acute or chronic illnesses or severe depression along with having HIV+ status were not included in the sample. During intervention if patients developed another disease then that patient was excluded from the sample.

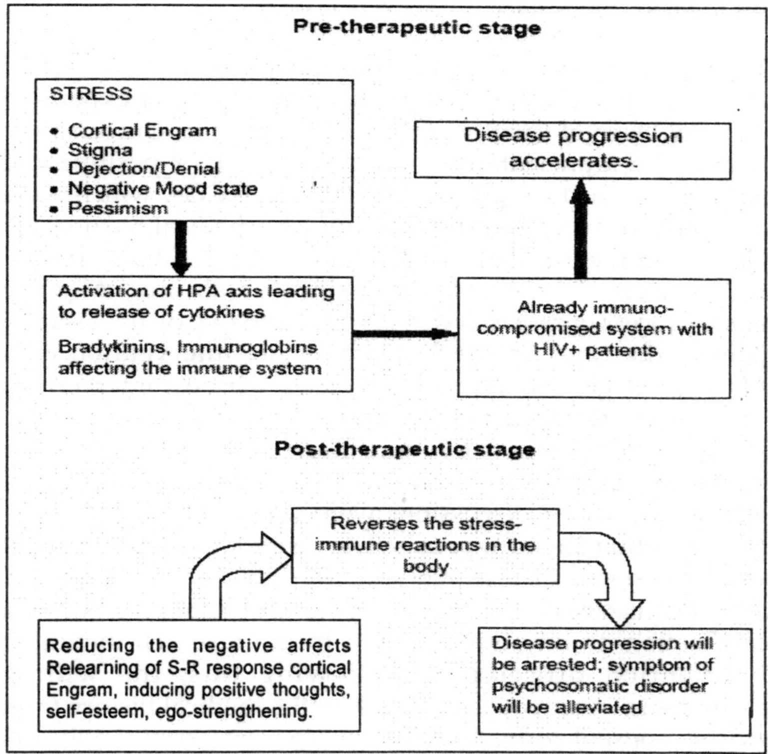

Fig. 19.1 : Pre-Therapeutic Stage and Post-therapeutic Stage

At the time of the first blood assay, the sample for the experimental group was 27, and control group was 18. But over 8 weeks period of intervention, six subjects discontinued and/or were excluded from the study. Finally by the post-test assay there were 21 participants in the experimental group. The control group, which was kept as a waiting list control, showed their disinterest to keep coming for the blood assays only from far off places and subsequently discontinued. During the second blood assays, only two of them showed up. In the final follow-up test, psychological test data, and blood assays could be collected only from 18 individuals. Finally, data collected from these 18 individuals were subjected to analysis.

Procedure

During the process of initiating the study, an ethics committee was formed at the university level comprising of experts in the field, Dean of Faculty of Medicine, the M. S. University of Baroda, the representatives (who are also HIV positive and participants in the study) from the two NGOs, which were interested to participate in the study. The medical history was taken from the selected individuals in order to find out that they have been confirmed as HIV+ individuals medically. The whole process of research was divided into five distinct stages; namely, the rapport building stage, pre-intervention data collection stage, the intervention stage, the post-intervention data collection stage, and the follow-up data collection stage.

During the rapport building stage the participants were invited to join a workshop in which they were briefed about hypnosis. Detailed discussions were carried out to clear any misconception about hypnosis. They were thoroughly briefed about the stages of research and were told why hypnosis is used for treatment. They were constantly encouraged to seek clarification on any issue related to the research including intervention procedures. Following this, the willing participants were requested to fill up the medical history form and the consent form. The Patient Consent Form (PCF) was filled up to get the patients' informed consent to participate in the research with the full knowledge of the objectives, procedures, and implications of the research. The patient medical case history form included questions about the history of the patient's HIV+ status (i.e., time since first detection of HIV+ status, type of medication, duration of medication, etc.). The form also included questions about the co-morbid problems, both physiological and psychological. The participants were also requested to provide information on CD4 count and plasma viral load.

In total, 45 participants were selected. The verbatim for eight intervention sessions were planned and standardized for its validity through expert validation. The group was divided into experimental and control group. The initial intervention started with 27 participants in the experimental group, with an apprehension that there may be drop-outs over time because of the nature of the disease. One session was given per week. Each session lasted for almost 90 minutes. But with preparation time and feedback time the average time per session was two hours.

The initial two sessions included progressive muscular relaxation, ego-strengthening, and self-confidence enhancement. It was followed by sessions to change from negative mood set to neutral mood set and then progressing to positive mood set. The suggestions and positive imageries were given for enhancing immune-competence and strengthening of the body to fight invaders in next few sessions. Visualization of a healthier, strong, immune competent self was provided through suggestion. At the beginning of each session participants were asked to give a feedback on whether the last session has affected their physical and psychological status any way and the feedbacks were systematically recorded.

All the sessions given to the clients were organized around the following steps :

1. General relaxation;
2. Breath watching;
3. Progressive muscular relaxation;
4. Ego-strengthening; and
5. Visualization.

The visualizations given were designed specifically for HIV/AIDS patients. As is known, hypnotherapeutic suggestions have to be tailor-made, customized, considering the problems faced by the client, goal of the session, symptoms to be managed. However, below are given gist of suggestions given to the subjects of the research. This has to be understood in the context and taken as examples only.

Example 1

"You are sitting in a hot balloon and moving ahead towards the top of the mountain . . . . Slowly, floating and flying you reach the mountain top, the peak of the mountain. You get down from the balloon. The morning sun is coming out from behind the mountain. The mountain peak is slowly getting bathed by soft sun rays. You are

wonder struck. You are soaked with soft and warm sun-rays. It slowly fills you with energy. Sun energy is entering all the tiny cells of your body and revitalizing them . . . . The soft sun rays are filling your body with comforting warmth. Now onwards, whenever you will feel weak and anxious, you will close your eyes and take deep breaths in and out. Along with that you can re-live the same experience. You will feel energetic and calm, serene because of this experience . . . ."

Example 2

During the progressive muscular relaxation, the suggestion was given that the body slowly gets energized from the fresh oxygen received by deep breathing and relaxation, and body stores up this energy.

> *"As you slowly travel down your own body, you are able to see the blood flowing like a river in your body through the veins and arteries. But there is a fight going on. The fight is between the white blood cells and the HIV virus. The white blood cells are coming together. In mass they are looking like dolphins. . . . The dolphins are smoothly swimming and gliding through your blood stream to gulp down the infected cells as if they are eating up small fishes. Your brain is continuously sending energy to these dolphins. The dolphins look aggressive and energized. Very smoothly and without facing any resistance they just keep floating, swimming. When they see any new virus infected cells, dolphins gulp them down. . . . Slowly and slowly, the number of infected cells is going down. Your body feels light and fresh."*

Example 3

"It is a rainy day. As you look down, you realize that the first drop of rain has just fallen on your feet. There is a tingling sensation spreading from that particular point to your whole body. This is the sensation of warmth, well-being and freshness. Surprisingly, the raindrops are warm and the warmth is flowing like a healing wave in your body. As the warm rain drops are bathing your skin you see slowly the skin rashes, the bruises, the itchy scaly skin and the weak

and fragile nails are getting changed. They are transforming slowly, changing slowly into normal healthy skin. . . . The rain is infusing more and more vitality, more and more energy into your body. . . . into all the body parts, even to all the tissues and tiny cells in your body. . . . You are feeling like a winner. Your self-confidence has been boosted hundred times. You now know that you have grown so strong from inside that it is difficult to infect you. You know you have now derived positive energy from the cosmic energy which will keep sustaining your good health and well-being through all odds."

After eight sessions of clinical hypnotherapy, the blood assays were conducted. The participants were again tested on psychological and physiological tests. Participants in experimental group were given CDs and audio cassettes, based on their demand and were asked to practice self-hypnosis for the coming four weeks. They were requested to report for follow-up after six weeks. During this period they were administered a multidimensional coping inventory (COPE) and the blood assays were conducted.

Blood Assays

Blood tests were conducted by Toprani Pathological Clinic, a nationally accredited laboratory and recognized by Medical Council of India (MCI), based in Vadodara and close to the place where participants were given the intervention. The participants were requested to report for the blood assays with an empty stomach and on all three occasions, the collection was completed between 8.30 a.m. to 10.30 a.m., thus the testing was done in highly standardized procedure so as to keep all the possible variations under control.

Measures

All participants were administered a set of psychological scales and inventories, including demographic information such as, age, sex, marital status, family members with whom they live, and number of children, HIV status of spouse and children, etc.

Multi-Dimensional Coping Inventory

Psychological scales and inventories included a multidimensional coping inventory (COPE) developed by Carver and Schier (1989). It incorporated 15 conceptually distinct scales which were developed on theoretical grounds or chosen on the basis of previous work which demonstrated their role in facilitating or impending adaptive coping in different context. Test-retest reliabilities for the dispositional version were obtained from two samples of participants over six and eight week periods and ranged from 0.42 to 0.89 for different scales. This indicates that the coping tendencies measured by COPE are reasonably stable. The measure comprised of dimensions such as, Active Coping, Planning, Seeking Instrumental Social Support, Seeking Emotional and Social Support, Suppression of Competing Activities, Turning to Religion, Restraint Coping, Acceptance, Focus on and Venting of Emotion, Denial, Mental Disengagement, Behavioural Disengagement, and Humour.

CD4 Count

The purpose of determining the CD4 count is to measure the strength of the immune system of the individual diagnosed with HIV infection. CD4 cells are a major target for HIV, which binds the surface of CD4 cells, enters them, and either reproduces or immediately killing them in the process. It may also remain in a resting state, reproducing later. The number of CD4 cells in the blood gradually declines as HIV disease progresses.

The CD4 cell count tells the doctor, (a) how strong is the patient's immune system, (b) how far HIV disease has advanced (the stage of the disease), and (c) helps to predict the risk of complications and debilitating infections. The CD4 count is most useful when it is compared with the count obtained from an earlier test. The CD4 count is used in comparison with the viral load test to determine the staging and outlook of the disease. Normal CD4 counts in adults range from 500 to 1500 cells per cubic millimetre of blood. In general, the CD4 count goes down as HIV disease progresses. Any single CD4 count value may differ from the last one even though the patient's health status has not changed. The pattern of CD4 count over time is more important than any single value. The patients' CD4 count should increase or stabilize in response to effective combination of anti HIV therapy (www. Aidonaids.com/English/for doctors/cd4-count.htm downloaded on 31 March 2008).

CD8 Count

CD8 cell is a type of white blood cell that is involved in fighting certain types of infection (i.e., HIV). The total CD8 cell count actually goes down immediately following infection (as does the CD4 cell count) for about 3-4 weeks—then over the course of the next month (roughly the second month of infection), the CD8 cell count increases (as does the CD4 count) to values higher than a typically seen in a HIV negative individual. During this period, the changes in CD4 : CD8 ratio is quite typical for HIV—though it can be very difficult to distinguish from other viral infections. The CD4 : CD8 ratio is an indicator of the overall level of the immune suppression or damage done by HIV. The lower the CD4 : CD8 ratio the worse the damage. The CD4 : CD8 ratio is rarely less than 1.0 in HIV negative individual, but may drop as low as 0.1 in patients with recent HIV infections or very advanced stage of the disease. There is almost substantial recovery of this ratio even without anti-retroviral therapy during the second-third month of HIV infection. The CD4 : CD8 ratio gradually decline over years of HIV infection in the absence of anti-retroviral therapy. With therapy (administered fairly early after infection) this ratio may again rise to above 1.0 or recovery rarely seen in patients with more advanced HIV infection to start on treatment.

Results and Discussion

The final sample being only 20, and the design being repeated measure design, it was decided to use paired t-test to compare the means of pre- and post-intervention scores and then post- and follow-up test scores to see the effect of the intervention.

Comparison of Pre- and Post-Test Mean Scores across the Dimension of Coping

Table 19.1 presents the mean, standard deviations and the results of paired t-test between pre- and post-test scores on the dimensions of COPE. The results suggest that in the post-intervention stage there was a significant increase in the use of all coping strategies except turning to religion, such as, acceptance, active coping, behavioural disengagement, mental disengagement, and planning compared to the pre-intervention stage. The PLWHA reported greater use of restrained coping and suppression of competing activities in the post-test. However, no difference was found across dimensions like turning to religion and reinterpretation and growth.

Table 19.2 presents the comparison of post- and follow-up test scores on different coping strategies. Active coping and alcohol abuse had reduced significantly over follow-up test scores in comparison to the post-test scores. Denial was reduced, and planning, and reinterpretation and growth as coping strategies increased in the follow-up test scores as compared to the post-test scores. However, there was no significant difference in all other coping strategies among the post-test and follow-up test scores.

Denial of reality of stressful event as a coping strategy has also improved as a result of clinical hypnotherapy. In case of the PLWHA, rather than denial of the reality of the stressful event it may be the reappraisal of the stressful event that may have reduced the threat of the stressful event. Carrico, Antoni, Duran, Ironson, Penedo, Fletcher, Klimas, and Schneiderman (2006) reported the efficacy of a cognitive behavioural stress management (CBSM) intervention in combination with medication adherence training (MAT) in 130 gay and bisexual men living with HIV infection. Greater reliance on denial coping at baseline was associated with decreased depressed mood at 10 weeks. They suggested that though denial may be an effective means of distress reduction in the short term, reliance on this coping strategy may result in a decreased capacity to effectively manage a variety of disease-related stressors in the long term.

Table 19.1 : Mean, Standard Deviations *r*, and Correlated 't-test' for Pre- and Post-test Scores on Dimensions of Coping (n = 20)

	Variables	*Mean*	*SD*	*t-value*	*Sig. (2 tailed)*
Pair 1	Acceptance (Pre-test)	9.2	3.91		
	Acceptance (Post-test)	11.85	3.15	-2.80	0.01
Pair 2	Active Coping (Pre-test)	11.55	2.91		
	Active Coping (Post-test)	13.65	2.91	-2.25	0.04
Pair 3	Alcohol/Drug Abuse (Pre-test)	2.7	4.40		
	Alcohol/Drug Abuse (Post-test)	8.25	5.24	-4.06	0.00
Pair 4	Behavioural Disengagement (Pre-test)	6.5	4.83		
	Behavioural Disengagement (Post-test)	10.85	3.54	-4.28	0.00
Pair 5	Denial (Pre-test)	8.05	4.06		
	Denial (Post-test)	12.05	2.82	-3.61	0.00
Pair 6	Focussed on venting of Emotions (Pre-test)	7.75	3.71		
	Focussed on venting of Emotions (Post-test)	12.1	2.85	-3.93	0.00
Pair 7	Humour (Pre-test)	6.3	3.03		
	Humour (Post-test)	9.75	3.49	-4.35	0.00
Pair 8	Mental Disengagement (Pre-test)	8.4	4.02		
	Mental Disengagement (Post-test)	11.4	2.56	-2.66	0.02
Pair 9	Planning (Pre-test)	9.85	3.56		
	Planning (Post-test)	12.6	3.30	-2.27	0.04
Pair 10	Reinterpretation and Growth (Pre-Test)	12.35	3.47	00	
	Reinterpretation and Growth (Post-Test)	12.35	3.47	00	
Pair 11	Restrained Coping (Pre-test)	8.35	3.96		
	Restrained Coping (Post-test)	11	3.73	-2.07	0.05
Pair 12	Suppression of Competing Activities Pre-test)	9.5	3.17		
	Suppression of Competing Activities (Post-test)	12.1	3.39	-3.06	0.01
Pair 13	Seeking Emotional Social Support (Pre-test)	6.85	4.25		
	Seeking Emotional Social Support (Post-test)	10.5	3.05	-3.53	0.00
Pair 14	Seeking Instrumental Support (Pre-test)	8.7	3.54		
	Seeking Instrumental Support (Post-test)	12.1	3.63	-3.30	0.00
Pair 15	Turning to Religion (Pre-test)	12	4.52		
	Turning to Religion (Post-test)	12.5	3.32	-0.50	0.63

Table 19.2 : Mean, Standard Deviations, and Correlated 't-test' for Post-test and Follow-up Scores on Dimensions of Coping (n = 18).

Pair No.	*Variables*	*Mean*	*SD*	*t-value*	*Sig. (2-tailed)*
Pair 1	Acceptance (Post-test)	12.22	2.86	1.68	0.11
	Acceptance (Follow-up)	10.94	2.39		
Pair 2	Active Coping (Post-test)	14.28	2.05	2.70	0.02
	Active Coping (Follow-up)	12.50	2.23		
Pair 3	Alcohol/Drug Abuse (Post-test)	8.33	5.40	4.02	0.00
	Alcohol/Drug Abuse (Follow-up)	3.11	3.68		
Pair 4	Behavioural Disengagement (Post-test)	11.00	3.51	1.46	0.16
	Behavioural Disengagement (Follow-up)	9.72	1.23		
Pair 5	Denial (Post-test)	12.56	2.33	2.31	0.03
	Denial (Follow-up)	10.94	1.89		
Pair 6	Focussed on venting of Emotions (Post-test)	12.72	2.22	1.91	0.07
	Focussed on venting of Emotions (Follow-up)	11.22	2.34		
Pair 7	Humour (Post-test)	9.83	3.67	-0.19	0.85
	Humour (Follow-up)	10.00	2.17		
Pair 8	Mental Disengagement (Post-test)	11.67	2.35	1.34	0.20
	Mental Disengagement (Follow-up)	10.72	1.90		
Pair 9	Planning (Post-test)	12.83	3.03	2.12	0.05
	Planning (Follow-up)	11.00	2.25		
Pair 10	Reinterpretation and Growth (Post-Test)	12.89	3.18	2.16	0.05
	Reinterpretation and Growth (Follow-up)	11.11	1.13		
Pair 11	Restrained Coping (Post-test)	11.28	3.64	0.95	0.35
	Restrained Coping (Follow-up)	10.28	1.56		
Pair 12	Suppression-of-Competing Activities (Pre-test)	12.22	3.28	1.28	0.22
	Suppression-of-Competing Activities (Post-test)	10.89	1.68		
Pair 13	Seeking Emotional Social Support (Post-test)	10.94	2.75	-0.76	0.46
	Seeking Emotional Social Support (Follow-up)	11.56	2.15		
Pair 14	Seeking Instrumental Support (Post-test)	12.67	3.34	2.02	0.06
	Seeking Instrumental Support (Follow-up)	10.56	2.43		
Pair 15	Turning to Religion (Post-test)	12.78	2.92	2.00	0.06
	Turning to Religion (Follow-up)	11.11	2.35		

Participants differed significantly in their post-test scores (m = 12.60) in planning as compared to their pre-test scores (m = 9.88). Planning as a coping strategy had improved because of intervention. The positive thought intervention had improved the support seeking behaviour of the participants. Both, the instrumental support seeking and emotional support seeking had significantly increased. The study conducted on HIV+ individuals and drug addicts report that who seek more support also receives more support. In this context, the increase in support seeking behaviour of PLWHA has positive implication in terms of possibility of more received social support which, in turn, is a great enhancement of quality of life and well-being in the life of HIV+ people (Wangehaum, 2003).

Suppression of competing activities as a coping strategy had increased significantly in the post-intervention scores (m = 12.10) as compared to the pre-intervention scores (m = 9.50). However, follow up scores failed to show a significant difference from post-test score.

Focus on and venting of emotions had improved significantly after the post-intervention stage. There was a significant difference between pre- and post-test scores; whereas, the follow-up score did not differ significantly from the post-test score. The participants in the study showed improved mental disengagement and behavioural disengagement as adopted coping strategies to fight with the situation as a result of positive thought intervention and relaxation. Additionally, there was an increase in their avoidance of the stressful thoughts concerning the disease. The post-intervention test (m=8.25) differed significantly from the pre-test scores (m=2.70); whereas, the post-test and follow-up test scores did not differ significantly implying the sustained effect of intervention.

There was a significant increase in the post-intervention scores on humour as a coping strategy (Post-intervention, m = 9.75) compared to the pre-intervention scores (pre-test scores, m=6.30). However, the follow-up test scores did not show a significant difference from the post- test scores. The increased use of humour as a coping strategy suggests the ability in the PLWHA to disengage themselves from self-disparaging thoughts. The results imply that positive thought induction through hypnotherapy has been very effective in strengthening positive coping strategies in PLWHA.

The Effect of the Intervention on Immunological Parameters

The effect of positive thought intervention on the immunological parameters of PLWHA has been analyzed by using paired sample t-test between the pre-post and post-follow-up scores. All the participants of the study were tested for their CD4 absolute count, CD4 percentage, CD-8 percentage, absolute CD8 count, proportion of CD4 to CD8 count, percentage of CD3 count and absolute CD3 count. They were also tested for the plasma viral load and cortisol level before and after the intervention. After the post-intervention blood assays, intervention sessions were ceased and instead, the participants were asked to regularly practice relaxation with the support of the pre-recorded instructions and music given in a Compact Disc (CD) for four weeks. Follow-up tests on the same parameters were taken for comparison with post-test scores. These are positive indicators of their emotional strength and stability which may enable them to overcome the stress and feeling of stigmatization. However, active coping, planning and reinterpretation and growth seek to be activated more as coping strategies when the PLWHA were going through the intervention schedules. This might indirectly indicate that importance of group therapy and support from similar others.

Table 19.3 presents the comparison of pre- and post-test scores. Results suggest that, post-intervention percentage of CD4 count, absolute CD4, and absolute CD8 count differed significantly (alpha = .01). However, the pre- and post-test scores on percentage of CD8 count failed to show significant difference. The comparison of mean scores suggested that the proportion of CD4 to CD8 count differed significantly between the pre- and post-test scores of the PLWHA. The mean scores

Table 19.3 : Results of Paired Samples Statistics for Immunological Parameters (Correlated 't' test) n=20

		Mean	*Std. Deviation*	*t' values*	*Sig (2-tailed)*
Percentage of CD4 Count	Pre Post	19.04 17.24	10.48 10.03	3.10	0.01
Absolute CD4 Count	Pre Post	348.55 433.70	234.21 336.29	-2.74	0.01
Percentage of CD8 Count	Pre Post	54.63 54.96	13.25 13.20	-0.38	0.71
Absolute CD8 Count	Pre Post	969.45 1293.80	473.35 574.42	-4.31	0.00
Proportion of CD4 to CD8 Count	Pre Post	0.42 0.37	0.35 0.30	2.67	0.02
Percentage of CD3 Count	Pre Post	121.26 78.10	191.22 10.65	1.03	0.32
Absolute of CD3 count	Pre Post	1414.70 1880.80	561.10 782.74	-4.27	0.00
Plasma Viral Load	Pre Post	137836.04 111924.37	356895.61 232174.40	0.45	0.66
Cortisol Level	Pre Post	12.98 15.21	4.22 7.22	-1.56	0.13

indicated that the proportion of CD4 to CD8 count had gone down significantly in the post-test results. No significant difference was found out between the pre- and post-test results of percentage of CD3 count in the PLWHA. The mean and standard deviation of post-test results showed that percentage of CD3 count had reduced in post-test results, but it failed to reach the significance level. Absolute CD3 count in post-intervention test results differed significantly from the pre-test scores. The mean CD3 count had increased in the post-test scores as compared to that of pre-test score.

Table 19.4 presents the comparison of post-test and follow-up test scores. There was no significant difference between the post- and follow-up scores percentage of CD4 count, absolute CD4 count, percentage of CD8 count, and the proportion of CD4 to CD8 count. These findings suggest that the follow-

Table 19.4 : Results of Paired Samples Statistics for Immunological Parameters (Correlated 't' test) n=20

		Mean	*Std. Deviation*	*t' values*	*sig*
Absolute CD4 Count	Post Follow-up	433.70 363.15	336.29 231.41	1.31	0.21
Percentage of CD4 Count	Post Follow-up	17.24 18.53	10.03 11.10	-0.61	0.55
Percentage of CD8 Count	Post Follow-up	54.96 50.45	13.20 16.48	1.81	0.09
Absolute CD8 Count	Post Follow-up	1293.80 979.95	574.42 476.11	2.65	0.02
Proportion of CD4 to CD8 Count	Post Follow-up	0.37 0.41	0.30 0.36	-0.85	0.40
Percentage of CD3 Count	Post Follow-up	78.10 74.07	10.65 19.75	0.86	0.40
Absolute of CD3 count	Post Follow-up	1880.80 1448.20	782.74 676.54	2.56	0.02
Plasma Viral Load	Post Follow-up	111924.37 136359.77	232174.40 457033.18	-0.33	0.74
Cortisol Level	Post Follow-up	15.21 13.34	7.22 4.63	1.29	0.21

up scores did not deviate significantly from post-test scores, which is indicative of the sustenance of the change brought in the parameters even after the cessation of actual sessions of intervention. Thus, the immune competence which was enhanced because of the positive thought induction had more or less sustained itself.

However, significant difference was found in the post and follow-up test reports in the absolute CD8 count and absolute CD3 count of PLWHA. A reduction in the marker cells—CD3 suggests that surface level marker T lymphocytes have reduced because of the intervention in long run. The fighter T cells CD8 had also reduced sharing an increase in CD4 to CD8 ratio which is an excellent indicator suggesting the enhancement of immune-competence.

These findings strongly suggest that the eight week long

positive thought induction intervention had been effective to reduce the diseases progression in the participants of the study. Campbell, Aurelius, Blowes, and Harvey (1997) pointed out that measurement of the CD4 lymphocyte count is widely used as a prognostic marker and guide for the institution of antiretroviral therapy in patients infected with HIV. These findings have very significant and relevant implications for the disease progression in PLWHA. Destruction of CD4+ lymphocytes is the major cause of the immunodeficiency observed in AIDS, and decreasing CD4+ lymphocyte level appears to be the best predictor of morbidity in these patients. Quantification of these cells, therefore, has been an important test in the staging and monitoring of patients infected with HIV. In assessing immune-competence, it is useful to identify decision points for treatment of AIDS or prophylaxis against various micro organisms and to assess therapeutic effect in clinical trial. Recently, the CD4 cell count has been used to actually define AIDS in HIV infected person. Throughout the course of HIV disease the total t-cell level remain fairly constant despite the fall in the CD4+ cell count. This is due to the concomitant increase in the CD8+ cells. The ratio of CD4+ to CD8+ cells is, therefore, a further important measure of disease progression in HIV infected patients.

The CD3 cells are present on the peripheral *t* cells, which are considered as markers of severity of infection along with other parameters. CD4 cells are *T* helper induced cells and increased CD4 cells in HIV+ people indicate an improved immune system, or enhancement of immune compliance. CD8 cells are white blood cells that fight against HIV. The CD8 cell count initially goes down and later on increases. The increase in CD8 cell is also an indicator of better immune compliance. The lower the CD4/CD8 ratio the worse is the damage for the PLWHA. Mean score of CD8 percentage count had increased in the post-intervention test and standard deviation had gone down. However, the change in the plasma viral load failed to meet the significance level although the mean score showed that the average plasma viral load had gone down in patients.

It has been suggested in the literature that stress management interventions can reduce symptoms of distress as well as modulate certain immune system components in persons infected with human immunodeficiency virus (HIV). These effects may occur in parallel with reductions in hypothalamic-pituitary-adrenal (HPA) axis hormones such as cortisol, which has been related in other work to a down-regulation of immune system components relevant to HIV infection. There has been significant increase in CD4 count in the post-test as compared to pre-test, whereas follow-up test report do not differ from post-test scores significantly. This trend implies that positive thought induction (hypnotherapy) has the potential to bring in positive change in the CD4 status of the PLWHA. This is supported by earlier studies of Antoni, Cruess, Cruess, Kumar, Lutgendorf, Ironson, Dettmer, Williams, Klimas, Fletcher, and Schneiderman (2000).

The absolute CD8 count has significantly increased in the post-test. There has been a significant difference in the post-test and follow-up test scores as well. In the 5th, 6th, 7th and 8th session of hypnotherapy, the participants were suggested to visualize that their ability to fight HIV is increasing, being enhanced. This may have implications for the increased absolute CD8 count. However, when the weekly intervention sessions have stopped and the participants were asked to practice relaxation as a follow-up, the CD8 cells decrease resulting in an increased CD4 : CD8 ratio which is an ultimate indicator of enhanced immune competence.

In both pre-post and post-follow-up comparison the counts of plasma viral load had not changed significantly. The trend showed that in post-test, the count had gone down as compared to the pre-test showing the lowering of viral load. However, in follow-up report, the count had gone up compared to post-test showing an increase in the viral load. Together, these findings suggest that active intervention through group hypnotherapy sessions, where positive thought intervention was done through relaxation, ego-enhancement, guided positive imagery, visualization, sensory imagery conditioning, etc., was more effective in increasing the immune competence and arresting disease progression as compared to the follow-up session, where the subjects were asked to practice self-hypnotherapy.

Conclusion

This research has put forward empirical evidence that positive thoughts have the power to change the functioning of the immune parameters: Relaxation, positive mood state, positive visualization, etc. enhance the immune competence which supports existing research (e.g., Keicolt-Glazer, 1995; Pert, 1997). The findings of the study suggest that clinical hypnotherapy enhances the use of positive coping strategies, both task oriented as well as emotion focussed strategies can be strengthened. Thus using clinical hypnotherapy stress level of the individuals can be reduced. The study reaffirms the mind-body connection. The 'molecules of emotion' (Pert, 1997) have been proven to have the power to control the immune parameters and diseased condition of the body.

This study also highlighted that once the PLWHA are able to break the stigma attached to the infection and the continuous denial of the existence of the infection were able to better cope with their disease. It has been noted that stigma, discrimination, and denial of HIV/AIDS is as important to the global AIDS challenge as the disease itself (Mann, 1987). Combating stigma and discrimination against PLWHA is most critical factor in the process of preventing and controlling the epidemic (Mawar, Sahay, Pandit, & Mahajan, 2005). PLWHA suffer the feeling of acute shame and a constant fear of being stigmatized by others, which is psychologically and consequently physically debilitating. The findings of the present study suggest that, may be the group therapy sessions, the exposure to other PLWHA, social support from the people with similar debilitating experiences reduced the internalized stigma, self-deprecating thoughts, mental engagement with diseased condition, and enhanced their focus on venting of emotions, cognitive reappraisal of the stressful situations and helped the PLWHA in more positive coping. A comparative understanding of the post-intervention and follow-up test scores further strengthen these interpretations. The PLWHA were meeting once in a week for the group hypnotherapy sessions. After the post-test assessment and during the follow-up period the regular group interventions ceased and the participants were presented with pre-recorded compact disc to practice individually at their own residences. The post-test and follow-up test scores did not show as much significant improvement as seen in the comparison of pre- and post-test scores. The positive effect of group intervention and support from people with similar life experiences can be studied as the reason behind this marked difference between the two phases (pre-post and post-follow-up). Further research would confirm the findings that group/support group therapy may have significant effect on the increased positive coping and immune competence of the PLWHA.

REFERENCES

Antoni, M.H., Cruess, S., Cruess, D.G., Kumar, M., Lutgendorf, S., Ironson, G.H., Dettmer, E., Williams, J., Klimas, N.G., Fletcher, M.A., & Schneiderman, N. (2000). Cognitive-behavioural stress management reduces distress and 24-hour urinary free cortisol output among symptomatic HIV-infected gay men. *Annals of Behavioural Medicine,* 22(1), 29-37.

Campbell, P.J., Aurelius, S., Blowes, G., & Harvey, D. (1997). Decrease in CD4 lymphocyte counts with rest: Implications for the monitoring of HIV infection. *International Journal of STD and AIDS,* 8(7), 423-426.

Carrico, A.W., Antoni, M.H., Duran, R.E., Ironson, G., Penedo, F., Fletcher, M.A., Kilmas, N., & Schneiderman, N. (2006). Reductions in depressed mood and denial coping during cognitive behavioural stress management with HIV-Positive gay men treated with HAART. *Annals of Behavioural Medicine,* 31(2), 155-64.

Carver, C.S., Scheier, M.F., & Weintraub, J.K. (1989). Assessing coping strategies: A theoretically based approach. *Journal of Personality and Social Psychology,* 56, 267-283.

Enumeration of T-Cell Subsets in Patients with HIV Infection, *Journal Watch: Medicine Matters.*http://aids-clinical-care.jwatch.org/cgi/content/full/1995/101/1#R1

Glaser, R., & Keicolt-Glaser. (2005). Stress induced immune dysfunction: Implications for health. *National Review of Immunology,* 5(3), 243-251.

Keicolt-Glaser. (2004). Hypnosis May Prevent Weakened Immune Status, Improve Health.htm, (STEP) sychoneuroimmunology and HIV; *Mind Body Connection & HIV.STEP PERSPECTIVE,* Volume 7, No. 2, Ohio-Columbia: Publication of the Seattle Treatment http://www.aegis.com/pubs/step/1995/STEP7204.

Kopnisky, K.L., Stoff, D.M., & Rausch, D.M. (2004).Workshop Report : The effects of psychological variables on the progression of HIV-1 disease. *Brain, Behaviour, and Immunity,* 18(3), 246-261.

Laidlaw, T.M., Kerstein, R., Bennett, B.M., Naito A., Henderson D.C.,

Dwivedi, P., & Gruzelier, J.H. (2004) Hypnotisability and immunological response to psychological intervention in HIV. *Contemporary Hypnosis,* 21, 126-135.

Langenfeld, M.C., Cipani, E., & Borckardt, J.J. (2002). Hypnosis for the control of HIV and AIDS related pain. *International Journal of Clinical and Experimental Hypnosis,* 50(2), 170-188.

Lazarus, R.S., & Folkman, S. (1984). *Stress, Appraisal and Coping.* New York: Springer.

Lutgendorf, S.K., Antoni, M.H., Ironson, G., Starr, K., Costello, N., Zuckerman, M., Klimas, N., Fletcher, M.A., & Schneiderman, N. (2007). Changes in cognitive coping skills and social support during cognitive behavioural stress management intervention and distress outcomes in symptomatic human immunodeficiency virus (HIV) — seropositive gay men. *Health Psychology.* 26(4), 473-480.

Mann, J. (1987). *Statement at an Informal Briefing on Global Programme on AIDS to the 42nd Session of the United Nations General Assembly,* 20 October, New York.

Mawar, N., Sahay, S., Pandit, A., & Mahajan, U. (2005). The third phase of HIV pandemic: Social consequences of HIV/AIDS stigma & discrimination & future needs. *Indian Journal of Medical Research, 122,* 471-484

Nott, K.H., & Vedhara, K.H. (2000). Psychoneuroimmunology and HIV Infection. In K.H. Nott & K. Vedhara (Eds.), *Psychosocial and Biomedical Interactions in HIV Infection.* London: Harwood Academic Publishers.

Nott, K.H., Vedhara, K., and Spickett (1995). Psychology, immunology, and HIV. *Psychoneuroendocrinology,* 20(5), 451-474.

Pert, C. (1997) *Molecules of Emotion: Why You Feel the Way You Feel.* Simon Schuster: Sydney.

Rucklide, J.J., & Saunders, D. (2002). The efficacy of hypnosis in the treatment of prutitus in people with HIV/AIDs: A time series analysis. *International Journal of Clinical and Experimental Hypnosis,* 50(2), 149-169.

Solomon, G.F., Temoshok, L., O'Leary, A., & Zich, J. (1987). An intensive psychoimmunologic study of long-surviving persons with AIDS: Pilot work, background studies, hypotheses, and methods. *Annals of the New York Academy of Sciences,* 496, 647-655.

UNAIDS (2005). *AIDS Epidemic Update: Special Report on HIV Prevention.* Report No. UNAIDS/05.19E URL http://www.unaids.org

Wangehaum, J. (2003). A study of Social support, Emotional Quotient and Spiritual Quotient among HIV Positive Individuals and Drug Addicts. Unpublished Masters Dissertation submitted to Department of Psychology, The M. S. University of Baroda, Gujarat, India.

World Health Organization (2003). Treating 3 Million by 2005. Making it happen. *The WHO Strategy.* Geneva: Author.

20

Experiences in Hypnosis

Stress Management and Psychosomatic Disease Situations

MUKESH TRIVEDI

Introduction

Stress is an inevitable part of everyday life. Life has become fast moving, more competitive and demanding. Difficulty or failure to keep pace results in stress. Stress is a biological term which refers to the consequences of the failure of a human or animal body to respond appropriately to emotional or physical threats to the organism, whether actual or imagined (Selye, 1956). It is "the autonomic response to environmental stimulus."

Stress could be major or minor. There can be social stress, business stress, financial stress, education related stress, relationship stress, or health stress. Social issues can cause stress, such as struggles with difficult individuals and/or relationship conflict, deception or breakup, and major events such as birth, death, marriage or divorce. Life experiences such as poverty, unemployment, depression, or insufficient sleep can also cause stress. Students and workers may face stress from exam, project deadlines, and group projects.

One can be affected by anyone particular type, or combination of more than one interrelated stressors. Expectedly, reaction to it varies from individual to individual and also as per the intensity of a situation. Mental build-up of the person concerned, counts as well.

Stress is not always harmful. Rather, some stress is necessary. It activates one, like nothing else does. That stress is positive stress. Some amount of stress increases adrenalin secretion and aids in improving performances. What, then, is negative stress? It is the stress which disturbs a person totally, upsets his concentration, his work schedule, his normal habits, and his mental equilibrium. Negative stress affects the body and also creates serious health problems. Long term, neglected stress can lead to depression and can result in general health problems such as ulcers, regular headaches, insomnia, constipation, hypertension, diabetes, asthma, stroke, vague pains in neck and lower back, permanent psychiatric illnesses and even cardiac problems.

Negative stress is sometimes referred to as "killer stress." Can stress really be fatal? The diseases it generates, can be killing agents, provided they are allowed to go uncontrolled and unchecked. Does it mean that once caught in the grip of stress there is no escape from its vicious hold? Not necessarily. Stress begins in the mind and then in time shows off on the body. The roots of high blood pressure, for example, might lie somewhere in one's inner self. Nerve-wrecking headache and subsequent development into heart attack are obviously physical symptoms. Stress and hence its ill effects can be managed under expert guidance. For managing stress the expert has to go deep into the mental condition of the patient, as well as his or her physical ailment. He has to be a physician, a psychotherapist and also a stress management expert.

Stress at Work

The stress problem does not trouble an individual only, it attacks and affects a group, a team or a particular section in an office as well. Handling such cases connected with the employees of an establishment is referred to as group stress management. Here a vital question can arise, "How can a whole group gets affected by stress?" This is an intensely competitive era, where two factors, timing and target play a crucial hand. When competition is hard, any innovation that comes first into the market, corners good clientele; hence, the need for right timing. Management's target is always to get the lion's share of the market. The staff in a business or corporate house remains under constant stress. Bosses press hard to keep a step ahead of rivals. It is also common knowledge, that when one is not mentally relaxed, one cannot concentrate fully on the task in hand. In such a case, production suffers; quality and marketing of production also suffers, contrary to the management expectations and objectives.

In the case of a group, stress moves quietly, noiselessly. But it does strike and with the passing of days, adds more and more to loss account. How then can group stress be managed? Rarely a single therapy works. Application of combination of therapies is needed.

Stress as a Cause of Psychosomatic Diseases

Physicians have long studied the connection between mind and body. One particularly interesting researcher in this area was Thomas Holmes who studied the association between stress and tuberculosis in the 1950s. Although lacking the sophistication of modern biostatistics, several of Holmes' studies suggested that persons who had experienced stressful situations, such as divorce, death of a spouse, or loss of a job, were more likely to develop tuberculosis and less likely to recover from it. Holmes (1956) consciously used the same scientific methods as his peers, devising a numeric scale that quantified stressful events and doing prospective studies with control groups. Although Holmes' work was rudimentary, his basic supposition may have been correct. Recent research, benefiting from advances in both immunology and biostatistics, suggests that stress may lead to decreased immune function and thus to clinical disease. As studies of stress and disease become more statistically sophisticated, it will be important to retain Holmes' emphasis on understanding the lives of individual patients (Holmes, 1978).

The interaction between psychosocial factors and the development of disease is attracting considerable attention

(Angell, 1985; Pelosi & Appleby, 1992). Much interest has been sparked by increasing knowledge of both neuroendocrinology and the immune system, which provides important insights into the ways in which mental stimuli produce physiologic changes (Plotnikoff *et al.*, 1991; Glaser, & Kiecolt-Glaser, 1994). Although the sophisticated tools necessary to answer these questions are of recent origin, the connection between the mind and disease has long intrigued both the general public and a subset of medical researchers.

The Therapies

Hypnosis, allopathic treatments, herbal medications, yoga, meditations, breathing exercises, massages, assertiveness training, visualization and biofeedback techniques are many ways of managing stress. They show significant detectable impact on the indicators of physical relaxation like respiratory rate, heart rate, oxygen requirements, muscle tension and controlling blood pressure. Hypnosis, which is often a less known and less practiced method of stress management, is one of the oldest and best techniques. It is neither a magical nor a mystical ritual but a more straightforward method in managing stress.

Hypnotherapy is the art as well as science of letting out emotions and feelings that are troubling individuals. It is a trance or deeply relaxed but focussed state. A hypnotherapist helps identify the causes for stress, a person's reaction to stress, gives stress reduction techniques and changes the person's approach in dealing stress in future. It also helps in ego strengthening.

Hypnosis can be used for reasons like simple relaxation, to more complex matters like pain relief during labour. It makes a person more confident and to face any obstacles with lot of courage in the future. Progressively relaxing muscles helps in lowering blood pressure, normalize pulse, respiration and perspiration.

Hypnosis is indicated for a wide range of unhealthy negative emotions, psychosomatic and stress-related disorders, including anger (damning), anxiety, asthma, allergies, behavioural problems (e.g. smoking, tics, over-eating and weight control), blushing, common and classic migraine, depression, guilt, hurt, hypertension, insomnia, irritable bowel syndrome, pain, phobias, physical tension, shame, skin disorders, (e.g. eczema), stress, speech disorders (e.g. stammering) and tension headache (Hartland, 1971; Palmer, 1993; Palmer and Dryden, 1995).

Rational emotive behavioural therapy or REBT helps in changing irrational self-inflicted beliefs to rational ones. It is a highly efficient method of stress management, which is an adjunct to hypnosis (Palmer & Dryden, 1995).

A Case Study

Of the several cases handled successfully in last five years, one case, typical of psychosomatic disease, is presented here.

A 42-year young lady presented with (i) Frequency of urination; (ii) Dysuria; (iii) Local irritation while passing urine; and (iv) Pain in and around vulva for the last 20 years.

Personal History—

—Education: Graduation with English literature.
—Used to work as a teacher till seven years ago.
—Father executive in MNC.
—Mother housewife.
—Has two younger brothers who are working with MNCs.
—Belongs to orthodox Brahmin family.
—Marital life: 20 years; not happy since day one of married life
—Husband General Manager in an MNC.
—One female child of 18 years of age.

Disease History

— Complete medical checkup was done two years back. All reports were normal. She was treated for urinary tract infection many times in last 20 years. Her urine culture was found normal every time except once two years ago.

Complete medical and clinical check up was done to assess the current status. All laboratory, radiological and clinical tests were conducted and found normal.

Provisional Diagnosis: As clinical tests were reported normal for the last 20 years, problem was considered as psychosomatic disease provisionally. In view of the history of long-standing emotional conflict in the context to married life, as brought out in the client's history, which seemed associated in time with an exacerbation of her symptoms of dysuria, and in view of many determining conflicts, it was decided that the patient should receive psychotherapy.

The Therapy

Stage 1

Relaxation Therapy by Meditation and Progressive Muscular Relaxation was conducted. It helped to ease, relax and prepare for therapy by parasympathetic system activation.

Stage 2

Cognitive behavioural therapy was utilized as its core premise is that activating events lead to negative automatic thoughts. These negative thoughts in turn result in disturbed negative feelings and dysfunctional behaviours. The goal is to reframe these irrational beliefs through structured sessions. By using belief system of the patient, she was further prepared for *Insight Generation* through psychoanalysis.

Stage 3

From a psychodynamic perspective, psychological dysfunctions are caused by unresolved unconscious conflicts of early development. Treatment focussed on bringing awareness to these unresolved conflicts and how they impact the patient's life. Psychoanalysis of some unresolved conflicts was facilitated by Age Regression. During meditation she was age regressed to the time, she was alright i.e., 20 years back to overview crucial points of this period, for insight generation.

Stage 4 (*Of insight generation*)

Age regression brought up deep seated issues of anger, and frustration on the surface. These issues were causing lot of distress which had physiological expression in terms of dysuria.

These issues were—

- —Love affair before marriage.
- —Could not marry 'him' due to parental pressures.
- —Forced marriage?
- —Present marriage—Adjustment?
- —Husband interested only in sex.
- —Attempt of abuse by father-in-law.
- —Felt violated?
- —Symptoms to avoid sex, 'Defense mechanism'?

Stage 5

Therapeutic Session was given for understanding the reasons of problem and acceptance of reality. The aim was to re-establish open communication in the relationship.

- —In hypnosis she was made to realize that she is fortunate that her health is good, and her husband still comes to her for his sexual needs. This is journey of life in which if you miss one train, you catch another and move on. The life is what happens to you when you are busy making other plans. Total four sessions, one per week, with above aim were conducted. Slowly patient started reducing the symptoms of dysuria. After six months, patient and her husband were contacted for feedback. Both were satisfied with their relationships and there were only occasional symptoms of dysuria.

Results, Discussion and Conclusion

The most striking finding of the case is that psychological conflicts can result in physiological expression, in this case as dysuria. Long ago, Auerback and Smith (1952) noted that "almost all patients with urinary frequency and urgency for which no physical causes can be found are women, and almost all are sexually repressed or even frigid, their symptoms originating situations of sexual frustration or temptation." Forced marriage, attempt of abuse by father-in-law and maladjustment with the husband reflect the similar pattern in the patient as observed by Auerback and Smith in their study. More recently, in a similar study on urinary disorder, Franzen *et al.* (2009) have concluded in their controlled research on patients that urinary incontinence among women is commonly associated with a number of different psychosocial problems as well as an expressed feeling of vulnerability.

There is sufficient evidence of the effectiveness of hypnotherapy in psychosomatic diseases. In a research, Flammer and Alladin (1997) undertook a meta study. They searched MEDLINE, PsycLIT and Dissertation Abstracts from 1887 to 2005. Studies were only included if they were reported in English, German or French. In addition, references from identified papers were screened. They concluded that hypnosis was a very effective treatment for patients with psychosomatic disorders such as tinnitus, insomnia, eneuresis, asthma, gastrointestinal problems, stress, chronic pain, osteoarthritis, chronic headache, conversion disorder, dermatitis and hay fever.

In present case the patient responded well as the sessions progressed. She was able to accept herself and the reality. Negative emotions, deeply rooted in subconscious, were addressed. The patient felt relaxed, and relieved of inner guilt as well as of the anger toward her husband. Follow up sessions after six months, and a year showed consistency and no signs of relapse.

REFERENCES

Angell, M. (1985). Disease as a reflection of the psyche. *N. Engl. J. Med.*, 312, 1570-1572.

Auerbach, A., & Smith, D.R. (1952). Psychosomatic Problems in Urology. *California Medi.*, 76 (1), 23-26.

Ellis, A., Gordon, J., Neenan, M., & Palmer, S. (1997) *Stress Counselling: A Rational Emotive Behaviour Approach.* London: Cassell.

Flammer, E., & Alladin, A. (2007). The efficacy of hypnotherapy in the treatment of psychosomatic disorders: Meta-analytical evidence. *International Journal of Clinical and Experimental Hypnosis,* 55, 3, 251-274.

Franzén, K., Johansson, J., Andersson, G., Pettersson, N., & Nilsson, K. (2009). Urinary incontinence in women is not exclusively a medical problem: A population-based study on urinary incontinence and general living conditions *Scandinavian Journal of Urology and Nephrology*, 43, 3, 226-232.

Glaser, R., & Kiecolt-Glaser, J. (1994) *Handbook of Human Stress and Immunity*. San Diego: Academic Press.

Hartland, J. (1971). *Medical and Dental Hypnosis and its Clinical Applications*. London: Bailliere Tindall.

Holmes, T.H. (1956). Multidiscipline studies of tuberculosis. In P. J. Sparer (Ed.), *Personality, Stress and Tuberculosis*. New York: International Universities Press.

Holmes, T.H. (1978). Life situations, emotions, and disease. *Psychosomatics,* 19, 747-754.

Palmer, S., & Dryden, W. (1995). *Counselling for Stress Problems*. London: Sage.

Palmer, S. (1993). *Multimodal Techniques: Relaxation and Hypnosis*. London: Centre for Stress Management.

Pelosi, A.J., & Appleby, L. (1992). Psychological influences on cancer and ischaemic heart disease. *BMJ*, 304, 1295-8.

Plotnikoff, P., Murgo, A., Faith, R., & Wybran, J. (1991). *Stress and Immunity*. Boca Raton: CRC.

Selye, H. (1956). *The Stress of Life*. New York: McGraw-Hill.

21

Use of Hypnotherapy for the Treatment of Paraphilia among Bisexual Men

VEENA GUPTA

Introduction

The ancient Indian writings from the Vedic and ancient period show that intense and passionate relationships between men and women have always existed in India. In early periods homosexuality was considered to be very natural and an inevitable emotional aspect of human sexual life. For this reason, homosexual relationships were accepted and not considered abnormal. Pradhan *et al.* (1982) noted that "homosexuality was not a condemned mode of sexual gratification when the temple sculptors of Konark and Khajuraho were depicting it in stone for all posterity to see." The attitude toward homosexuality however changed in the nineteenth century and is now considered unnatural (Vanita & Kidwai, 2000).

The phrase "Men who have Sex with Men" (MSM) refers to those men who engage in sex relationships exclusively with other men (Homosexuality) or who engage in sex relations with either men or women (Bisexuality). In the global programme on AIDS conference in Geneva (1992-93) governments accepted the behavioural phrase "men who have sex with men" as a depoliticized euphemism. The phrase "men who have sex with men" is a collective social identity for all men who have sex with men irrespective of how they might identify themselves (Pandya, 2008).

Men who have sex with other men in India are diverse in their sexual identities. Some identify with the modern 'gay' or 'bisexual' identity while others with indigenous sexual identities like 'Koti'/'Durani'—feminized male, usually a sexually passive partner; or 'Panthi'/'Giriya'–masculine male and usually a sexually active partner. 'Double-decker'/'Dupli' (DD) refers to those who penetrate their partners and are penetrated by their partners. 'Panthi'/'Parikh' or 'Giriya' and 'DD' are labels and usually not 'identities' (Pandya, 2008).

The National AIDS Control Organization (NACO), through its counterparts in the States/Union Territories, is mapping high risk behaviour populations in India. The agency has put the categorized data on MSM at NACO website.

Paraphilia

The paraphilias are sexual dysfunctions characterized by recurrent, intense sexual urges, fantasies, or behaviours that involve unusual objects, activities, or situations and cause clinically significant distress or impairment in social, occupational, or other important areas of functioning (Brannon, 2002). The paraphilias include exhibitionism (exposure of genitals), fetishism (use of nonliving objects), frotteurism (touching and rubbing against non-consenting person), pedophilia (focus on prepubescent children), sexual masochism (receiving humiliation or suffering), sexual sadism (inflicting humiliation or suffering), transvestic fetishism (cross-dressing), and voyeurism (observing sexual activity).

The essential features of a paraphilia are recurrent, intense sexually arousing fantasies, sexual urges, or behaviours generally involving :

1. Non-human objects;
2. The suffering or humiliation of oneself or one's partner; and
3. Children or other non-consenting persons, that occur over a period of at least 6 months.

For some individuals, paraphiliac fantasies or stimuli are obligatory for erotic arousal and are always included in sexual activity.

In other cases, the paraphiliac preferences occur only episodically (e.g. perhaps during periods of stress), whereas at other times the person is able to function sexually without paraphiliac fantasies or stimuli. The behaviour, sexual urges, or fantasies cause clinically significant distress or impairment in social, occupational, or other important areas of functioning.

Paraphiliac imagery may be acted out with a non-consenting partner in a way that may be injurious to the partner (as in sexual sadism or pedophilia). The individual may be subject to arrest and incarceration. Sexual offences against children constitute a significant proportion of all reported criminal sex acts, and individuals with exhibitionism, pedophilia and voyeurism make up the majority of apprehended sex offenders. In some situations, acting out the paraphiliac imagery may lead to self-injury (as in sexual masochism). Social and sexual relationships may suffer if others find the unusual sexual behaviour shameful or repugnant or if the individual's sexual partner refuses to cooperate in the unusual sexual preferences. In some instances, the unusual behaviour (e.g. exhibitionistic acts or the collection of fetish objects) may become the major sexual activity in the individual's life. These individuals are rarely self-referred and usually come to the attention of mental health professionals only when their behaviour has brought them into conflict with sexual partners or society.

Exhibitionism

The paraphiliac focus in exhibitionism involves the exposure of one's genitals to a stranger (Abouesh & Clayton, 1999). Sometimes the individual masturbates while exposing himself (or while fantasizing exposing himself). If the person acts on these urges, there is generally no attempt at further sexual activity with the stranger. In some cases, the individual is aware of a desire to surprise or shock the observer. In other cases, the individual has the sexually arousing fantasy that the observer will become sexually aroused. The onset usually occurs before the age of 18 years, although it can begin at a later age. Few arrests are made in the older age groups, which may suggest that the condition becomes less severe after the age of 40 years.

Frotteurism

The paraphiliac focus of frotteurism involves touching and rubbing against a non-consenting person. The behaviour usually occurs in crowded places from which the individual can more easily escape arrest (e.g. on busy sidewalks or in public transportation vehicles). He rubs his genitals against the victim's thighs and buttocks or fondles her genitalia or breasts with his hands. While doing this he usually fantasizes an exclusive caring relationship with the victim. However, he recognizes that to avoid possible prosecution, he must escape detection after touching his victim. Usually the paraphilia begins by adolescence. Most acts of frottage occur when the person is in age range of 15-25 years after which there is a gradual decline in frequency.

Voyeurism

The paraphiliac focus of voyeurism involves that act of observing unsuspecting individuals, usually strangers, who are naked, in the process of disrobing, or engaging in sexual activity (Abouesh & Clayton, 1999). The act of looking (peeping) is for the purpose of achieving sexual excitement and generally no sexual activity with the observed person is sought. Orgasm, usually produced by masturbation, may occur during the voyeuristic activity or later in response to the memory of what the person has witnessed. Often these individuals have the fantasy of having a sexual experience with the observed person, but in reality this rarely occurs. In its severe form, peeping constitutes the exclusive form of sexual activity. The onset of voyeuristic behaviour is usually before the age of 15 years. The course tends to be chronic.

Gender identity disorders are characterized by strong and persistent cross-gender identification accompanied by persistent discomfort with one's assigned sex.

It is important to note that notions of deviance, standards of sexual performance, and concepts of appropriate gender role can vary from culture to culture.

Objectives of the Study

The main aim of the study was to find out the ways and mechanisms for therapeutic intervention for bringing about behaviour change for paraphilias among five bisexual men of Vadodara city. The main objectives of the study were :

1. To identify the underlying issues of the clients;
2. To identify the high risk behaviour for these clients; and
3. To bring about behaviour change (reduction) in high risk behaviour.

Methodology

The present study was conducted upon five MSMs who were in contact with Lakshya Trust, Vadodara. Lakshya Trust is a community-based organization working on various issues addressing and advocating the social, economical, legal, mental and sexual health issues of sexual minorities i.e. gay, lesbian, bisexual and transgender populations of Vadodara, Surat and Rajkot cities of Gujarat. For the study, a prior permission was taken from the management of Lakshya Trust and a schedule of one session per week was arranged with the group. The group was not charged for the psychotherapeutic services. The entire group was called in for group counselling session.

In the first session, history was taken using a history-taking format, issues were identified, usual responses to the issues involved were listed and the coping patterns to deal with the issues were identified. The issues reflected from the history-taking format were having multiple partners for sexual relationships, more than two sexual penetration in a week, no/irregular use of condoms with regular as well as casual partners, sex with total strangers, group sex activities and no/very low concern for self and personal health. Personal interview with all the clients individually also reflected these issues: seen as Sex Symbol; comments from the neighbours and local people; approached for sexual relationship only; harassment from cheaters and delinquents; physical abuse; fearful of going out anywhere with the family members especially with female figures of the family because of fear of any obscene comment from other people and their approach to family members for sexual relationships (the extent can go up to social phobia); far from newspapers and news channels because of their constant reporting about homosexual behaviour and orientation without or very low understanding of sensitivity of the issue; fearful of family members for their non-acceptance, constant comments, and consistent force to prove that the homosexual relationship and orientation is unnatural, dirty, and abnormal; torture, violence, abuse and harassment of physical, mental, sexual and economic nature from/by the family members and outsiders also; no importance in family due to sexual preference and feminine mannerisms; no social, emotional, and economic support from anyone; etc. Also, narrations of some of the behaviours not socially sanctioned (term used by two of the clients individually) are the exposure of one's genitals to a stranger, touching and rubbing against a non-consenting person (particularly men) and observing unsuspecting individuals, strangers, known persons who are naked, in the process of disrobing, or engaging in sexual activity. If we refer to DSM IV-TR, then there were occurrence of Gender Identity Disorder as well, which is characterized by strong and persistent cross-gender identification accompanied by persistent discomfort with one's assigned sex.

In the second session, the diagnosis was done and individual issues were discussed in detail. Out of the five clients, four had exhibitionism, three had frotteurism and all the five had voyeurism. Based on the similar age, similar experiences and their agreement, a group was formed and thence onwards therapy sessions were conducted in group setting only. The group norms of confidentiality, regularity of time and attendance were established by the clients. The detailed discussion of issues led to probing of their feelings and the defense mechanisms adopted by them. There were feelings of guilt and shame; deep hurt, rage and anger; constant fear; consistent guilt for feminine behaviour; confusion about self identity and sexual identity; helpless and hopeless from life; wish to leave everything and run away from everyone; feel like committing suicide as a solution for all their issues; wish to kill others who comment or harass them; wish to remain/live alone, wish that parents and relatives die so that they do not get affected; want to fight with the "outside world"; strong feeling of rage and revenge; avoidance—tend to avoid almost everybody who is known to them or their family; feelings of sadness and experience of extreme restlessness; difficulty in getting sleep; continuous negative thoughts; constant irritation and also experience of extreme irritability etc. The adopted ways to deal with the issues were increased alcohol intake; increased cigarette smoking; throwing and breaking things and articles; listening to and singing songs; keeping quiet and silent till some time and then experience sudden burst-outs; overly love and attention to family; staying away from family; verbal fights with peers; staying away from the particular places in anticipation of any kind of problem/ row; suppress anger and wrath, then experience more increased problems; increased sexual activity; get disinterested from sexual activities; reading books; going out to distant places where known people are not around; neglecting or avoiding fights and focussing upon recreational activities; watching movies and going out for stroll alone or with like minded people; and if the situation becomes unbearable, then, meeting the counsellor. The goals of the therapy sessions were decided which were to know the ways for dealing with negative feelings; to learn relaxation and positive thinking; to reduce high risk behaviour and to reduce the incidents of exhibitionism, voyeurism, and frotteurism. It was consensus in the session that the negative responses coming from the society at large cannot be changed but the response to those reactions of society can be managed. Hence, the need of basic understanding of self, self-confidence and self-esteem, and positive approach in day-to-day living were decided to be addressed in the therapy sessions.

In the third session, a detailed understanding of hypnotherapy was given and all the queries related to effectiveness of hypnotherapy were attended. Questions like hypnotizability and mechanisms of relaxation were answered. The issues of external locus of control, low self-esteem, self-concept and self-confidence were discussed in detail for insight generation. Inputs from the group were invited and proper understanding of self-concept was brought in.

In the fourth session, simple suggestions for relaxation were given to the entire group. Progressive muscular relaxation and deep breathing exercise were adopted for induction of relaxation. The entire group was given the task of administering deep breathing exercise on self, everyday before sleeping.

In the fifth session, deepening techniques were administered. Active progressive muscular relaxation (PMR) was adopted as deepening technique. Therapeutic suggestions were given based on the creative skills that they had for strengthening of the self, self-concept and the self-confidence. Suggestions like appreciating the self for the creativity, openness and the strength were given. Ego-strengthening was done and positive suggestions were given based on the positive defense mechanisms adopted and on the other positive attributes of the clients. The entire group was then asked if they had any queries about PMR, which were addressed and they were asked to practice PMR daily before sleeping and/or after waking up in the morning. The clients already reported of better memory and better sleep.

In the sixth session, the clients were provided with the basic principles of behavioural learning (conditioning and relearning) and rationales for specific procedures to modify undesirable response patterns. This helped them develop a sense of control and participation in the treatment. Developing pleasant images to use in trance inductions were difficult with this group of clients because of multiple instances of unpleasurable experiences they have had on a daily basis. However, all of them had reported a passion for travelling and going to distant tourist places where no one recognized them. This was taken as a clue and pleasant imageries based upon these experiences were made. The imageries developed were going to a mountain/hill area, viewing the sunrise, seeing the water fountains and flowing river. The sunrise and experiencing the pleasant sun rays was taken as an archetypal symbol of protection and care. The water fountain and flowing river were used as archetypal symbols for sex and sexual experiences; the intensity of water fountain, the force of flowing river, and then the river becoming calm and quiet. Therapeutic suggestions were given to the entire group to recognize the irrational justifications that they offer for their behaviour, and to alter other distorted thinking patterns especially for sexual behaviour. Hypnotherapeutic suggestions (like recognizing the common behaviour pattern of sex relationships and more subtle way of expressing one's own sexual desire) were also given to replace fantasies of exposing themselves with fantasies of more acceptable sexual behaviour while indulging into the sexual act.

In the seventh session, therapeutic suggestions were given for even deeper state of relaxation and a little control over self-behaviour and impulses so as not to offend anyone else and hence protect themselves from any kind of social trouble. Systematic decrease in the sensation seeking behaviour using hypnotic imagery (of not getting enough excitement and pleasure from the acts of exhibitionism/voyeurism/frotteurisms; while experiencing enough excitement and pleasure from the acts of sexual relations with one's own partner) and framing of statements with positive consequences was utilized. By the end of seventh session, the clients were able to relax themselves whenever they practiced PMR and deep breathing. They had also generated an insight about their underlying feeling of rage and contempt for the society at large. One of the clients spoke about this and had catharsis. He was given proper time to let his feelings out and after he calmed down and was ready for further talk, this issue was discussed with the group in detail. They all recalled the account of their own similar experiences. And slowly the discussion revealed a deep rooted dislike for the self and rejection of the self. Since, the time of the session was already over, this was scheduled for the next session's discussion.

In the eighth session, a detailed discussion for self-rejection and self-dislike took place. Since all of them were familiar with the Hindu mythological scripture *Ramayana,* the incident of Rama leaving for jungles for 14 years and people following him requesting him not to go away till the riverfront was taken into the hypnotic session. When Rama told the people—all the men and women return back to their homes, and then all the third gender people stayed back at the riverbank only. When Rama was returning back after completing 14 years of his renouncing his palace, he saw some people still staying at the riverbank; he stopped there to ask them who they were. They recognized him as their Lord and told him that he never told them to go back to their homes, so they stayed there only. Rama was delighted to see their devotion and gave them the goodwill that other people for their devotion and generosity will worship them. Therapeutic suggestions were given for self-acceptance, self-love and for attaining more health oriented behaviour and protecting the self from risks pertaining to one's own behaviour.

In the ninth session, therapeutic suggestions were given for attaining enlightenment and solving queries related to the self. A permissive and accepting therapeutic atmosphere was maintained that permitted the clients to occasionally open their eyes for reassurance and then return to the images. In between the several brief trances used during this session, feedback, encouragement and explanations were provided.

In the tenth session, therapeutic suggestions were given for improving the quality and way of life style (like realizing the sense of self and self responsibility, recognition of the needs and the ways to fulfil them by working positively and continuously, and more importantly, being able to take decisions for the self and for the related individuals if need be) along with attaining more control in the life events, hence addressing the need for locus of control.

In the eleventh session, suggestions of the sixth session were repeated.

In the twelfth session, suggestions from the seventh session were repeated.

In the thirteenth session, suggestions from the eighth session were repeated.

In the fourteenth session, suggestions were given for adopting better life skills and dealing constructively with the stresses and frustrations.

In the fifteenth session, suggestions were given for dealing positively and constructively with the issues one may encounter in further life.

Each therapeutic session was of about 90 minutes duration, once every week. After every session, the feedback from the participants was taken and their queries were attended to.

Results and Discussion

All homosexual men, like heterosexual men, are raised in a homophobic society. Such societal homophobia mobilizes other psychological processes that extend beyond the development of prejudice, stigma and discrimination. For example, one client reported suffering such derogatory terms as '*gudd*', 'sister', 'homo', or '*halwa*' since childhood. Later, he attributed the same words to himself and it was very stressful. One of the most commonly seen adaptation strategies amongst men who have sex with men is internalized homophobia i.e. incorporation of negative feelings into their self-image.

After fifteen sessions of hypnotherapy, there was observable change in their behaviour, notably in terms of self-acceptance and their ability to self-control in not involving in paraphilia. The results (no incident/occurrence of exhibitionism, voyeurism and frotteurism in three months subsequent to the sessions—the number of incidents came down from 9-10 incidents a week to no incident for 3 months continuously) indicated that there was a significant change in behaviour in the group by the end of the sessions. Also, there was reduction in number of casual sexual partners and hundred per cent use of condom in sexual relationship; hence significant change in high risk sexual behaviour.

Follow up of the participants after two months indicated relapse of one participant for voyeurism and relapse of one participant for high-risk sexual behaviour.

Follow up of the participants after one year indicated the practice of modified behaviour by the three participants and all of them were aspiring and working effectively for self-growth and development.

REFERENCES

American Psychiatric Association. (2000). Diagnostic and Statistical Manual of Mental Disorders. 4th Edition. Washington, DC: Author.

Abouesh, A., & Clayton, A. (1999). Compulsive voyeurism and exhibitionism: A clinical response to paroxetine. *Archives of Sexual Behaviour,* 28, 23-30.

Brannon, Guy E. (2002). Paraphilias. *Medicine Journal,* 3.

NACO. (2004). Annual Report 2002-03, 2003-04 National AIDS Control Organization, Ministry of Health and Family Welfare, accessed at http://www.nacoonline.org/publication.htm accessed on 10/29/2004.

Pandya, A. (2008). *Voices of Invisibles: Coping Responses of Men Who Have Sex with Men (MSM).* Retrieved 20/11/2008 www.strength basedstrategies.com/.../12 per cent20PandyaFormatted.pdf.

Pradhan, P.V. *et al.* (1982). Male homosexuality: A psychiatric study of thirteen cases. *Indian J. of Clinical Psychiatry,* 24(2), 182-186.

Vanita, R., & Kidwai, S. (2000). *Same Sex Love in India: Readings from Literature and History.* Delhi: MacMillan India Ltd.

PART III
Philosophical Perspectives on Consciousness

22

Transcending the Normal Limit

The Nyāya-Vaiśesika Reflections

V. N. JHA

cancalam hi manah Kṛsna pramāthi balavaddrdham/
tasyāhan nigrahan manye vāyor iva suduṣ karam//[1]

'O Krishna, mind, indeed, is fickle; it is so strong, so aggressive, and powerful that it is very difficult to control it, as difficult as the wind.'

mana eva manusyānām kāranam bandha-mokhsayoh/
bandhanam visayāsaktir muktyai nirvisayam manah//[2]

'Mind, indeed, is the cause of both, the conditioning and the deconditioning of the self. The conditioning means mind's attachment to its objects and in the deconditioned state the mind becomes objectless.'

There are two states of human beings: (a) the conditioned (*baddha*) state; and (b) the unconditioned or deconditioned (*mukta*) state. The conditioned state is the normal state in which we all are situated in this moment and the unconditioned or deconditioned state is our original state towards which our journey is on, through different forms of lives.

To deal with the normal state, we human beings are given a world of our experience, a part of which is internal and another part is external. We internalize both and behave with them all through our lives.

For the process of internalization, we are given five external sense organs and one internal sense organ. Eyes, nose, ears, touch and tongue are external sense organs and mind is postulated as the internal sense organ. When the external senses come in contact with the external world, there arises the perception of the external world and we perceive the inner world through our mind.

Mind Performs Two Functions

(1) It establishes contact of the self with the external world through the external senses on one hand; and
(2) It reveals the inner world directly on the other[3]. The mind also creates awareness of the existence of both the worlds, external and internal. Although the mind does not have direct access to the external world in normal condition, it does have direct access to the knowledge of the external world.

Mind is an instrument which is used by the self to internalize both the external as well as the internal world[4].

Self is a distinct spiritual substance which is neither our body, nor senses nor our mind. It is the self which alone can have consciousness, at the same time self is not consciousness. Self is the locus of consciousness. Self is the knower, the agent, the initiator, and the enjoyer. In all its roles, self uses mind as an instrument[5].

But since in ordinary conditions a self remains conditioned, there are bound to be limitations in its roles. It can perceive the world, no doubt, but only under certain conditions.

Eyes reveal colour; nose reveals smell; ears reveal sound; skin reveals touch and tongue reveals taste. But all this happens under certain conditions. Not only that the eyes reveal only colour and nose reveals only smell and so on, but they reveal respective qualities only under certain conditions. For instance, eyes can reveal colour only if there is sufficient light; they can reveal colour only if the observer is attentive and not absent-minded; only when the eyes are not defective; only when the object is at a visible range; only if the locus of colour is also visible; under such and many more such conditions the eyes can reveal colour[6]. The same is the story with other senses too. They too reveal their respective objects under a limited condition.

Mind is the only common factor without which no knowledge is possible[7]. Unless the self uses the mind consciously no knowledge will occur to him. As the popular saying goes:

anytra-manā abhūvam na kincid adrākṣam

"I was absent-minded and hence I could not see anything."

Any normal human-being is found encountering this state.

Thus, perception is restricted by several factors which are either in the perceiver's instruments such as senses and mind, or in the object of perception or in the external factors acting as auxiliary causes of perception. It is in this sense, normal human beings are conditioned by limitations. We all are in this state in the present moment.

But this is not our real or original state. The Nyāya-Vaiśesika System of Indian Philosophy has postulated the real nature of self as unconditioned one. In that state the self is a pure spiritual substance (*nirguna-dravya*).

The conditioned self, therefore, wants to discover or get back that original state which is his deconditioned state. The Indian philosophical systems believe that this is possible through transformation[8].

In a transformed state the limitations of the conditioned state are loosened. The glimpses of this transformation can be had even from our normal experience. We have normal perceptions with five external senses through normal six types of contact called *laukika-sannikarsa* and also super-normal perception through three types of super-normal contacts called *alaukika-sannikarsa*. The *alaukika-sannikarsas* are *jnāna-laksaṇa-pratyāsatti, sāmānya laksaṇa-pratyāsatti* and *yogaja-sannikarsa*[9].

When we see a piece of sandal wood from a long distance and we say that it is fragrant, this is a perception of smell. But how could it happen without bringing the sandal wood in contact with the nose? Here, the Indian logicians explain this perception by introducing the idea of a super-normal perception.

The contact between the nose and the sandal wood in this case is not a normal one but supernormal. It is the remembrance of one's previous experience of smell of the sandal wood which is acting as the contact between the nose and the sandal wood. This is our day-to-day experience which needs to be explained and this cannot be explained without postulating a super-normal contact. Such contact is called *jnāna-laksaṇa-pratyāsatti*[10].

Similarly, when we infer fire on the mountain from seeing the smoke on it, it implies that we know the invariable relationship (*vyāpti*) between smokes and fires. But how could this happen? It is not possible to physically see all smokes and fires of the world, including the past and future smokes and fires. Then how can we say: wherever there is smoke there is fire? But again, it is our day-to-day experience that we infer fire on the basis of smoke. To explain this, the Indian logicians suggest that we have to transcend this limitation by postulating a super-normal contact between our eyes and all smokes and all fires. This is done by saying that since the universal in smokes namely, "smoke", is only one and the universal in fires namely, "fire", is also only one, even if we see one instance of smoke and one instance of fire, we are seeing, as a matter of fact, all smokes and all fires through the contact of those universals. In this way, such universals like "smoke" and "fire" themselves are playing the role of connecting our eyes with all individuals belonging to their respective classes. This super-normal contact is called *sāmānya laksana-pratyāsatti*[11]. This is another instance of transcending the normal limit of perception even within the normal range of our experience.

Still another instance of transcending the limit is the perception of the transformed selves like the *yogins*. In the perception of *yogins* all limitations of normal human perceptions are transcended. What is achieved through the external senses can be achieved by mind directly. Thus a *yogin* can see colour by closing his eyes directly by his mind. What is considered to be beyond the range of sensual perception (*atīndriya*) is believed to be directly perceptible by a *yogin*.

Although a gross substance is visible in normal perception, atomic substances are not so. But a *yogin* can see even that. Objects of the past and future are beyond the range of normal perception, but they are very much within the range of yogic perception. In transcending these limits, only one instrument is required and that is the mind. But why does the mind not cross the limit in ordinary perception but crosses in the yogic perception only? Obviously, the *yogins* develop extraordinary properties (*yogaja-dharma*) in association with which the mind can transcend all limitations of ordinary perceptions. To develop that, one has to take recourse to the *Yogaśāstra* of Patanjali. Once a person starts practicing the yogic methods, he starts transcending the limits because a gradual transformation starts occurring in him.

The Indian logicians have classified the transformed selves i.e. *yogins* into two categories: (a) those who are in the process of transformation (*yunjāna*); and (b) those who have already reached the height of transformation (*yukta*). The persons in the first category will gradually transcend the limitations of perception and those who are transformed will finally transcend those limitations for ever[12].

In order to make it understandable and in order to create hope for transformation through the practice of yogic methods the Nyāya-Vaiśesika system cites examples of ranges of perception in various species of living beings. For instance, we cannot see in the darkness but cats can see; we cannot see an object if the object is beyond the range of normal perception, but vultures can see from a long distance (*yojana-śata* 'hundred *yojanas*')[13]. We also know how the kingfisher takes out fish from a huge distance by diving deep into the water; the examples can be multiplied.

What all three examples suggest is that there are variations in the perceptions of living beings. Even within human beings there are variations of capacities, some of them are natural and some of them are developed through rigorous practices. For example, while a part of intelligence is natural, the power of remembrance can be increased through the traditional methods of *samsthā-grahana* (the mode of acquisition of the Vedic texts). Similarly, one can increase one's physical capacity through exercises.

Therefore, there is nothing impossible in developing a transformed state of self through the yogic practices.

One cannot argue that there should be an upper limit to any transformation and beyond that it is impossible to transcend the upper limit. For instance, one can acquire lightness of one's body by removing fat through exercises or medicine and can become a champion in jumping competition, but by no means through such practices one can jump an ocean or Mount Everest[14].

Jayanta Bhatta, the Kashmiri logician of the ninth century AD, says that this argument may be true with regard to the acquisition of physical excellence, but no such argument is tenable with regard to the transformation of mental capacity. Through the yogic method an impure and agitated mind is transformed into a pure and calm mind and once the mind is purified and becomes calm there is no limit which can put any challenge to it for its transformation. The yogic practices will keep on purifying the mind like the fire purifies the gold. As the gold shines brighter and brighter so also the mind will keep on taking self to higher and higher states by removing gradually all impurities such as *rāga* (excessive attachment), *dvesa* (hatred), *ahamkāra* (ego) etc. This is how the yogis pass through the state of *yunjāna* and reach the state of *yukta*. Once they reach that state they transcend all limitations which an ordinary human being is likely to encounter. A *yogin*, therefore, can have mental perception of any object[15].

According to Indian logicians, a *yukta* variety of a *yogin* can see even *dharma* and *adharma* which have been declared as something beyond the range of human mind by Kumārila, the propounder of the Bhātta school of *Pūrvamīmāmsā*.

Kumārila did not accept any yogic perception and this position of Kumārila was contested by the Indian logicians and the yogic perception was established[16].

A yogin can perceive an object of past, present and future[17].

To create a belief and hope in this fact Jayanta Bhatta presents an ordinary example of intuition. He says that it may be an experience of many that on some day a sister intensely thinks of her brother and says that her brother will come tomorrow and it is corroborated more than once by the fact that her brother does come on the same day. How to explain this extraordinary perception of the sister when there is no source to know the coming of the brother? It is merely her mind which has informed her that her brother will come tomorrow[18].

So, it is clear that even an ordinary human being can know the future, what to talk of *yogis* who have undergone a very intense exercise to reach this state. Therefore, one should not have any disbelief or doubt regarding the possibility of transformation in self by transcending the ordinary limitations of ordinary perceptions by following yogic practices. By the practice of yogic methods one can reach different heights. Yogic practices generate extraordinary capacities (*yogaja-dharma*) through which one can transcend ordinary limitations of ordinary human beings, the Indian analytic reflections corroborate this fact.

What is necessary to achieve this is the control over our mind and gradual purification of mind in order to bring the mind to a state of calmness. It is the agitated mind that causes all our sufferings. An agitated mind is an impure mind and it blocks the reality to appear in its true form and that paves the way for the enemies like greed (*lobha*), craziness (*moha*), egoistic attitude (*ahamkāra*) etc. to create their habitat in each one of us. Therefore, in the diagnosis and remedial action-plan of Patanjali the immediate goal of ordinary human beings should be to achieve *yoga* which is defined as *citta-vrtti-nirodha* 'merging the mind into its source'[19].

The ultimate aim of human life should be to discover one's own Form or State and to be permanently in that State.[20]

This is possible only through *yoga*.

In the journey towards that goal, however, human beings will receive additional incidental results (*ānusangika phala* or *avāntara-phala*) such as different kinds of *siddhis* including entering into other's body (*para-śarīrāveśa*)[21].

But, Patanjali has warned that the aim of Yogaśāstra is not meant for generating *siddhis*. Not only that, if one indulges too much in developing that faculty there is likelihood that the practitioner may be tempted to indulge in immoral acts.[22] Thus, for those who have decided to go for the ultimate aim of life i.e. *ātma-sākṣātkāra*, these *siddhis* are going to be hindrances.

Nevertheless, if these abilities are developed through the practice of yogic methods and used for the service of man it must be encouraged. As long as there is *viveka* in man and he is capable of making a distinction between good and bad, any knowledge is good for humanity.

Hypnosis or *yoga-nidrā* is also a kind of *siddhi* and if it is used with a sense of service, I think, one must appreciate it and welcome it.

REFERENCES

1. *Bhagavadgītā*, 6.34.
2. *Trīpurātāpanyupanisat, 5.6.*
3. *Nyāyasūtra*, 1.1.4.
4. *Sukha-duḥkhādy-upalabdhi-sādhanam indriyam mahaḥ*, Tarkasamgraha, edited by Ramachandra Jha, p. 13, Chowkhamba, 2003.
5. *Nyāyasiddhānta-muktāvalī*, Verses, 47-49.
6. *Nyāya-vārttika* on *Nyāyasūtra*, 1.1.4
7. *Manorūpendriya-janyam sarvam eva jnānam*, Nyāyasiddhānta-muktāvalī on Verse no. 51.
8. *Duḥkha-janma-pravrtti-dosa-mithyājnānānām uttarottarāpāye tad-anantarāpāyād apavargah*, Nyāyasūtra, 1.1.2
9. *Nyāyasiddhānta-muktāvalī*, Verse no. 63.
10. *Ibid.*, Verse no. 64-65.
11. *Loc. cit.*
12. *Nyāyasiddhānta-muktāvalī*, Verse no. 65-66.
13. Jayanta Bhatta's *Nyāyamanjarī*, Part I, p. 268.
14. *Ibid.*, pp. 272-274.
15. *Loc. cit.*
16. *Ibid., pp.* 270-71.
17. *Yatra asya parah prakarsah te yogino gīyante/darśanasya ca paro'tiśayah sūksma-vyavahita-viprakrsṭa-bhūta-bhavisyadādi-visayatvam*, Nyāyamanjarī, p. 268.
18. *Nyāyamanjarī*, pp. 272-74.
19. *Sva-kārane layah*, Vyāsa-bhāsya on *Yogasūtra* 1.2.
20. *Tadā drasṭuh svarūpe avasthānam, Yogasūt*ra 1.3.
21. *Yogasūtra*, 3.39.
22. *Samādhau upasargāh vytthāne siddhayah*, Yogasūtrá 3.38.

23

The Varieties of Religious Experiences of William James and Unification of Ennobling Experiences in *Turya*

RUPA VYAS

The Varieties of Religious Experience was first presented as a series of lectures at the University of Edinburgh in 1901. To prepare for the talks, Harvard psychologist William James had read widely in the religious classics, including the personal accounts of various saints and mystics.

William James was a scientist to begin with and ended being a pragmatist philosopher at the end. The detour included being anatomist and a psychologist. He must have been a materialist too, since he argued about the utility of the spiritual experiences. Probably his is the first rational and objective inquiry into spiritual experiences and, one of the many attempts of his times to persuade the scientifically-minded that mystic experience is actual; it is no illusion or hallucination.

James harped on the abstract quality like immediate luminousness of spiritual experience while also dwelling on parameters such as philosophical reasonableness and utilitarian value of moral helpfulness. Thus James is a correct blend of science and spirituality, so much so that he disregards—as medical materialism—the medical evidence of Fox, the Founder of Quaker Movement, being a schizophrenic. James said, "We find such persons in every age, passionately flinging themselves upon their sense of the goodness of life, in spite of the hardships of their own condition. From the outset, their religion is one of union with the divine." This is, indeed, replicated in the Beautiful Mind of Nobel Prize winning schizophrenic of our century. He describes such individuals as seeing God, "not as a strict Judge, not as a Glorious Potentate, but as the animating Spirit of a beautiful harmonious world, Beneficent and Kind, Merciful as well as Pure."

James recognized a pattern in experiences. It tended to happen when people were so low that they just 'gave up', the vacuum of hope providing space for revelation. The religious literature is full of stories along these lines, in which the constrictions and negative aspects of the ego are finally discarded; one begins to live only for others or for some higher goal. The compensation for becoming dependent upon God is a letting go of fear, and it is this that makes it a liberating experience. It is the fearlessness and sense of absolute security. It can be simply the belief in an unseen order, to which our task was to "harmoniously adjust ourselves".

James cites in detail about the experiences of St. Paul's, St. Augustine's and Teresa of Avila. He quotes a passage from St. Teresa's autobiography, in which she talks about her visions. At the time some suspected she was seeing the devil, not God, but she protested that what she saw could not be just the work of the imagination, since it had made her a much better person ("uprooting my vices, and filling me with a masculine courage"). Teresa also made a distinction between imaginings and spiritual reality, pointing out that while pure imagination weakens the mind and soul, 'genuine heavenly vision' revitalizes and strengthens the subject. In Teresa's case, she felt that her visitations guided her to a better order in the world around. These 'visitations' may have come from inside a saint's own mind, or they *may indeed have been from God*. What was sure was that they could transform a life.

There are numerous—innumerable such instances in Indian tradition. We may take Narsinh Mehta as just one illustration. It is said: Narsinh Mehta was a worshipper of Lord Shiva. Pleased with him, Lord Shiva took him to witness the divine dance—*Krishna Lila.* Witnessing the divine celestial event, Narsinh got so absorbed that the torch that he was holding got finished and started burning his hand. Not even the pain or the smell of burning flesh could distract him. He returned from the experience as a transformed person.

From the recent past, we have Sri Ramkrishna Paramhans. He was known to undergo spontaneous trance. One such experience is that of his seeing flying a pair of swans in the sky that put him into a deep spontaneous trance. Reading the details of this will at once convince us that it was none other than *Turya*.

James observes "a person can be transformed by forces apparently beyond their normal consciousness." But while psychology defines these forces as 'unconscious' i.e., within the self, in a spiritual mystical experience, the incandescent luminosity may be seen as coming from Union with Divine—that is how *Turya* is described. It is an experience that states that I am one with the Whole—*Aham Brahmasmi.*

We all want to connect with something 'more', whether that something is great inside us or an external Higher Power, and altered state of consciousness provides a generic ground to experience the better things which come from going by faith in the experience of Fourth State (*Turya*) instead of our more natural state of rationality and reason alone. "Not God", James states, "but life, more life, a larger, richer, more satisfying life, is, in the last analysis, the end of all experiencing."

This is a humble proposition that is bound to be challenged on the grounds of a "different experience" by so many others. A rose will smell the same by any other name. We revert to rational materialistic criterion of James: all spiritual experiences have an ennobling quality and judged by this utilitarian criterion alone; all that is ennobling and emancipating happens during *Turya* state.

Conclusion

Altered states of consciousness are the natural attributes of all human beings, though many have had no access to them at all. *Turya* as described in the classical Indian tradition may indeed be the generic ground as well as the ultimate destination of all the varieties of quests. It may as well be a method and the goal. It is there that the observer and observed merge.

REFERENCE

James, W. (1902). *The Varieties of Religious Experiences—A Study in Human Nature.* New York: Longmans Green & Co.

24

The Freudian Unconscious
A Philosophical Exploration

RANJAN K. PANDA

Introduction

This chapter attempts to delve into the Freudian notion of unconscious which is central to the study of his psychoanalysis. Freud explicates the nature of unconscious referring to various conditions of human subjects and their experiences with regard to the psychic structure, dream experience, and sexuality. The unconscious signifies the absence of consciousness. Does this mean that the unconscious and conscious constitute two different structures of the mind? Does the Freudian notion of unconscious try to eliminate consciousness from the discourse of psychoanalysis and psychology? In other words, does psychoanalysis as science reduce the human subjectivity into the realm of the physical? I will discuss these questions with the help of two major interpreters of Freud's notion of unconscious. They are: Jonathan Lear[1] and John Searle[2]. According to Lear, the Freudian notion of unconscious does not commit to any kind of Cartesian ontological dualism. Rather, it shows the unconscious as real and connected to the psyche. The Searlean interpretation, on the other hand, shows that there is an intentional link between the unconscious and the conscious. This relationship is formed by intentionality which is an intrinsic property of consciousness.

The Notion of Consciousness : A Behaviouristic Discourse

Rudy Krejci in one of his papers titled "Re-emergence of the Concept of Consciousness in Twentieth Century Science and Philosophy"[3] draws attention to three important revolutionary ideas in the mechanistic paradigm of nineteenth century science. They are: First, Darwinian Theory of Evolution, which is against the notion of "a universal design with man on the top", and advocates "the concept of survival of the fittest as a new mechanistic selector in the development of cosmic matter; second, Karl Marx explaining the history of human societies referring to dialectical development of cosmic matter; and the third, the Freudian psychoanalysis for the study of human personality". The notion of unconscious being central to psychoanalysis maintains that "man is not being in the charge of himself but rather a victim of unconscious drives and two forces; the self preservative and the sexual drives whose primary interests are the optimal satisfaction of both of them. Thus, man is unable to control himself and becomes a true object of scientific study".[4] The science of mind is interested in developing physicalistic theory of the mind. The mind is treated as a physical entity. And the behaviour is causally identified with the neurophysiological functions of the brain. In other words, the mind is a physical phenomenon caused by the neurophysiological functions of the brain. Thus, human behaviour can be explained with the help of a comprehensive study of the brain.

Krejci believes that the scientific study of man excludes certain intrinsic features such as self-consciousness, self-knowledge, intentionality, introspection, etc. The exclusion of these features in the Freudian psychoanalysis, especially in the experimental psychology, would reduce the mind to the theoretical framework of behaviourism. The human voluntary actions, for behaviourists, are caused by the certain dispositions of the body. Anxiety, the power of instinct, sexual drives, etc. are unconscious phenomena which manifest themselves in response to the stimuli. In other words, human behaviours are manifestations of the *repressed* mental states or the *latent* preconscious ideas.[5] The experimental research in psychology investigates the inner workings of the human mind. The behaviouristic approach defined psychology as science of (*objective*) behaviour.[6] Its objectivity is grounded in the systematic study of cognitive processes and human behaviours.

The Behaviourists reject the autonomy of the mind. They claim that the human behaviour (both voluntary and involuntary) is sufficient to explain human mind. The mental states, such as intention, desire, belief, hopes, fears, etc. are simply an invention for the explanation of human behaviour. "By 'behaviour', the behaviourists mean the publicly observable, measurable, recordable activity of the subjects at issue: bodily movements, noise emitted, temperature changes, chemical released, interaction with the environment and so forth."[7] The behaviour is the source of knowing the mind. We do not observe mental phenomena, but they are measured by the observable behaviours. The behaviour is always in response to the reception of certain stimuli. The reception of stimulus from the environment and the manifestation of behaviour are caused by certain unobservable *dispositional properties*. These dispositions are part of the organic structure of the body. They are built into the structure and intrinsic to the organism. Human behaviour is determined by the dispositional properties of the brain. Brain functions are measured in connection with human behaviour. Behaviour is causally identified with the dispositional states of the brain, i.e., corresponding to a particular behaviour there must be a dispositional state in the brain. We generalize about dispositions by observing the constant occurrence of the same type of behaviour in typical external condition. This helps us in arriving at general causal laws for the explanation of human behaviour.

The mental phenomena like desire, belief, sensation, feeling, fear, imagination etc. are the manifestation of the dispositional properties of the brain. The brain being a physical organ causes these behavioural effects. Jenny Teichmen, following Skinner, writes, "So called conscious action and reflex action is that the latter is the result of evolution and the former is the result of environment; in other words, the distinction has nothing to do with internal mental states. Internal mental states are fictions."[8] Behaviourism, in a way, rules out the reality of the mind as a necessary condition for explaining behaviour. Moreover, it only looks for the behaviour *per se* as real along with the physical conditions that are causing the behaviour.

Freud's Notion of Unconscious

The Freudian notion of unconscious provides a theoretical support to explain the complex human behaviour. The existence of dispositions and their functions are unobservable. They exist in the realm of unconscious. The unconscious refers to thoughts, motives, beliefs, etc. which are inaccessible to the conscious mind. The agent only knows that he is acting but he fails to know why she/he acts like that. For instance, let us discuss about a moment of Mr. R's life that Freud mentions. "He (Mr. *R*) is walking along a road on which he knows his lady-friend will later be travelling in a carriage. He removes a stone from the road so that the carriage will not be damaged. A bit later he feels compelled to go back to replace the stone in the road."[9] Here, in this passage, Mr. *R*, the agent, is not aware of *why he puts the stone back in the road*. In Freud's analysis, Mr. *R* is suffering from *reflexive breakdown* that shows the inconsistency and incoherence in the patterns of beliefs, attitudes, emotions, intentions, and action. As a result, he exhibits *irrational* behaviour, i.e. *removal* and *replacement* of the stone. So far as removal is concerned, Mr. *R* shows love and concern towards his lady-friend, whereas replacement of stone again indicates Mr. *R's* anger. It is important to note that as a person, he is *unaware of* the reason of the second action.

The agent has no access to the realm of unconscious. The unconscious, according to Freud, constitutes the *primary processes* of the mental life, whereas the conscious-mind constitutes the *secondary processes* of the mental life. This split of primary and secondary processes indicates a conceptual split. Does this conceptual split create any dualism between the unconscious and the conscious mind ? Davidson points out that the whole idea of articulating action would give an impression of a *second mind* that would have a *quasi-independent structure.*[10] This is similar to the conscious mind that articulates and rationalizes an action.

According to Davidson, every action that is performed has a reason. Davidson writes, "In each case of reasons for the action tell us what the agent saw in the action, they give the intention with which he acted, and thereby give an explanation of action. Such explanation, as I have said, must exist if something a person does is to count as the action at all."[11] In this regard, the action performed by an unconscious mind must also have the power of rationalization and articulation. It is a paradox that the agent is not able to *see* why he is doing so.

Lear does not agree with Davidson's interpretation of action. Following Freud, Lear argues that the anger shown in the case of *replacement of the stone* gives an impression of the *repressive* experiential content that has gone into the *preconscious* state of the mind. As a result, Mr. *R* is unable to know why he is motivated to perform a hostile action. Moreover, it is also necessary to examine the process of development of emotional life of Mr. *R*. Freud finds that any kind of disruption in the development of emotion could be reason for exhibiting irrational signs. The emotional response like *the replacement of stone* is a motivated action. It is a *reaction; just an outburst,* but not a conscious decision.[12] Fear and anxiety are intrinsic to the emotional mental life. The responses corresponding to fear and anxiety are due to the emotional orientation of a person. According to Lear, the *replacement of stone* is the expression of anxiety of Mr. *R*.

Defining the nature of anxiety, Lear further illustrates Freud's ideas. He writes, "It is difficult to capture the activity accurately. Freud discovered that anxiety is not simply an emotional state that overcomes us; it is a state we can learn to induce in ourselves. This learning is not a conscious process, and producing anxiety is not an action. Although it is a mental activity, it is not outcome of beliefs and desires."[13] There are two things Lear tries to clarify: (1) showing anxiety is a mental activity inherent to emotion, and (2) that which is mental is not necessarily conscious. In the process of development of emotion one unconsciously accumulates anxieties in the form of repressed states. These repressed states get manifested without the agent consciousness. In other words, the anxious behaviour exhibited by the agent is not intended. Hence, he is unaware of why he does it. Following Freud, one can say that the agent is thus unconscious about the entire process of formation and articulation of action. It is because the process is active at a primitive level than in the level of the formation of desire and belief. Nevertheless, Freud maintains that anxiety can be induced as a defense mechanism. That is to say, one 'learns to trigger the anxiety in himself but he is not conscious of why he does this.'[14] Thus anxiety is part of the unconscious mental life.

The unconscious as primary process of mental life is inaccessible to the agent. The agent can consciously deliberate or reflect on thoughts and intended action. This reflection is otherwise known as introspection. Accessing the repressive states of unconscious mental life is impossible because one is lost in the process of conscious deliberation. This loss is due to the pleasure seeking attitude or the sexual drives of the person. In the extreme case of hysteria, the person loses the reflective attitude due to physical pain. And these elements disturb and disrupt the entire reflective process. As a result the person *forgets all about it.*[15]

The repressive states do appear in the form of dreams. Freud has given importance to the interpretation of dreams. The repressed thoughts and wishes in the unconscious mind are manifested in the dreams. Moreover, the connection between dream experience and the unconscious states is arbitrary. Impressions are accumulated in a discrete manner. These impressions form ideas. Lear writes, "These ideas form connecting clusters, and they tend to form around 'nodal points'."[16] There could be several nodal points that are mechanically connected with each other and 'their association shows how ideas are *condensed* and transmitted in many directions'. Lear further points out that, "In unconscious mental activity, Freud argues, psychic energy moves across these loose associations of ideas."[17] If that is so, the process of radiation is caused by the 'pressure and intensity of psychic energy'. This energy is displaced along the associative paths. But the process of displacement depends upon how the ideational elements are *condensed*. The manifestation of these condensed ideas in dreams and conscious experiences are nothing but shows the mode of gratification of sexual drive or hidden wish. Thus, these desires and wishes are not consciously articulated. They are indirect expression of unconscious thoughts.

However, according to Lear, the manifestation of the unconscious thoughts forms a kind of mechanism. The mechanistic process indicates the flow of psychic energy or the process in which the unconscious thoughts find mode of expression. The mode is not due to the intentionality of the self or conscious-mind. Rather, the unconscious forms its own mechanism and gets manifested in the behaviour. Lear also maintains that Freud was not interested in developing the causal relation between psychic energy and neural energy. But the whole process of formation, condensation and getting rooted as nodal point is an indication of formation of dispositions which are essential element of behaviouristic explanation of the mind. The behaviourists do not believe in the presence of Cartesian self and also deny psychoanalysis. The self and self-reflection, in Freudian psychoanalysis is explained referring to two notions: ego and super-ego respectively. These concepts are developed in the process of interaction with the world. They are rooted in the primitive notion of the psyche.

Searle on Ontology of Unconscious

Searle disagrees with Lear's interpretation of Freud's notion of the unconscious. Searle makes two important points here: (i) the notion of unconscious can be discussed with reference to the consciousness; (ii) the unconscious behaviour cannot be completely unintentional, i.e. the intentionality is present in both rational and emotional behaviour. I would like to illustrate the second point and then move about discussing the first point.

According to Searle, consciousness is central to the explanation of the human mind. It has many features that constitute the mental life. They are: intentionality, phenomenality, subjectivity, aspectuality, familiarity, unity, etc. He speaks of a dozen of such features which provide a structure to consciousness; intentional mental states. Intentionality being an intrinsic feature of consciousness helps in explicating the entire structure of the mental life. It shows the relationship between the mind and the world, and also forms the network of mental states that forms the mind.

Actions or conscious behaviours are intended. They are caused by the intentional mental states of the mind. Belief, desire and intention are intentional states referred for the explanation of the action. An analysis of the performance of an action would show not only the sequence in which the intentional states are connected, but also the psychological mode in which the action is performed. An action is considered effective if and only if it fulfils the condition of satisfaction, i.e., the fulfilment of an expectation that results from the performance of the action.

Furthermore, an action, according to Searle, is constituted of two components: one is the intention of doing it and other is the intentional object. The two components are related with each other in the sense that former results in the latter. As Searle interprets the Oedipus complex, 'Oedipus intended to marry Jacosta.' After marrying Jacosta, he came to know that he married her mother. Can we say Oedipus action is intentional? For many what is important is how an action is defined. Searle says that it is misleading to claim that description can alone give a clear picture of intentional action. He writes: "It is misleading to state these facts about actions in terms of descriptions of action because it suggests that what matters is not the action but the way we describe the action, whereas, according to my account, what matters are the facts that descriptions describe."[18]

Searle admits that there can be mental actions possible without movement of the body. Because, whenever I intend to do some action, I can very well form what would be my expected and possible results and what are the procedures to be adopted. He says, "mental acts are formally isomorphic to the cause of physical act . . . ."[19] It is not, therefore, the case that physical movements are basic to human actions. One can do an action by refraining from a physical movement. Searle does not want to reduce intention to belief and desire, rather he maintains that our intentional actions possess both belief and desire. From the beginning if the agent forms a determination that he will do that work, and then he believes that he will do the action. Besides he also desires to do the same. The following is the schema of action which includes belief and desire; 1. I will do *A*, 2. Belief that I will do *A*, 3. Desire to do *A*, 4. Desire *X* will cause: I will do *A*. In other words, thoughts are involved in causing action.

However, for Searle, to say that some of the thoughts are unconscious and they are unconsciously causing behaviour is to deny the *aspectual character* of mental states. The aspectuality shows that the content of thought and experience is intentionally related to the mind. The mental states bear an intentional content in them. Searle says, "The notions of thinking and experiencing are notions which imply the presence of aspectual shapes and that in turn implies accessibility to consciousness. The link, then, between intentionality and consciousness lies in the notion of an aspectual shape. To be intentional, a state or process must be thinkable or experiential; it must have an aspectual shape under which it is, at least in principle, consciously thinkable or experiential. It must be a sort of thing that could be the content of a conscious thought and experience."[20] Every mental representation is accessible from a point of view, whether they are unconscious or conscious. The point of view is subjective. The subjectivity here is an epistemological mode in which the content of representation is linked with the state of experience. This intentional link shows how the unconscious thoughts are potentially intentional and they can be brought to consciousness. Thus the subjective experience of the content of mental states cannot be exhaustively or completely characterized solely in terms of third person point of view. In this regard, both unconscious and conscious mental states are in some sense *irreducibly subjective*.[21]

The behaviouristic explanation of the unconscious does miss out this point. Behaviourism not only treats the dispositions as behavioural evidences located in mental life, but also treats it as part of the unconscious. This is quite analogous to the algorithmic process shown in the case of automata processing information. A computer processes the information with the help of algorithm and hardware. The algorithm is syntax. And syntax, according to Searle, is not sufficient to explain the entire linguistic activities. It needs semantics too. The mental content is semantic content structured by intentionality of the mind. Thus, content is part of thought and experience. A computer does not experience things. The mind or the mental life of human being contains both unconscious and conscious mental states. They are all intentional. For, "the dispositional analysis of unconscious mental phenomena is not a disposition to behaviour, rather if disposition is a right word then unconscious states are disposition of conscious thoughts".[22]

Moreover, the ontology of unconscious and conscious mental states is entirely neurophysiological. The neurophysiological functions of the brain are not necessarily intentional and conscious. But brain has the causal power to make unconscious mental states conscious. The conscious experiences and representations which go into the realm of unconscious and pass on into the realm of consciousness do not lose their aspectuality or any of its structural features. In this regard, for Searle, the unconscious and the conscious are real and part of the mental life.

To conclude, the unconscious as part of psychoanalysis does not eliminate the notion of psyche or the mind. Searle while critiquing the mechanistic and behaviouristic theorization of the mind brings back the notion of consciousness and intentionality to the discourse of the study of psychoanalysis. Although Lear denies the notion of dual structure of the mind, i.e. the conscious and the unconscious, still he believes that the mind is not intrinsically intentional.

Intentionality is not a necessary feature of mind. He also nullifies the causal link between the psyche and neurophysiology. Thus, the ontology of unconscious is not clearly defined in Lear's interpretative framework. Searle, on the other hand, discusses the ontology of unconscious in a naturalistic paradigm. Consciousness and the unconscious are not mystical phenomena. Rather, they are connected to the neurophysiological functions of the brain. Moreover, he differs from the behaviouristic theorization of the mind. Behaviourism is not clear about the nature of disposition as such. Disposition remains mental phenomena without bearing any kind of consciousness, which shows the physicalistic inclination of behaviourism. Physicalism in the name of scientific study of the mind does reduce the mind to the certain mechanical states and processes. As a result, the mind is treated as an epiphenomenon. Searle, on the other hand, does not low down the scientific temperament of Freudian psychoanalysis. Rather, he has shown that psychoanalysis for developing method for psychotherapy need not subscribe to strict scientism which is emphasized by the behaviourists and physicalists. Introducing an irreducible notion of the mind, along with its intrinsic features, Searle gives a picture of structure of consciousness. This notion of consciousness does not give a phenomenological investigation of subjective self-awareness, but a naturalistic account of intentionality, aspectuality, self-reflexivity which would help in explicating the nature of the unconscious in psychoanalysis. The unconscious may be an indiscernible layer of the mental life but can be traced with the conscious intentionality.

REFERENCES

1. Jonathan Lear, *Freud*, London: Routledge, 2005.
2. John Searle, *The Rediscovery of Mind*, Massachusetts: The MIT Press, 1992.
3. *Philosophy of Mind and Philosophy of Psychology, Proceedings of Ninth International Wittgenstein Symposium*, Vol. 11, Ed. Roderick M. Chisholm, Johann Chr. Marek, John T. Blackmore, and Adlof Hubner,

(Vienna: Holder-Pichler-Tempsky, 1985), pp. 65-72.

4. *Ibid.* p. 65.
5. *Ibid.*p. 65.
6. Giovanni Jervis, "The Unconscious", *Cartographies of the Mind: Philosophy and Psychology in Intersection*, Eds. M. Marraffa, M. De Caro and F. Feretti, (Dordrecht: Springer, 2007), p. 147.
7. Paul Churchland, *Matter and Consciousness*, Massachusetts: The MIT Press, 1989, p. 88.
8. Jenny Teichmen, *Philosophy and the Mind*, Oxford: Basil Blackwell, 1988, p. 9.
9. See, Lear, *op. cit.*, p. 24.
10. *Ibid.*, p. 25.
11. Lear refers to Davidson's interpretation of action to show the paradox involved in explaining action. *Cf.* Davidson, "The Paradox of Irrationality", in R. Wolleheim and J. Hopkins (Eds.) *Philosophical Essays on Freud*, Cambridge: Cambridge University Press, 1982, p. 292..
12. See, Lear, *op. cit.*, p. 37.
13. *Ibid.*
14. *Ibid.*
15. *Ibid.*, p. 67.
16. *Ibid.*, p. 106.
17. *Ibid.*, p. 107.
18. John Searle, *Intentionality: An Essay in Philosophy of Mind*, Cambridge: Cambridge University Press, 1983, p. 101.
19. *Ibid*, p. 103.
20. John Searle, "Consciousness, unconsciousness and intentionality" *Philosophical Issues*, Vol. 1, Consciousness (1991), pp. 51-52.
21. *Ibid.*, p. 55.
22. *Ibid.*, p. 58.

25

Nature of Consciousness and *Turiya* in Different Schools of Thought

GEETA M. ADWANIKAR

Everyone knows what consciousness is until one attempts to define it. Consciousness denotes a state of awareness of one's own self and one's environment. This is the common understanding. The word *Turiya or Turya* is used as synonymous to the fourth state of consciousness in Indian philosophy. Dictionary meanings are so varying that one is almost confused in understanding the concept.

Meaning of *turiya* is variously described as the fourth, mighty, a quarter, and in the Vedantic philosophy it is described as fourth state of the soul in which it becomes one with *Brahman* or the Supreme spirit[1]. This definition conveys much more than 'consciousness.'

Consciousness is defined as awareness, conscious thought and feeling as a whole, state of being conscious. Self-consciousness in standard dictionaries[2], English-Sanskrit dictionaries[3] gives broader meaning of the word consciousness as *jnana, upalabdhi, chetana, sanjnya, vedana, anubhava, bodhah, pratibodhah*. These words are specific to the Sanskrit language and hence, they do not appear in standard English dictionaries.

Concepts

The meaning of these Sanskrit words become the cornerstone in the understanding of the concepts of consciousness.

Prajna—intelligence, understanding, intellect, wisdom, *buddhi.*
Chit—to be conscious of, observe, notice, see, animating principle of life, thought, intellect, soul, *atma, chidabhasa*—individual soul, *jivatma.*
chetas—consciousness, sense, thinking soul, mind, heart, soul.

These Sanskrit words convey a broader understanding of consciousness which is a reality inherent in existence. It is the energy, the motion that creates the universe and all that is in it.

Vedanta, the last portion of the *Vedas* consists of different *Upanishads.* They are philosophical discussions on—*one reality;* that is substratum for the pluralistic phenomenon of the material world and its manifestations[4]. All the things in this world that are seen and experienced by us have their origin in one source. They are sustained and resolved into that source alone. This reality means *Turiya* in the words of *Vedanta.*

Constitution of Consciousness

Human existence is inevitably a matter of encounter with reality; he must be related with other objects and persons in the external world for having any sort of life at all. Cognition is inherent in man's being. The world around has unavoidable cognitive dimensions. The world is revealed to him in ordinary perception. The notions of utility and practical efficiency are what normally guide not only his behaviour but his cognitions as well. More than mere encounter with the "objective world", understanding of the "lived world" becomes important in philosophy as well as in science. The bodily activities and mental processes both may be described as "the constitution of consciousness".[5]

Upanishads

There are more than hundred *Upanishads,* discussing the reality of existence. *Mandukya Upanishad* belongs to *Atherva Veda, Brahman Bhaga* and is the shortest among the principal

Upanishads. It has only twelve *mantras* and analyses the entire range of human consciousness in the three states of waking (*jagrat*), dream (*swapna*) and dreamless sleep (*sushupti*), which are common experiences of all. *Mandukya Upanishad* asserts that the absolute reality is nondual and attributeless (*nirguna* and *nirvishesha*) which is distinct from the other three and is amenable to realization. *Mandukya Upanishad* is probably the very first scriptural literature where life has been considered in its totality and after exhaustive observations the masters had come to their conclusions.

Gaudapadacharya (520-620 A.D.) elucidates the original *mantras* of the *Mandukya Upanishad*. It has 215 verses explaining the 12 *mantras* that constitute the *Mandukya Upanishad*. It points out the line of inquiry and the enunciation of truth provided by the *mantras*, by rearranging the ideas of the *Upanishads* into a pattern which can easily convey the central points of the scriptures in his *Karika*.[6]

Turiya in Mandukya Upanishad

Aum is the sound symbol signifying the ultimate reality. In *Mandukya Upanishad, Aum* is described as all pervasive, conscious principle, fundamental truth. All that is past, present and future verily is *Aum*. This forms the substratum which is unchanging in all the three periods of time. That which is beyond the three periods of time is also *Aum*.

सर्वं ह्येतद् ब्रह्म, अयमात्मा ब्रह्म,
सोऽयमात्मा चतुष्पात् ॥2॥

In the second *mantra*, it is emphasized that *Aum* is Brahman as the spiritual centre in the individual and also representing the spiritual reality behind the world of plurality. The names and forms that constitute the world are mere superimpositions upon the all pervading consciousness. In vedantic inquiry through a process of detachment and observation of the body, mind and intellect, the student is guided to the spiritual centre latent in himself. This process of the rediscovery of the *Self—the*

Atma, includes the realization of the all pervading divinity which is unconditioned and unborn. And it has four quarters: *jagrat, swapna, sushupti and turiya.*[7]

The seventh *mantra* of the Mandukya *Upanishad* describes *Turiya* as

नान्तःप्रज्ञं न बहिष्प्रज्ञं नोभयतः
प्रज्ञं न प्रज्ञानघनं न प्रज्ञं नाप्रज्ञम ।
अदृष्टमव्यवहार्यमग्राह्यमलक्षणम्
अचिन्त्यमव्यपदेश्यमेकात्मप्रत्ययसारं
प्रपञ्चोपशमं शान्तं शिवमद्वैतं
चतुर्थं मन्यन्ते स आत्मा स विज्ञेयः ॥7॥

Na antah prajnam—It is not that which is conscious of the internal subjective world,
na bahishprajnyam—nor that which is conscious of the external world,
na ubhayatah prajnam—nor that which is conscious of both,
na prajnana ghanam—nor that which is a mass of consciousness,
na prajnam—nor that which is simple consciousness,
na aprajnam—nor is it unconsciousness.
adrishtam—it is unseen by any sense organ,
avyavaharyam—beyond empirical dealings,
agrahyam—incomprehensible by the mind,
alakshnam—uninferable,
achintyam—unthinkable, beyond thoughts,
avyapadeshyam—indescribable, beyond description,
ekatma pratyaya saaram—traceable through unbroken self awareness,
prapancha upashamam—negation of all phenomenon.
Shantam—the peaceful,
sivam, advaitam—the auspicious and the non dual. This is considered as the fourth (*Turiya*).
Atma sah vijnehyah This is the *Atma* and this is to be realized.[8]

In this mantra, the reality has been explained using the *swaroopa lakshana, tathasta lakshana* and *nishedha lakshana.*

Essence of Life

Life consists of existence (the material) and consciousness (the energy). These two, are like two sides of a coin which cannot be separated.

A human being lives his life in contact with the external objects gaining experiences. The moment the physical structure has ceased learning experiences, we call that body "dead." The life principle governing all the experiences is pure consciousness, the *Atma,* the *Brahman.* Consciousness is the capacity to know that I AM, or I EXIST, direct and intuitive knowledge which everyone possesses. But this is limited to the body. *Upanishads* make a distinction between this limited knowledge of the self and the essential nature of self which is unlimited by time, space or object. It is the connecting link between all that exists. This has been described in *Vivekchudamani* (Verse 130) as *Eshontaratma Purushah Puranah.*

Delinking oneself from the limitations of the body sense is the first step on the path of self-realization. The Self is all consciousness, always liberated, uninvolved witness. Knowledge of the presence of the other objects and persons in this world is conditioned knowledge, filtered and modified through the sense, mind and memory.

All entities are by their very nature unattached like the space. There is not the slightest variety (plurality) in essence, in them in any way, at any time. This is how all the reality would appear viewed from the state of *Turiya.* It can be stated in other words, as seeing the unity in diversity.

Consciousness in Gaudpadakarika

Gaudpadakarika discusses distinct difference between the "mind in sleep" and "mind in self-realization." In deep sleep the mind is only withdrawn or drowned in ignorance but in case of self-realization, that very mind becomes alive to the awareness without any objects of external or internal world. This state of the mind, unbound by the time and space, is *Pure Consciousness,* also called *Turiya.*[9]

This state is explained further as a mind redeemed from its attachment and maintained away from the object of its distractions—attains its state of changeless purity. This is being realized by the wise as undifferentiated, birthless and nondual.[10]

Gaudpadakarika (1-10-15) mentions the characteristics of *turiya* as that all pervading, capable of the cessation of all miseries, powerful, immutable, nondual, among all entities, effulgent. . . . This state is not affected by cause and effect, and is omniscient.

While answering a question on consciousness, Swami Chidananda of Divine Life Society, referred to Descartes, a French philosopher, who had said, "I think, therefore, I am." But *Vedanta* says, "I am, therefore, I think." If I did not exist, thought itself would be impossible, so I come first. Pure existence and consciousness go hand in hand; then, all the process of thought and all other things are made possible.

The ego goes through constant rotation of three states of consciousness, i.e., waking, sleep and dreaming. These three states of consciousness operate upon a substratum which is permanent ground of pure consciousness, *turiya,* in the *Vedanta* which alone is the reality and there are no other states of consciousness. All projections are of one and only pure consciousness which is not conditioned by time and space. And this is the nature of self. "I" am unconditioned and unqualified by any thing.[11]

Gaudpadakarika appears to expound the truth that the three states of the phenomenal self are unreal and illusory and that the fourth one *turiya,* (which is Gaudapada's name for the *Upanishada's chaturtha*) alone is real.[12]

Here, it is stated that pure consciousness alone is the reality and there are no other states of consciousness.

Minor Upanishadas

Dr. Shweta Kaluskar in her research on the minor *Upanishads* finds several references to four states viz. *Jagrat, Swapna,*

Sushupti and *Turiya* in the minor *Upanishads* like *Saryopanishad*, *Kaivalyopanishad*, and *Annapurnopanishad* mostly borrowed from the earlier *Upanishads* like *Mandukya*.

In *Saryopanishad, turya awastha,* is described as "essence of consciousness" which manifests itself as three states—who is a witness of the states, itself devoid of the states, positive or negative and remains in the state of non-separation and oneness.[13]

In *Aitareya Upanishad*, there is reference to Rishi Vamadeva's experience of consciousness in him, in the pre-natal stage. It is recorded that he could see the development of the various organs of his body and the beginning of their functions.[14]

Kaivalyopanishad in its 14th and 18th *mantras* describes pure consciousness. The former says that after having slept and temporarily enjoyed the reviving pause from the agitations and sorrows of the waking and dream, individuality does not once forever get extinct, but is revived again to play its part either as a waker or a dreamer. The latter says that all that constitutes the enjoyable, the enjoyer and the enjoyment in the three realms .... different from them all "I" am, the Witness, the ever auspicious Pure Consciousness. None of these activities would be possible without this Consciousness. Now, to identify ourselves with Self (Witness) is to train ourselves to be a witness of all physical perceptions, mental feelings and intellectual thoughts. This "attitude of witness" (*sakshibhava*) to all that is happening at different layers of my personality is possible for me, only so long as these things are happening in them. When the objects fade away, the witness in me becomes "the faculty that gave me the capacity to witness." This Pure Consciousness with no objects (*chinmatra*) is the Supreme Self, unconditioned and free, immaculate and perfect which is the reality behind the universe.[15]

Sri Shankaracharya in the *shloka* 136 and 137 of Vivekchudamani refers to the "Witness" in the following manner: Different from *Prakriti* (*avidya*) and its transformation, of the nature of pure intelligence, devoid of any qualities, illuminates all the material world which has forms. The formless *atma* shines through the waking and other states as their witness and is referred to as the "I " who is oneself.[16]

Dwait (Vaishnava) Concepts of Four States of Consciousness

Madhvacharya (1238-1317) was the chief proponent of *Tattvavàda* (True Philosophy), popularly known as *Dwaita* or dualistic school of Hindu philosophy. *Turiya* represents consciousness free from material influence. The idea is that consciousness, of which the *atman* is constituted, exists in our wakeful state of material experience, as it continues during sleep. In sleep, we dream and experience the mental realm, whereas during our waking state the physical plane has more bearing on our lives.

The self is independent of the body and mind. If the physical and mental realms were to shut down, the self would continue to exist. This we know from our experience in deep sleep. Realizing this involves entering the *turiya*.

According to the *Dwaita* philosophy, *turiya* is the ultimate reality which is referred to as God and is explained in *Bhagavata Purana* (11.15.16) and describes as *Bhagavan* with the words *turiyakhye* (the fourth).[17]

Maharishi Mahesh Yogi's Description of Consciousness

Maharishi Mahesh Yogi describes *turiya* as follows: "Founders of Vedic tradition discovered the capacity of human mind to settle into a state of deep silence while remaining awake and therein to experience a completely unified simple and unbounded state of awareness called pure consciousness (*turiya* in their terms). This is distinct from sleeping, dreaming or waking state. The experience was not on the level of thinking or theoretical conjecture or imagination but on the level of direct experience "insight", like that Newton or Einstein experienced on their discoveries of the new laws."

The Veda is a sequential flow of the process of the oneness of pure consciousness giving rise to diversity. Vedic science is to be understood as a body of knowledge based on direct experience of the sequential unfoldment of the unified field into the diversity of nature. As one gains the knowledge of the natural laws on the intellectual level, one begins to live by that natural law in daily life, in most spontaneous way. This is the basic application of the Vedic science in practice.

According to Maharishi Yogi, each state of consciousness has a corresponding state of physiologically functioning which can be correlated by laboratory data.

1. Deep sleep—*sushupti chetana*
2. Dreaming—*swapna chetana*
3. Waking—*jagrat chetana*
4. Restful alertness—*Turiya* (transcendental consciousness, *Bhavatita Chetana*)
5. Cosmic consciousness—*Kaivalya*
6. God consciousness—*Bhagvat chetana*
7. Unity—*Brhami chetana*

Each higher state consciousness is characterized by increasing alertness, comprehension and fulfilment; each state has a corresponding stage of nervous system functioning. As higher states develop in brain physiology, a more coherent functioning is established even while engaging in specific activities. The increased coherence leads to coordination of all other systems into an integrated whole. This holistic functioning of the individual human physiology gives rise to the extraordinary property of self-awareness in human consciousness.[18]

Neurological View

Dr. Bibek Maiti talks about two components of consciousness as awareness and arousal (wakefulness). While discussing unconsciousness, he puts it as "abnormalities of consciousness comprise a continuance ranging from full alertness to total unresponsiveness. The different levels of unconsciousness are confusion, delirium, drowsiness, stupor, semi-coma and coma."[19]

Dr. Maiti has categorized the various states of awareness while Maharishi, Mahesh Yogi enumerates the levels of consciousness. If normal awareness is considered on the scale of ten, Dr. Maiti goes down the zero point and Maharishi Mahesh Yogi goes up from that point towards a more rarified and active awareness or the consciousness. It would be interesting to see that in both the cases, the awareness or the consciousness is considered as separate from the autonomic or involuntary functions of the body and its various levels are identified.

Life is a continuous homogeneous whole. The wave of individual life on the ocean of life arises without breaking the continuity and all pervading status of eternal, absolute Being.

All the innumerable laws of nature carrying out the process of creation, evolution and dissolution in different parts of the universe are the diverse expressions of the one eternal cosmic life. The entire creation is the expression of cosmic life.[20]

The word absolute Being means the state of life which is neither active nor passive. It is clear that the metabolic process which keeps the body alive and maintains its coordination with mind in the relative field of existence could be brought physiologically to a state of restful alertness, life could be placed on the level of Being.

It can be said that awareness depends upon the state of nervous system. When the nervous system is active in the waking state, the mind has no opportunity to dissociate itself from the surrounding world. When the nervous system is tired, the mind has no chance to use its conscious capacity, and awareness is lost in deep sleep. If the nervous system could be brought to a state where it could hold the mind so that it neither uses its conscious capacity to experience outer object nor yet completely loses its awareness—that is, if the mind could simply remain conscious without being conscious of anything in the outer world—it would attain a state of pure awareness where it is neither active nor passive. This pure awareness is the state of Being. Simultaneously, the nervous system gains the state of restful alertness which becomes the meeting place for relative and absolute state of life. The nervous system, as far as its ability to produce awareness is concerned, is on the plane of Being, the field of eternal existence. This would be the state of perfect health in mind and body.[21]

Analogies from Science

Nobel Laureate Dr. Brian Josephson, Professor of physics, Cambridge University, England, while commenting on transcendental meditation (TM), says that: "Two subjects have relevance to what is going on in TM. Quantum Mechanics is very significant in that, because of it, people realized for the first time that it was necessary to take consciousness into account in describing nature. Before that time, it was thought that one could have a purely objective picture of nature. In quantum mechanics, it was recognized that when we make an observation we always disturb a system. Although it would be necessary to take consciousness of the observer into account, in practice, physicists have tried to live consciousness out as much as possible. But, I think we must go deeper into the role of consciousness. What goes on is clearly a matter of ourselves as well as the world around us, and we must unite all approaches.

In thermodynamics, two things are important—energy and entropy. When a system becomes more ordered in the language of thermodynamics, its entropy becomes less. But living systems have the ability to stop disorder. All around a living system are forces that tend to introduce disorder; yet, living systems can reverse this tendency. What occurs may be something like the increase of order that accompanies reduction of temperature as in a refrigerator. This analogy may be a way of explaining the increase of orderliness in the brain brought about through the TM technique."[22]

Dr. Laurence Domash, professor of physics and an authority on semiconductors talks about the changes in consciousness. In the study of nature, there is common thing of phase transition. When we take natural system and lower its temperature, we find that in general, the entropy decreases steadily. In addition, it tends to make sharp jumps at certain points. When we cool down water vapour, there comes a point where it converts into liquid water. When we cool liquid water further, there comes a point where it crystallizes into ice. These changes from gas to liquid and from liquid to solid are phase transitions.

It is very interesting to think of a change in the mind that is experienced subjectively as an expanded state, a very silent state, and that is described physiologically in terms of great rest, orderliness and coherence in the brain waves. The idea that TM, as seen in physiological studies brings about a phase transition—a new state of consciousness—is beginning to connect with other facts about the nervous system, also from a fundamental level. The nervous system is capable of phase transition and that nature repeats itself in this context may turn out to be very powerful ideas.

If simple physical systems like water and helium and superconductor and magnet can exhibit phase transitions, then, as vastly complex as the human nervous system can also exhibit phase transition.[23]

Conclusion

What sages have been saying for ages and otherwise men trying to explain, remains an enigma to be predicated by words. But, one thing is certain that there is some life force, active and alive, with the human system or in spite of it. It is matter of experiencing than verbalizing the nature, from gross to subtle and material to ethereal and from physical to metaphysical.

The debate on the nature of consciousness continues since the Vedic times. The newer context of understanding it through the quantum mechanics model has added another dimension. Indian philosophical view is, however, unchanged. Consciousness is awareness with various states, the fourth one being highest and termed as *turiya,* a state of *aham brahamam,* omnipresent and omniscient. Our stand is, any attempt by the scientific community to represent consciousness via a model should take into consideration of philosophical aspects too.

Only an integrative model of consciousness based on science and psycho-philosophical-biological aspects can be fully representative.

REFERENCES

1. V.S. Apte, *The Practical Sanskrit English Dictionary*, 1980, Pune.
2. *Webster's New World Dictionary*, 1986 and *The Little Oxford Dictionary*, 1983.
3. V.S. Apte, *English Sanskrit Dictionary*, 1997.
4. Swami Chinmayananda, *Mandukya Upanishad* with Karika, Mumbai, 1998.
5. S.K. Ramachandra Rao, Vidyalankara Prof, *Consciousness in Advaita*, (Study of Consciousness Preject-Fascicule-1, pp. 53-55, IBH Prakashana, Bangalore, 1979.
6. Swami Chinmayananda, *Mandukya Upanishad* with Karika, p. 17, Mumbai, 1998.
7. *Ibid.*, pp. 22-25.
8. *Ibid.*, pp. 61-62.
9. Swami Gambhirananda, Eight *Upanishads*, Vol. 2. Verse No. 35; *Adwaita Prakarana*, pp. 307-8, Adwaita Ashram, Pithoragarh, Himalayas. 1992.
10. *Ibid.*, 4th chapter, Karika, Verse No. 80, *Alatshanti Prakarana*, pp. 384-385.
11. Swami Chidananda, *Truth, Mind-Soul-Consciousness*, Q & A at Mar Lu Ridge, Maryland, USA., p. 12, Divine Life Society, Sept. 14, 1990.
12. S.K. Ramachandra Rao, Vidyalankara Prof, Consciousness in *Advaita, Study of Consciousness Project*-Fascicule-1, p. 15, IBH Prakashana, Bangalore, 1979.
13. Dr. Shweta S. Kaluskar, *Some Minor Upanishads of Atherveda*; A thesis, The M.S. University of Baroda, pp. 85-92.
14. Swami Chinmayananda, *Aitareya Upanishad*, pp. 77-78, Central Chinmaya Mission Trust, Mumbai, 1992.
15. Swami Chinmayananda, *Discourses on Kaivalyopanishad*, Central Chinmaya Mission Trust, 3rd edition.
16. Jagadguru Sri Chandrasekhara Bharati Swaminah, Vivekchudamani (with an English translation of Sanskrit commentary) pp. 50 & 64.
17. This reference is taken from the Internet search.
18. Maharishi Mahesh Yogi, The Science of Being and the Art of Living, Part 2, Chapter 2, p. 72. International SRM Publication, London.

19. Dr. Bibekananda Maiti, *Morbid Anatomy and Pathophysiology of Coma—Questions and Answers*. J. Indian Med. Association, Vol. 88, No 1, January, 1990.
20. Maharishi Mahesh Yogi, *Creating An Ideal Society*, p. 50. A Maharishi European Research University Press Publication, No. G 1112, 1977.
21. *Ibid*. p. 198.
22. Nobel Laureate Dr. Brian Josephson, Mind-Matter Unification Project in the Theory of Condensed Matter research group.
23. Prof. Lawrence Domash, Prof. of Physics, Maharishi International University.

26

The Nature of Transcendental Consciousness in Mandukya Upanisada

SHILENDRA S. SHARMA

Introduction

Since the dawn of any serious human reflection and deep thinking, the nature of consciousness and its relation to non-conscious has remained an important and hitherto unsolved problem of rational and empirical investigation of mankind.[1] In Indian philosophical and psychological context this is a fundamental subject, and from *Ṛg Veda* to the latest schools of *Nyaya* and *Vedanta,* important philosophical discourses on consciousness are found. This covers "*Bhutachaitanyavada*" of *Carvaka Darshan* to all-pervading and all-inclusive transcendental consciousness of *Upanisads* and *Vedanta* philosophies.[2] However, since the time of *Ṛg Veda,* it is realized that consciousness cannot be regarded as a function of any physical entity. It must have its own independent ontological existence and, at the same time it should not have the ultimate distinction from non-conscious. This can be elaborated by an example, say, if *X* knows *Y*, then *X* and *Y* cannot be totally distinct and independent to each other, because in that case there cannot be any explanation of interaction between them and also the possible epistemological awareness of *Y* to *X*. Moreover, it is also true that we cannot proceed through one sided metaphysical abstraction for finding the true nature of consciousness. Neither can we divide the entire realm of existence into X knower nor Non *X* (*Y*) that which is known because such a division would be totally arbitrary.

Hence, in Indian metaphysical context, the consciousness is defined as transcendental in nature and *Upanisadas* name it as *'Atman'*. This is also equated with *Brahma* and the equation

(Atma = Brahma = Absolute Reality)

becomes the fundamental equation of Upanisadic and Vedantic ontology.

This fundamental consciousness is explained as the basis of all reality and is not identical to the concept of human consciousness. The concept of human consciousness appears rather late in cosmic evolution.[3] The all-inclusive nature of transcendental consciousness is explained in detail in *Upanisads* and particularly in *Mandukya Upanisada,* which is the shortest *Upanisada*. In it, the transcendental consciousness is explained by the metaphysical symbol of *Om* (An ontological sign which contains the denotation with all—that—there is). Though *Om* is a well-known symbol of Indian philosophy and culture, it finds its fullest explanation in *Mandukya Upanisada*. In this chapter, an attempt has been made to bring out the metaphysical and epistemological reconstruction of transcendental consciousness with some contemporary references.

Transcendental Consciousness as All-Inclusive Reality

In entire Upanisadic philosophy, the reality is considered as one and it is known as non-dual *Atma* or *Brahma*. This nature is stated clearly in the very first *mantra* of *Mandukya Upanisada* as[4]:

"ओमित्येतदक्षरमिद सर्वं तस्योपख्याख्यानं भूतं भवद्विष्यदिति
सर्वमोङ्कार एव यच्चान्यत्त्रिकालातीतं तदप्योङ्कार एव।"

The *aksara Om* is everything (There is a special symbol for *Om* in Hindi/Sanskrit script). All that is in past, present and future is *Om* and what is beyond the stream of time is also *Om*.

It is clear from above *mantra* that the concept of consciousness is defined with relation to time and also in trans-temporal reference. The relation of consciousness in time is emphasized in Eastern and Western thoughts. Kant explains time as inner sense.[5] Godel considers time in terms of the relativity of simultaneity.[6] Penrose, on the other hand, explains the flow of time as justified only with reference to consciousness.[7] The position of *Mandukya Upanisada* is clear from the beginning. The consciousness is transcendental and it not only transcends the phenomenal world but also includes itself in it, means, that which is manifested—*Karyarupa* is *'Om'* and that which is *avyakruta*—unmanifested is also *'Om'*.[8] Hence consciousness is described with metaphysical identity with *Brahma* as[9]

"Sarvahytad Brahmyamatma Brahma Sayamamtma".

Above *mantra* says "all that which exists, is *Brahma*." In this context, *'Sarva khalu Idam Brahma'*, becomes the chief cosmo-ontic principle, and *'Aham Brahmasmi'* becomes main spiritual as well epistemological maxim. *Brahma* has four *padas*. But it does not mean that it contains any type of parts like the Absolute of Hegel[10]. It does not have parts like cow's four legs but it has parts like a Kasharpana.[11] *Brahma* has absolute identity with world and all that which is phenomenal.

Now, the question is, how does this all inclusive transcendental consciousness account for empirical consciousness? And what is the metaphysical meaning and epistemological states of empirical consciousness? The answers are elaborated in the subsequent narration of Upanisada.

Three States of Empirical Consciousness and its relation with Transcendental Consciousness

Normally any empirical-consciousness can be defined in three states:

(i) The state of awakening (*Jagruti*);

(ii) The state of dream (*svapna*); and
(iii) The state of dreamless sleep (*sushupti*).

In *Mandukya Upanisada* these three states are denoted by the three *matras* of *'Om'* to give possible field of experience of the related state of consciousness.

Mandukya Upanisada defines turn by turn these three states of consciousness:

First the *'Jagruti'* state is defined as[12]

जागरितस्यानो बहिष्प्रज्ञः सप्ताङ्ग, हर्मान विशतिमुखः
स्पूलमुग्वैश्वानरः प्रथम पादः ।

The *'Svapna'* state as[13]

स्तप्नस्थानोऽन्तःप्रज्ञाः सप्ताङ्ग एकोन विशांति मुख
प्रविषिक्त मुलतेज्ञत्से द्वितीयः पादः ।

and *'Susupti'* state as[14]

यत्र सुप्तो न कंचन कामं कामयते न कंचन स्वप्न पश्यति
तत्सुषुप्तम्। सुषुप्तस्थान एकी भूतः प्रज्ञानधन एवानन्दमयो
हयानंद मुर्क्य तोमुखः प्राज्ञस्तृतीयः पादः ।

Here, these three empirical states are explained in a general metaphysical reference. Awakening state is not a objective question which can be answered in the context of brain states or related psychological references. Here, the term which is used is *'sthan'* or 'field'. What is the possible field of experience for a finite consciousness? As no agnosticism is possible in the current framework, the answer would be the whole universe. So the *jagrut* state is described by the term *"Vaishwanar"*. *Vaishwanar* has seven parts and nineteen mouths and the description of this is mythological as well as epistemological. It is not only subjective consciousness which is the metaphysical abstraction, but also whole field of cognition which is metaphysically being abstracted. So, the result is the transcendental consciousness which is all-inclusive and not the pure abstract consciousness like the *purusa* of *Samkhya*. The *Shankara Bhasya* makes this clear as[15]

> *"Anyatha hi svadeh parichhina eva pratyagatma Samkhyadibhirive ḍrsta"*

Thus, the *'Jagrutisthan'* provides the description of whole universe and not only of the personal cognitive knower which resides in each individual body. The cosmic aspect of consciousness is being emphasized here.

Same is the case with *'Svapnasthana'* description. It is not simply the narration of the state of dream which is generally considered as subjective and unreal. As the owner of *'Jagruti'* is described by Vaishanara, the owner of *'Svapna'* is described by *"Hiranyagarbha." "Hiranyagarbha"* is stated as the cause of the universe in *Ṛg Veda.*[16] *'Sushupti'* is generally interpreted as the causal background of this entire manifestation which is described as beyond *sat* and *asat* in the *Nasadiya Sukta* of *Ṛg Veda.*[17]

From a cosmic point of view, the three empirical states of consciousness can be interpreted as:

(i) The *'Jagrutisthan'* is the entire manifested universe together with a cosmic observer.
(ii) The *'Svapnasthan'* is the entire formal ground of the universe with the formal conditions of the universe.
(iii) The *'Sushuptisthan'* is the metaphysical background of fact and form, and remains somehow in undescribable form in normal cognitive discourse.

These states are not final or ultimate. There is the highest transcendental consciousness which is beyond these three states.

Transcendental Consciousness

The fourth *pada* of *Om* represents the *'Turiya'* state of consciousness which transcends above three, empirical states. It is described as[18]

नानाःप्रज्ञं न बहिप्रज्ञं नोभयतःप्रज्ञं न प्रज्ञानधन न प्रज्ञं नाप्रज्ञम् ।
अदृष्टमव्यवहार्यम ग्राहयमलक्षणमेयमव्यपदेश्यमेकात्मप्रत्ययसारं
प्रपंचोपशमं शान्त शिवमद्वैतं चतुर्थ मन्यन्ते स आत्मा स विज्ञेयः ।

This state is neither *'anatahprajna'* or subjectively determined, nor *'balisprajna'* or objectively determined, not even a combination of subjectivity or objectivity. It is neither cognizable nor non-cognizable[19]. It cannot be described by any positive predications as all predications are determinations and all determinations are negations, and, therefore, limitations. Hence, the inevitable methodological situation for the description of ultimate reality in *Upanisada* is *"Neti-Neti"*[20]. This is called *'Prapanchopashama'* as it includes all that which is factual, formal or the metaphysical ground of both.

This transcendental consciousness is not totally distinct from three empirical conscious states. Otherwise the metaphysical imperative of *Upanisadas* for its realization would be meaningless.[21]

Conclusion

The entire discussion presupposes the meaningfulness or justification of metaphysical discourse. But this is inevitable, particularly, in the situation where pure physicalistic world-view is to be rejected. This metaphysical abstraction seems far-reaching but in reality this is not the case. Suppose we have a piece of metal before us, it can be explained in many discourses including chemical and economics. But there is a cosmological discourse too, where the origin of that metal is to be sought in the explosion of a Super Nova and that in turn indicates the formation of galaxy and also origin of the universe. This does not become unscientific. In the same way, there are many explanatory discourses of our consciousness. But this metaphysical or spiritual discourse refers to transcendental consciousness in which *Atma* is to be included in *Atma* by *Atma* as described in this *Upanisada*[22] as *"Shantam Shivam Advaitam"*.

This *'Samvishan'* of *Atma* into *Atma* by *Atma* with the three fold ontological identity is the main theme of the justification of transcendental consciousness.

REFERENCES

1. This stands correct, at least in the beginning for Indian philosophy. In Western philosophy the rational philosophical inquiry begins in the search of objective explanation of the cause of universe. Ancient Greek philosophy, from Thales to Protogorus, including all pre-Socratic thinkers, asks questions and demand explanations about the cause of the World. *Cf.* W.T. Stake, "A Critical History of Greek Philosophy" Dover Publication Chapter I.
2. Swami Madhavacharya—*Sarvadarshan Sangrah*. Chaukhamba Prakashan, Banaras. Chapter I. The *Carvaka Darshan*. Here, the materialistic view has been presented and up to this day including all recent identity theories for mind-body interaction and strong artificial intelligence, there is nothing metaphysically new which is presented and it includes the very fundamental idea that the consciousness is nothing but the outcome of that which is un-conscious and in the case of the life on earth, it is the by-product of organic compound. These all are forms of materialism and contain nothing ontologically new which is not in *Carvaka Darshan*. On the contrary, sometimes it appears that Carvakas are more honest in their materialistic commitment or physical explanation on the riddle of consciousness.
3. Radhakrishanan S. (1962). *Indian Philosophy*, Vol. II, Chapter X.
4. *Mandukya Upanisada*. M.L. Gita Press, Gorakhpur.
5. Kant I. (1998). Critique of Pure Reason, Translated by Paul Guyer. Cambridge University Press.
6. Godel Kurt (1949). Idealism and relativity of simultaneity in Albert Einstein: *A Philosopher—Scientist*. Open Court Pu. Co. Ed. Schlipp. A.
7. Penrose Roger (1990). *Emperor's New Mind*, Oxford Uni. Press; Shadows of Mind, Oxford Uni. Press.
8. *Mandukya Upanisada—Shankarbhasya*, Gita Press, Gorakhpur.
9. *Ibid*.
10. M.2, Hegel G.W.F. (1961). *The Science of Logic*, George Allen & Unwin, London.
11. *Shankarbhasya* of M.2. As a one rupee coin contains four 25 paise coins.
12. *Mandukya Upanisada* M.3
13. *Ibid* M.4
14. *Ibid* M.5
15. *Ibid Shankarbhasya* M.5
16. *Ṛg Veda*. 'Hiranyagarbha Sukta', 10.1201.
17. *Ṛg Veda*—Nasadiya Sukta, 10.129.1.
18. *Mandukya Upanisada* M.7.
19. In *Ken Upanisada*, the *Brahma* is stated as which is neither '*jneya*' nor *ajneya*'.

20. *Bṛhadaranykopanisada* 1.4. The state of *aksara* in *Yajnavalkya,* Gargi Śamvad is described in the same way of negative description i.e, by stating what it is not in the place of what it is.
21. *Mandukya Upanisada—Shankar Bhasya* M.7.
22. *Ibid.,* M.12.

27

Nature of Consciousness in Single and Double Reflection Theory in *Tattva Vaisharadi* and *Yogavartika*

C. B. VADHER

Introduction

In Indian philosophy, the concept of consciousness plays an important role in subjective and objective determination and description of reality. The acceptance of non-material existence of consciousness is the fundamental basis of Upanisadic metaphysics and spirituality.[1] In all metaphysical systems, which incorporate epistemology and ontology as its ingredients, the role of consciousness is viewed from a twofold dimensions :

(i) Consciousness as a knower which plays the part of subjectivity in epistemological discourses.
(ii) Consciousness as an ontological category which is beyond space and time and any type of distortion or *vikara*.

When both these discourses are put in a combinational structure, it creates a situation of paradoxical explanation. In any epistemology, where knowledge is a result of a knowing process, the complete transcendence of the ontological status of consciousness is very hard to maintain. Yet, there are attempts in the history of Indian philosophy for the ramification of this perplexing situation. For example, in the dualistic epistemology of *Nyayavais'esika Darshana,* the consciousness is explained as a property (*Guna*) of a substance called *atma* and the knowing subjectivity comes in the direct connection with an epistemological process based on the distinction between knower and known.[2] However, there are many epistemological and ontological shortcomings in this position. The main shortcoming is that the ontological status of consciousness as an independent category is not preserved.

Epistemologically, the solution of this situation is indicated in the philosophy of *Samkhya Yoga*. In *Saṃkhya Yoga,* the consciousness itself does not play direct role in the process of knowledge. In other words, no knowledge can occur directly in the state of transcendental consciousness known as *purusa.* It means, again that the basic ontological independence of consciousness, known as *purusa* cannot be maintained.

Hence, to come out of this perplexing situation *Saṃkhya Yoga* philosophy introduces the concept of *vritti. Vritti,* or as it is translated in English as modification, is the transformation of *citta* in the form—*akara* of the knowable subject. This stand is explained in *Yogatattva-Vaisharadi* of Vacaspati Misra and *Yoga Vartika* of Vijnanabhiksu.

Single Reflection Theory of Vacaspati Misra

Vacaspati Misra states his single reflection theory in the *Yogatattva Vaisharadi.* Commentary of *Yoga Sutra* 1.1.7.[3] says, "*Pratyakshanumana agamah pramanani.*"

In above *sutra, Vritti* is connected with knowledge i.e. *prama.* Therefore, it is important to define and interpret the meaning of *prama. Prama* is not defined either in Yoga Sutra or Vyasa Bhasya. Vacaspati Misra gives the definition of *prama* as,[4] "*Anadhigat tatvabodhah pourusheyyo vyavhar hetuh prama.*"

Above sutra indicates that with the help of *purusa, akhanda vritti* is in a continuous knowledge (*prama*). Now, the question is, how *purusa,* which is totally transcendental to any function or existence of *prakriti* can have a role in the knowing process? To answer this question Vacaspati Misra puts forward his single reflection theory.

Citta is manifestation of *prakṛti* in its course of evolution. Since, *citta* in itself, without the role of *purusa* cannot play the role of knower, it is necessary that the *citta* has the properties of modification according to the subject under consideration. This modification of *citta* is known as *vritti*. But for the origin of *vritti*, there must be some transcendental connection between *citta* and *purusa*. So, Samkhya Yoga postulates the concept of *pratibimba* of *purusa* in *citta*, which makes *citta* capable of modification. In this context Vacaspati Misra states[5]:

बुद्धिदर्पण पुरूषप्रतिबिम्बसङ्क्रान्तिरेव बुद्धिप्रतिसंवेदित्वं पुंसः। तथा च दीशिच्छायाऽऽपन्नया बुद्धया संसृष्टा शब्दादयो विषया भवन्ति दृश्या इत्यर्थः।

According to Vacaspati Misra, the reflection occurs only once, and because of this reflection, modification of *citta* becomes possible and it starts behaving like conscious entity. Without this *pratibimba* (reflection), there is no *vritti* and so there is no knowledge in the sense of general epistemology.

Single reflection theory indicates the complete independence of *purusa* from *prakṛti*, and ultimate dualism between *purusa* and *prakṛti*. Against this Vijnanabhiksu gives theory of double reflection in purpose of filling the gap of the dualism of *samkhya* and *yoga*.

Double Reflection Theory of Vijnanabhiksu

Vijnanabhiksu states double reflection theory in Yogavartika. As the name suggests, there are two reflections in his theory. First occurrence of reflection is almost same just like the case of the single reflection theory of Vacaspati Misra, i.e., for the modification of *citta* in the form of *vritti* with the epistemological capacity of the generation of cognition, the reflection of *purusa* in *citta* is necessary. However, this single reflection theory makes the knowledge of material world only possible, not the knowledge of *"chetaney"* or consciousness. In other words, the reflection of *purusa* in the *citta* is not the *"pauruseya bodha"* or *"prama."* For this to happen another reflection is required. Hence, the second reflection is of *purusa* in the *purusa* itself. It is known as *"purusa-reflected-citta-vṛitti*[6]:

चेतने तावद् बुद्धिप्रतिबिंबमवश्यम स्वीकार्यम अन्यथा कुटस्थनित्यविभू चैतन्यस्य सर्वसंबंधा सदैव सर्ववस्तु सर्वेज्ञायेत . . . . यथा च चितेबुद्धिप्रतिबिंबमेवं बुद्धावपि चित्तप्रतिबिंबं स्वीकार्यम्म्यथा चैतन्यस्यमानानुपपत्ते।

The second reflection which occurs in Purusa is, in a sense, reflection of selection. In any cognitive knowledge, there is an element of a perception with the first cognitive apprehension of "I know the pot." "I know the pot" requires a difference between knower and known in the terminology of *Samkhya Yoga* which is provided by double reflection theory in the *Yoga Vartika* of *Vijnanabhiksu*.

This double reflection theory attempts to account for the subjectivity of cognitive knowledge and also for the justification of the cognitive knowledge of the known object.

Conclusion and Critical Epilogue

In the entire history of the different interpretations of *Yoga Sutra* and *Vyasa Bhasya*, the mainstream lies with the commentary of Vacaspati Misra and *vartika* of Vijnanabhiksu. No doubt, there are works like *Rāja-Martandavritti* of Bhoja.[7] But above two are generally considered as the classical works on the interpretation of yoga philosophy so far as the philosophical side of *Pātanjali Rajayoga* is concerned. However, it is also a fact that both of these interpreters have their own philosophical stand. Vacaspati Misra, though known as *sarvatantra svatantra*, his basic trend is toward *Advaita Vedānta* of Sankara while the basic philosophical position of Vijnāna-bhiksu is toward the synthesis of Samkhya and Vedānta in the form of *Avibhāgādvaita*. In an attempt of synthesis, Vijnānabhiksu strongly criticized the position of Sankara Vedanta—particularly its principle of *Māyā-Vadā*.[8]

Apart from historical interpretations, if the situation is viewed from a conceptual point of view regarding the consistency of epistemological discourses, the entire notion of "reflection" requires an appropriate ramification. Certainly, in this discourse, the meaning of the term *"pratibimba"* or "reflection" does not contain any optical reference in itself.[9]

The single reflection theory imparts a one-way ontic possibility of having a reflection in *citta* of *purusa* which is in no way either "aware" or "effected" with such an epistemological situation. This is neither epistemologically nor ontologically consistent if the position of both *"bimba"* and *"pratibimba"* are to be taken as independently existing two separate ontological categories. And if the views of double reflection theory of Vijnanabhiksu is to be taken seriously, then the whole programme of providing the transcendental ontological status to consciousness as an onward developmental stage from *Nyaya* and *Bauadha* philosophy itself becomes highly obscure. So, the way out from this situation is the adoption of *bimb-pratibimba vada* in the stream of *Sankara Vedanta* where the reality of *"pratibimba"* and its substratum is to be taken at the level of empirical reality and not as ultimately real.

REFERENCES

1. The denial of materialistic world view is the fundamental ontological position of *Upanisada*. cf. *Indra-Prajapati samvada* in *Chhandogya—Upanisada* as well as *Bhṛgu-Varuna Samvada* in *Taittiriya Upanisada* states the transcendence from *dehatmavada*.
2. Radhakrishnan S. (1962). *Indian Philosophy*, Vol. II. Oxford University Press: Oxford. Chapter II. 'The logical real in Nyaya.' *Nyayasidhhanta Muktavali* by Vishvanatha Panchanana Chaukhamba Press, Varanasi.
3. *Yoga Sutra* 1.1.7. Before this *sutra* there is a classification of *Vritti* in 1.1.6 as *"pramanaviparyay vikalp nindrasmriti."* It is also noteworthy that *vritti* itself is not explicitly defined.
4. Vacaspati Misra (2004). *Patanjali Yogasutra*—with *Vyasa-Bhasya* and *Yogatattava Vaisharadi* with Gujarati translation. Sanskruta Sahitya Academy, Gandhinagar, p. 25.
5. *Patanjali Yoga Darsanam* (1998). Chaukhamba Prakashan, Varanasi, p. 37.
6. *Ibid.* (1998), p. 32. In the justification of his stand Vijnanabhiksu states the view of Bhasyakara as *"Buddhe pratisanvedi purush"*, pp. 22-23.
7. Raja Martanda Vritti (1987) *Bhoja-Vṛtti*. M.L. B.D. New Delhi. This work, though puts out some important interpretation of the implicative side of Yoga, in the realm or pure epistemology and metaphysics, there is no real advancement in it.
8. Radhakrishnan, S. (1962). *Indian Philosophy*, Vol. II, George Allen & Unwin, London. Chapter X, "the Advaita Vedanta of Sankara." In

his *Vijnana Mrita Bhasya* on *Brahma Sutra,* Vijnanabhiksu gives the Quotation from *Padma Purana* in the effect of the Criticism of *Mayavada* as *"Prachhana Baudha."*

9. The reflection of a material object in a non-transparent object in the presence of light states the reality of both of these objects at the same level of physicality. Generally this does not hold for *Purusa* and *Prakriti.*

Index